SKLAR, Richard L. Corporate power in an African state; the political impact of multinational mining companies in Zambia. California, 1975. 245p map tab bibl (Perspectives on Southern Africa) 74-81440. 12.00. ISBN 0-520-02814-7

Sklar (*Nigerian political parties*, 1972) provides an excellent case study of converging values between the managers of multinational corporations and the bureaucratic elites in the new states of Africa. The evolution of the copper industry in Zambia from white settler government to accommodating growing demands of Zambian nationalist ideology reveals how multinationals have survived under such a wide variety of regimes. The agility of mining companies headquartered in South Africa to successfully adapt to the demands of Zambian nationalism also underscores the commitment of company managers to the corporation over any single form of government. Recommended for serious upper-division students of multinational corporations or political transformation studies of the new states. There appear to be few studies beyond scattered journal articles that have attempted Sklar's task of explaining the politics of adaptation of large-scale multinationals. The book is impressively researched and well written by one of the best

Africanist scholars. Good index, bibliography, and visual aids. Some material is now dated due to developments in Portugal but that does not affect the basic thesis of the book.

CORPORATE POWER
IN AN AFRICAN STATE

PERSPECTIVES ON SOUTHERN AFRICA

CORPORATE POWER
IN AN AFRICAN STATE

The Political Impact of
Multinational Mining
Companies in Zambia

Richard L. Sklar

UNIVERSITY OF CALIFORNIA PRESS
Berkeley · Los Angeles · London
1975

To Eve

University of California Press
Berkeley and Los Angeles, California

University of California Press, Ltd.
London, England

Printed in the United States of America

Contents

Preface

Among recent trends in social science, the revival of political economy is widely and wisely acclaimed. The present study looks toward, but does not attain, the interdisciplinary estate of political economy. It is mainly focused upon the activities of an industrial enterprise; yet it largely depends upon traditional methods of political analysis to interpret the evidence that is presented. As a social scientist, I strongly favor the development of synthesizing interdisciplinary studies such as political economy. However, I am also convinced that strictly political analyses of business corporations are essential to the quest for increasingly realistic approaches to the study of modern society.

Scholarly works relating to the Zambian (formerly Northern Rhodesian) copper industry and its social environment are justly renowned among students of modern Africa. This study is particularly indebted to the works of economists, historians, and sociologists. Yet it does not present an account of their theories, and it is highly selective in its report of their factual findings. Nor does this study pretend to compete with leading works of political and economic journalism, notably, Richard Hall's *The High Price of Principles*, an informed commentary on Zambia's struggle to promote racial justice in Southern Africa, and Antony Martin's *Minding Their Own Business*, a vivid account of Zambia's 51 percent nationalization of her giant copper industry. This book is specifically written for two groups of people, namely, political scientists and concerned laymen. However, political scientists themselves may wonder at the paucity of standard political information presented in these pages, which give the barest outline of political groups and organizations. Three individuals—the president of Zambia and two leading businessmen—are extensively quoted from published sources, but they are not otherwise analyzed as political personalities. Nor does this study inquire into questions of a bureaucratic or organizational nature, including decision-making within the industry and the crucial administrative arrangements for governmental supervision.

Basically, this study is concerned with the changing relationship between two entities—the African people of Zambia and the mining industry that has dominated the economy of this territory for most of the present century. Other entities, in particular, colonial governments, European settlers, and various sovereign states, have profoundly affected the relationship under consideration. Each, like the mining industry, has made its permanent impact upon the territory and its people. Yet the political impact of the mining industry since Zambia's emergence as an independent state is a matter of unstructured controversy and largely arid ideological disputation. It needs to be studied objectively as a factor that may profoundly affect the future of Zambia. At the same time, such an investigation may also shed light upon the adaptation of international business enterprises to postcolonial conditions in Africa.

Recently, political scientists have awakened to the awesome implications of giant business on an international scale. In political parlance, the term "international capitalism" may now be analogous to international communism. Among the distinctive institutions of international capitalism, the multinational corporation is preeminently significant as a repository of values and interests that might transcend the existing political order of sovereign states. The present study attempts to assess the political viability of this institution as an agent of economic and social development in a hostile ideological environment. It is also concerned with the capability of transnational business groups to alter the ideological configurations of newly developing countries in accordance with the long term interests of such groups. Finally, it seeks to demonstrate the efficacy of class analysis in preference to other, in particular, institutional, approaches to the study of multinational corporate expansion.

Research for this study was initiated in 1966, when I took up an appointment as senior lecturer in political science at the new University of Zambia. I explained the intent of my research—a wide-ranging and often roundabout investigation of the political influence of the mining companies within Zambia and upon Zambian foreign relations—to executives of the companies concerned, namely, the Anglo American Corporation and Roan Selection Trust. These persons and their associates in Britain, South Africa, and the United States generally appreciated the intellectual significance of this kind of research and gave me many courtesies, including their time, candid opinions, access to important documents, and assistance in planning and carrying out my research in Lusaka, the Copperbelt mining region, Johannesburg, London, and New York. I left Zambia in 1968, but, for various reasons, could not complete the manuscript until 1973. Meanwhile, great changes had taken place in the copper industry, most notably its 51 percent nationalization in 1970. Fortunately, in addition to basic documents, valuable commentaries by scholars and journalists have been published, establishing the factual foundations of numerous topics that are treated in this book. In 1972 I returned to Zambia for three weeks of intensive research, during which time I once more enjoyed the full cooperation of the mining companies.

I am indebted to many people in the companies, the Zambian government, and other walks of life for their help along the way. However, special acknowledgements are due to three individuals who opened many doors for me and gave me valuable advice on procedures in addition to the benefit of their substantive knowledge. I am most grateful to Denis Acheson of AMAX Zambia Inc. (previously, RST Management Services Limited), Winifred Armstrong of American Metal Climax, Inc., and Peter Leyden of Anglo American Corporation (Central Africa) Limited. I am also pleased to acknowledge the courtesies and contributions of Norreys Davis at the Copper Industry Service Bureau, J. W. H. Moore at the RST Group Archives, Eric Bromwich, Alfao Hambayi, and Richard Hobson of AMAX Zambia Inc., M. S. McCrum of Anglo American Corporation (Central Africa) Limited, Edward Marks, formerly economics officer at the American Embassy in Lusaka, D. R. De Vletter at the Zambian Ministry of Mines, Lawrence Mutakasha of MINDECO, and Allan Robertson at the United Nations. In Los Angeles, I have been aided by the knowledge and encouragement of Hans A. Ries, formerly vice-president of Continental Ore Corporation.

My understanding of the modern business corporation as a political institution was decisively shaped years ago by the profound teaching of Professor H. H. Wilson at Princeton University. The potential value of research on the political influence of foreign business corporations in Africa was first suggested to me by the late Professor Harwood L. Childs, Professors Dennis Austin, Robert H. Bates, Dennis Dresang, and William Tordoff graciously read my manuscript. Their comments were most helpful, but they

cannot be blamed for my shortcomings or mistakes. I am grateful
to Mrs. Beatrice Gould for her expert and cheerful typing of the
entire manuscript. Sound editorial advice was provided by Alain
Hénon and Shirley Warren of the University of California Press,
and Marya Holcombe. My wife, Eve, read and checked the proofs.
Finally, acknowledgments are due to the University of Zambia for
funding several research trips to the Zambian Copperbelt and one
trip to South Africa, to the UCLA Political Change Committee for a
summer research grant in 1969, and to the UCLA Academic Senate
and African Studies Center for funding my research trip to the
United Kingdom and Zambia in 1972.

ONE

Introduction

AIMS OF THE STUDY

Political science does not as yet have a theory of the modern corporation comparable to the theory of the firm in economics. As Grant McConnell has written, "the existence of the modern corporation does not accord with long-standing conceptions of political organization, and no theory exists by which it can be reconciled with such conceptions."[1] Adolf A. Berle's dictum that the corporation is "essentially, a nonstatist political institution" was intended by its author to spur the quest for theory and mark its starting point.[2] Some of the issues that are implicit in Berle's conception have since been clarified.[3] But events do not wait upon the appearance of theories; the problem of corporate power has burst upon the study of international politics, where it is basic to the debate about capitalist imperialism[4] and highly relevant to inquiries into the possibility of a world at peace.[5]

1. Grant McConnell, *Private Power and American Democracy* (New York: Vintage Books, 1966), p. 129.
2. Adolf A. Berle, Jr., *The Twentieth Century Capitalist Revolution* (New York: Harcourt, Brace & World, 1954), p. 60; and Berle, *Power Without Property* (New York: Harcourt, Brace, 1959), pp. 17–24.
3. See Edward S. Mason, ed., *The Corporation in Modern Society* (Cambridge: Harvard University Press, 1959); Andrew Hacker, ed., *The Corporation Take-Over* (Garden City, N.Y.: Anchor Books, 1965); John Kenneth Galbraith, *The New Industrial State* (New York: Houghton Mifflin, 1967); Edwin M. Epstein, *The Corporation in American Politics* (Englewood Cliffs, N.J.: Prentice-Hall, 1969); and Richard J. Barber, *The American Corporation* (New York: E. P. Dutton, 1970).
4. The imperialism thesis has been expounded by Paul A. Baran and Paul M. Sweezy, "Notes on the Theory of Imperialism," *Monthly Review* 17 (March 1966): 15–31; and Paul M. Sweezy and Harry Magdoff, "Notes on the Multinational Corporation," *Monthly Review* 21 (October 1969): 1–13; see also Stephen Hymer, "The Multinational Corporation and the Law of Uneven Development," in *Economics and World Order from the 1970's to the 1990's*, ed. Jagdish N. Bhagwati (New York: Macmillan, 1972), pp. 113–140; and Peter B. Evans, "National Autonomy and Economic Development," in *Transnational Relations and World Politics*, ed. Robert O. Keohane and Joseph S. Nye, Jr. (Cambridge: Harvard University Press, 1971), pp. 325–342. A representative rebuttal to the imperialism thesis is presented by Neil H. Jacoby, "The Multinational Corporation," *The Center Magazine* 3 (May 1970): 37–55.
5. See Kenneth N. Waltz, "The Myth of National Independence," in *The Interna-*

In 1960, David E. Lilienthal, statesman and business executive, introduced a term for corporations "which have their home in one country but which operate and live under the laws and customs of other countries as well." He referred to them as "multinational corporations."[6] Since then, the phenomenon of multinational enterprise has been investigated by economists, legal scholars, and many others.[7] In 1973, the United Nations commissioned an expert study of the impact of multinational corporations on world economic development and international relations.[8] Research from the vantage point of political science is needed to establish an adequate empirical basis for theoretical findings.[9] The present

tional Corporation, ed. Charles P. Kindleberger (Cambridge: M. I. T. Press, 1970), pp. 205–223; Chadwick F. Alger, "The Multinational Corporation and the Future International System," *The Annals of the American Academy of Political and Social Science* 403 (September 1972): 104–115; Hobert P. Sturm and Francis D. Wormuth, "The International Power Elite," *Monthly Review* 11 (December 1959): 282–287.

6. David E. Lilienthal, *The Multinational Corporation* (New York: Development and Resources Corporation, 1960), p. 1.

7. The term "multinational enterprise (or corporation, or firm)" is variously defined by relevant authors. Raymond Vernon has noted the following characteristics of major American multinational enterprises: "Each . . . turns out to be a parent company that controls a large cluster of corporations of various nationalities. The corporations that make up each cluster appear to have access to a common pool of human and financial resources and seem responsive to elements of a common strategy" (*Sovereignty at Bay: The Multinational Spread of U.S. Enterprises* [New York: Basic Books, 1971], p. 4). According to Vernon, other significant attributes include size allowing for sales in excess of $100 million, activities abroad other than mere exporting or licensing, and a geographical spread over more than two countries. For Jack N. Behrman, a multinational enterprise is "one that attempts to integrate operations and centralize policy control" while conducting business within a number of national economies (*National Interests and the Multinational Enterprise: Tensions among the North Atlantic Countries* [Englewood Cliffs, N.J.: Prentice-Hall, 1970], pp. 1–2). This corresponds to Samuel P. Huntington's conception of a "transnational organization"—one that "carries on significant centrally-directed operations in the territory of two or more nation-states" ("Transnational Organizations in World Politics," *World Politics* 25 [April 1970]: 336). See also John H. Dunning, "The Multinational Enterprise: The Background," in *The Multinational Enterprise,* ed. John H. Dunning (London: George Allen and Unwin, 1971), pp. 16–17; Isaiah A. Litvak and Christopher J. Maule, "The Multinational Firm: Some Perspectives," in *The Multinational Firm and the Nation State,* ed. Gilles Paquet (Don Mills, Ontario: Collier-Macmillan Canada, 1972), p.22. The latter volume also contains a valuable bibliography of works on multinational enterprise (pp. 167–182).

8. This followed the publication of a special study prepared under the auspices of the United Nations Department of Economic and Social Affairs, *Multinational Corporations in World Development,* UN Doc. ST/ECA/190 (New York, 1973); see also the brief study by the UN Economic Commission for Africa, *The Multinational Corporations in Africa,* Africa Contemporary Record Current Affairs Series (London: Rex Collings, 1972).

9. Three recent case studies of multinational corporations by political scientists

study suggests a conceptual approach to the political analysis of multinational business enterprise on the basis of a single intensively researched case.

This book is about a big industry in a small and newly developing country. In recent years, the Zambian mining industry has accounted for slightly more than 12 percent of world copper production, on a par with the output of Chile and greater than that of any other copper exporting country. Among metallic mineral production industries in Africa, this one ranks second only to the gold

MAP 1.

Zambia shown in the context of Central and Southern Africa.

in Latin American settings should be noted: Theodore H. Moran, "Transnational Strategies of Production and Defense by Multinational Corporations: Spreading the Risk and Raising the Cost for Nationalization in Natural Resources," *International Organization* 27 (Spring 1973): 273–287; Adalberto J. Pinelo, *The Multinational Corporation as a Force in Latin American Politics: A Case Study of the International Petroleum Company in Peru*, Praeger Special Studies in International Economics and Development (New York: Praeger, 1973); Charles T. Goodsell, *American Corporations and Peruvian Politics* (Cambridge: Harvard University Press, 1974).

MAP 2.

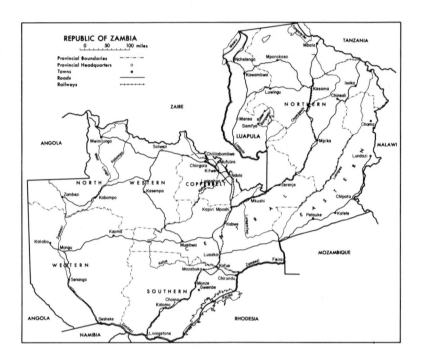

Zambia showing towns and provinces; also rivers, lakes,
major roads, and railways. By courtesy of the Ministry of
Development Planning and National Guidance, Lusaka.

mining industry of South Africa.[10] It is the mainstay of Zambia's
economy; in fact, it is the sole significant source of national wealth.
Despite its large area (290,000 square miles), Zambia's population
was little more than 4 million in 1969. Nearly 750,000 were found to
dwell in the urban districts of Copperbelt Province, a conurban
region of seven major towns within an area that is about 90 miles in
length and 30 miles wide adjacent to the Zaire pedicle. Another
500,000 live in urban areas, including the capital city of Lusaka
(pop. 238,000), along the railway line that runs 500 miles from the

10. William Hance, *The Geography of Modern Africa* (New York: Columbia University Press, 1964), p. 468.

Copperbelt to the Victoria Falls of the Zambezi River. Under colonial and white-settler rule, the development of rural Zambia (called Northern Rhodesia during the colonial era) was neglected while rural communities were being exploited as a source of cheap labor for the mines and other urban undertakings. For many years and various reasons, as noted below, Zambia's great industry operated within a technologically modern enclave that was able to develop and generate wealth without significant benefit to the vast majority of Zambians.

Since the attainment of national independence in 1964, Zambian leaders have sought to revolutionize the social effects of this industry's operation. In the past, their small country had been an asset to the great industry; now the industry would become more of an asset to the country. Henceforth, it would be used to develop the country as a whole so as to reduce the long-term danger of domestic conflict between relatively privileged interest groups and an impoverished majority. In 1969 the Zambian government chose 51 percent nationalization as its major means to control the conditions and effects of mine production. As a result, joint ventures or partnerships have been formed between an agency of the state and two multinational corporations, based in South Africa and the United States respectively. The present study is concerned with the adaptation of the mining companies to the passing of colonial rule and the resulting establishment of new operating conditions both before and after nationalization.

Following a brief survey of the historical, political, and economic background in this introduction, chapter 2 examines the corporate structure of the mining industry and the nature of the two multinational corporations that have, through subsidiaries, entered into partnership agreements with the Zambian government, namely the Anglo American Corporation of South Africa and American Metal Climax of New York. Questions of right and justice in the economic sphere underlie the issues of economic reform discussed in chapter 2, which also presents an assessment of the distribution of financial benefits and costs resulting from the nationalization agreements. Chapter 3 considers the control of processes that determine the size of the financial pie that will be divided between Zambia and her partners in the mining industry. The central question arising here is Zambia's continuing dependence upon external powers, including other states and business entities outside of

Zambian jurisdiction, for the performance of such crucial functions
as pricing, marketing, mining development, and the establishment
of copper-related manufacturing enterprises. Chapter 4 is concerned with the claims of labor and other demands upon the industry to promote the cause of social justice within Zambia. Chapter 5
considers demands upon the industry to alter an established pattern of foreign commercial relationships for ideological reasons. A
viable partnership cannot disregard Zambia's profound commitment to the cause of African liberation in Southern Africa. On the
other hand, the multinational corporations concerned will not
conduct their business outside of Zambia in accordance with Zambian ideological precepts. A theoretical solution to this potentially
divisive ideological problem is formulated as the "doctrine of
domicile" in chapter 6, which goes on to ponder the balance of
power between the corporate enterprise system and the Zambian
state.

The issue of corporate versus state power may be analyzed cogently in various ways, and it may be appropriate to mention three
distinct conceptual approaches that appear in the literature on this
subject but are not adopted in the present study. First, an approach
in terms of institutional analysis would examine the properties of
the corporations concerned and their relative strengths and weak-
nesses vis-à-vis the state. This approach accords with common
sense and follows the tradition of Berle and other prophets of
corporate power.[11] It is implicit in the formulations of Raymond
Vernon,[12] and it promises to be most productive in political science
research.[13]

A second approach, roughly behavioral in nature, would
examine political relationships within the companies themselves—what Earl Latham has termed "the body politic of the corporation."[14] This approach corresponds to the idea of "private

11. ". . . the modern corporation may be regarded not simply as one form of
social organization but potentially (if not yet actually) as the dominant institution of
the modern world." Adolf A. Berle and Gardiner C. Means, *The Modern Corporation and Private Property*, rev. ed. (New York: Harcourt, Brace & World, 1968), p. 313;
cf. Peter F. Drucker, *The New Society* (New York: Harper, 1950), p. 27.
   12. Vernon, *Sovereignty at Bay*.
   13. See Huntington, "Transnational Organizations in World Politics."
   14. Earl Latham, "The Body Politic of the Corporation," in *The Corporation in
Modern Society*, ed. Mason, pp. 218–236. A design for this approach is elaborated in
Michael Z. Brooke and H. Lee Remmers, *The Strategy of Multinational Enterprise:
Organization and Finance* (New York: American Elsevier Publishing Company, 1970).

government";[15] it would also be consistent with a functional inquiry into the "political" aspects of "economic" institutions. I regard the latter approach as a step backward from Berle's dictum that the corporation itself is a political institution. However, all inquiries into the political life of business institutions examined in this case would surely produce valuable knowledge about the extent and exercise of corporate power.

Third, an approach in terms of group theory perceives multinational corporations as international interest or pressure groups.[16] The pluralistic assumptions of group theory are well suited to the autonomy of multinational corporations, and this approach is especially conducive to the study of issues involving conflicts of interest. The logic of this approach is also consistent with the abstract conception of international politics as a system of action; multinational corporations may be conceived as "structural components of systems of world politics."[17] It should be noted, however, that the premises of "systems theory" and related approaches in political science tend to deemphasize the importance of "power" as an analytical idea.[18]

I take the position, maintained by Robert S. Lynd, that power is fundamental to the order of society and that it should be conceived as a property of social structure.[19] Power is manifest in group and institutional behavior. Yet it is a mistake, in my view, to identify organized groups or institutions as the basic elements of social structure. Deeper analysis will reveal the bearing and thrust of underlying interests and social forces that motivate the activities of groups and institutions.

In Zambia, as in other newly developing countries, the national effort to establish effective domestic control over the means required for social reconstruction has given rise to conflicting forces.

15. McConnell, pp. 119–154.

16. Jonathan F. Galloway, "Multinational Enterprises as Worldwide Interest Groups," *Politics and Society* 2 (Fall 1971): 1–21.

17. G. Modelski, "The Corporation in World Society," in *The Year Book of World Affairs 1968*, ed. George W. Keeton and Georg Schwarzenberger (London: Stevens, 1968), p. 78.

18. See, for example, Morton A. Kaplan, "Systems Theory," in *Contemporary Political Analysis*, ed. James C. Charlesworth (New York: The Free Press, 1967), p. 161; and Karl W. Deutsch, *The Nerves of Government* (New York: The Free Press, 1966), p. 124.

19. Robert S. Lynd, "Power in American Society as Resource and Problem," in *Problems of Power in American Democracy*, ed. Arthur Kornhauser (Detroit: Wayne State University Press, 1959), pp. 1–45.

Bureaucratic and technocratic elitism, nurtured by the state, has arisen to challenge the democratic ideals of the nationalist party in power. Either the party will restrain the pretensions of technocratic elitism, or technocratic elitism, sheltered by the influence of multinational corporations, will transform the populist party into a willing instrument for capitalist development. The struggle between elitist and popular power looms as the central issue of Zambian political development.

THE ZAMBIAN SETTING

Historical Background

The forebears of present-day Zambians formed numerous kingdoms, large and small, in central Africa between the sixteenth and nineteenth centuries.[20] During the nineteenth century, powerful kingdoms were sustained by the Lunda, Bemba, and Ngoni peoples in northern and eastern Zambia, and by the Lozi of southwestern Zambia. Official publications have listed some one hundred tribal groups,[21] many of whom are closely related, and thirteen separate language groups. Four languages—Ci-Bemba in the north, Ci-Nyanja in the east, Ci-Tonga in the south, and Si-Lozi in the west—are widely spoken and understood. In Zambia today, English is "the sole official language . . . [it is] the language of documentation, of political pronouncements at national level, of business and technology, and of all education above lower primary level."[22]

The earliest non-African intruders were Arab traders, principally slave dealers, and Portuguese travelers, who traded for slaves and ivory. Beginning in 1850, the famous Scottish missionary and explorer, David Livingstone, traveled widely throughout central Africa until his death in the vicinity of Zambia's Lake Bangweulu in

20. A succinct outline of precolonial Zambian history is presented by H. W. Langworthy, "Pre-Colonial Kingdoms and Tribal Migrations, AD 1500–1900," in *Zambia in Maps*, ed. D. Hywel Davies (London: University of London Press, 1971), pp. 32–33; also Andrew Roberts, "Migrations from the Congo," in *A Short History of Zambia*, ed. Brian M. Fagan (Nairobi: Oxford University Press, 1966), pp. 101–120; and Mutumba Mainga, "The Lozi Kingdom," in *A Short History of Zambia*, pp. 121–127.

21. See W. V. Brelsford, *The Tribes of Zambia*, 2d ed. (Lusaka: Government Printer, 1965), pp. 151–152.

22. H. W. Langworthy, "Languages and Tribes," in *Zambia in Maps*, ed. Davies, p. 34.

1873. Livingstone's example and ideas stimulated many other missionaries and traders (from Britain in particular) to spread the gospel and to promote "legitimate commerce" in Africa as an alternative to the devastating slave trade. Missionaries and a group of Scottish businessmen, who were dedicated to the eradication of slavery, were largely responsible for the establishment of a British protectorate in Nyasaland under direct Imperial administration.[23] Elsewhere in central Africa, including the vast territory to the west of Nyasaland, credit for the extension of British authority was due mainly to the ardent imperialist and powerful financier, Cecil John Rhodes. In 1889, Rhodes's newly formed British South Africa Company obtained a royal charter to govern an indeterminately vast region north of Bechuanaland. The territorial limits of this grant were fixed by subsequent agreements between the British government and other sovereigns, specifically, the governments of Germany and Portugal, and the King of the Belgians.

South of the Zambezi River, the Chartered Company consolidated its position by defeating the militaristic Matabele nation in 1893. However, Rhodes's inept and abortive attempt to foment a revolution in the Transvaal republic in 1895 led the British government to favor the establishment of separate administrations for territories within the sphere of the charter north of the Zambezi.[24] Consequently, by the turn of the century, British central Africa consisted of four separate political entities: a protectorate, outside of the Chartered Company's sphere, in Nyasaland; two separate protectorates, within the Chartered Company's sphere, in North-Eastern and North-Western Rhodesia; an embryonic colony, under mixed company, Imperial, and settler rule, in Southern Rhodesia. In 1911, North-Eastern and North-Western Rhodesia were amalgamated to form the protectorate of Northern Rhodesia, with its capital at Livingstone, where the railway from Southern Rhodesia passes over the great gorge of the Zambezi below the Victoria Falls. Southern Rhodesia became a self-governing colony in 1923, when its electorate chose this option in preference to union with South Africa. The following year, administrative authority in Northern

23. A. J. Wills, *An Introduction to the History of Central Africa*, 2d ed. (London: Oxford University Press, 1967), pp. 118–119, 168–184; and A. J. Hanna, *The Beginnings of Nyasaland and North-Eastern Rhodesia, 1859–95* (Oxford: The Clarendon Press, 1956).

24. L. H. Gann, *A History of Northern Rhodesia: Early Days to 1953* (London: Chatto & Windus, 1964), pp. 77–78.

Rhodesia was transferred from the Chartered Company to the Imperial government.

During the period of company administration extensive prospecting by pioneer firms and individuals failed to result in as great a discovery of mineral wealth in Northern Rhodesia as had been anticipated. The most successful new mining enterprise was the lead and zinc mine at Broken Hill, approximately one hundred miles south of the region that would become known as the Copperbelt. The railway reached Broken Hill (now Kabwe) in 1906; it was extended to link up with the Congo railways in 1909 as a result of initiatives by British financiers who were involved in developing the newly discovered and extremely rich copper beds of Katanga. This stimulated the settlement along the line-of-rail of a small but significant group of European farmers, who produced maize and beef for both the Congo mines and lesser markets in Northern Rhodesia.

Compared with the Katanga mines, where ores containing copper oxide averaged 15 percent copper, the orebodies in adjacent areas of Northern Rhodesia, averaging 3 to 5 percent copper, were much less attractive. This appraisal was revised during the latter 1920s, when immense deposits of sulfide ore were discovered at workable depths beneath the topmost layers of oxide ore. The technical and financial implications of this discovery have been explained thus:

> Sulfide ores can be fed directly into smelting furnaces after the crushing and concentrating process, whereas with oxide ores a leaching process is necessary to extract the copper. In the twenties the cost of processing sulfide ores was much lower than handling oxide ores of equal copper content. Thus, the discovery of extensive sulfide ores opened up a highly lucrative investment opportunity in Northern Rhodesia.[25]

This breakthrough led to the formation of the mining companies that are considered in this book (identified in chapter 2) by financiers who had acquired prospecting concessions from the British South Africa Company.[26]

25. Robert E. Baldwin, *Economic Development and Export Growth: A Study of Northern Rhodesia, 1920–1960* (Berkeley and Los Angeles: University of California Press, 1966), p. 31.
26. The various groups and leading personalities are identified in Gann, pp.

Previously, in 1922, the Chartered Company had decided that in order to stimulate mining development, it would deliberately seek to promote the formation of strongly capitalized mining finance companies which would be able to conduct systematic exploration programs and create operating companies as required to develop promising discoveries. Such enterprises would be granted "exclusive prospecting rights over large areas" on condition of their spending minimum annual sums on prospecting.[27] In return, the Chartered Company would be entitled to a shareholding in any mining company that might be formed as well as royalty payments on all future mineral production. When, in 1924, Chartered relinquished its administrative responsibilities to the Crown, its ownership of mineral rights throughout Northern Rhodesia (apart from exceptional areas in which the company had transferred such rights to early concessionaires) was preserved. These potentially lucrative rights were confirmed by the British government despite their origin in dubious concessions and "treaties" that company agents had obtained in meetings with African traditional rulers during 1889–1890.[28] The value of these rights became apparent when the mines of the Northern Rhodesian Copperbelt entered production. In 1925 the Chartered Company's income from mining was "a paltry £12,781; by 1937 it had risen to £311,000 per annum; in 1964 it was estimated by the Northern Rhodesian government that by then the company had received a total of £70 million after tax in royalty payments."[29] Concomitantly, a mine labor force, consisting of relatively privileged European workers and a far greater number of African workers, emerged to form the nucleus of several towns that give the Copperbelt its distinctive urban character. In 1920 the European population of Northern Rhodesia was a mere 3,000; by 1950 it had risen to 36,000, inhabiting the Copper-

---

117–124, 204–209. Basic sources include the following: Kenneth Bradley, *Copper Venture* (London, 1952); J. Austen Bancroft, *Mining in Northern Rhodesia* (London: The British South Africa Company, 1961); Theodore Gregory, *Ernest Oppenheimer and the Economic Development of Southern Africa* (Cape Town: Oxford University Press, 1962), pp. 384–452; Francis L. Coleman, *The Northern Rhodesia Copperbelt 1899–1962: Technological Development up to the End of the Central African Federation* (Manchester: Manchester University Press, 1971).

27. Bancroft, p. 23.

28. The methods of these "concession hunters" are discussed in Richard Hall, *Zambia* (New York: Praeger, 1965), pp. 61–86.

29. Peter Slinn, "Commercial Concessions and Politics during the Colonial Period: The Role of the British South Africa Company in Northern Rhodesia, 1890–1964," *African Affairs*, 70 (October 1971): 365–384.

belt, commercial farms as well as towns adjacent to the line-of-rail, and the farming communities around Abercorn (now Mbala) in the north and Fort Jameson (now Chipata) in the east. During this period, the country's known African population increased from 950,000 to 1,700,000.[30] The vast majority of Africans lived by sub-sistence farming, although it should be noted that African farmers were not encouraged to engage in commercial production and they were systematically excluded from the farmlands that were most suitable for commercial agriculture within a belt "extending in most areas about 20 miles on each side of the railway."[31]

Before the late 1920s, spokesmen for the white settlers of South-ern Rhodesia were averse to the idea of political union with the impoverished northern protectorate. However, the discovery of an immensely valuable buried treasure of red metal in the Copperbelt and the resulting growth of European settlement north of the Zambezi converted many Southern Rhodesian settlers to the cause of expansion. Moreover, political trends in South Africa, spe-cifically the electoral defeat of the pro-British Smuts government by a coalition led by Afrikaner nationalists in 1924, prompted the newly self-governing Southern Rhodesians to turn away from thoughts of union with South Africa toward the idea of a "Greater Rhodesia," securely under the control of English-speaking whites. In Northern Rhodesia, the much smaller community of white settlers remained cool to Southern Rhodesian schemes for amal-gamation until 1930, when Lord Passfield, colonial secretary in the British Labor government, declared that in Northern Rhodesia and Nyasaland, as in other East African dependencies, "the interests of the African natives must be paramount" and should prevail whenever they conflicted with the interests of immigrant races. The enunciation of this doctrine did not affect official policy in Northern Rhodesia; the doctrine itself was soon qualified to reas-sure white settlers. Nonetheless, from this time on, Northern Rhodesian whites were ever more disposed to favor political union with Southern Rhodesia.[32]

"Greater Rhodesia," the dream of those who hoped to consoli-date the domination of English-speaking whites in British Central

30. Wills, App. 4.
31. Baldwin, pp. 147–150, 159.
32. To be sure, Northern Rhodesians were always wary that Southern Rhodesia would exploit any such union to reap disproportionate benefits from the copper-rich north. In turn, Southern Rhodesian whites had misgivings about the reliability

Africa, became a reality in 1953. Once again, the resurgence of Afrikaner political strength in South Africa—this time, the Nationalist electoral victory of 1948—served to galvanize sentiment for the creation of a "strong British bloc" north of the Limpopo.[33] During the course of discussions between 1948 and 1951, it became evident that Britain would insist upon a federal form of union in order to minimize Southern Rhodesia's potential control over the established rights of Africans in the two northern protectorates. Southern Rhodesians were attracted to the idea of union with Northern Rhodesia mainly by the prospect of access to the tax revenue that was generated by the copper industry. Certainly, there was no desire on the part of Southern Rhodesia to unite with Nyasaland, but the British government had decided to transfer its financial responsibility for Nyasaland to the Greater Rhodesians, and would not countenance any proposal to the contrary.[34] In Northern Rhodesia, the Europeans embraced federation as a way to attain political independence without African majority rule. Ultimately, in 1953, a new state, the Federation of Rhodesia and Nyasaland, was brought into existence.

It lies beyond the scope of this discussion to analyze the ambiguous policy of "partnership" between racial communities as it was professed and practiced by the white leaders of the federation. A fair summary might emphasize both the overwhelming reality of racial discrimination and the erratic implementation of incremental reforms.[35] Doubtless, federation did promote the flow of material benefits to all sections of the population. Yet the distribution of

---

of arrangements to maintain white supremacy in the north; they were inclined to favor a partition of Northern Rhodesia so that Southern Rhodesia might amalgamate with the railway strip and the Copperbelt only. Gann closely examines these and related questions in portions of *A History of Northern Rhodesia*. See also Edward Clegg, *Race and Politics* (London: Oxford University Press, 1960), pp. 50–70; and Colin Leys, "The Idea of Amalgamation," in *A New Deal in Central Africa*, ed. Colin Leys and Cranford Pratt (New York: Praeger, 1960), pp. 1–10.

33. Gann, p. 400.

34. T. R. M. Creighton observes that Southern Rhodesian leaders were prepared to accept Nyasaland in the proposed federation "if this were Britain's price for the copperbelt" (*The Anatomy of Partnership* [London: Faber, 1960], p. 38).

35. Searching appraisals are presented in the following works: Colin Leys, *European Politics in Southern Rhodesia* (Oxford: The Clarendon Press, 1959); Creighton, *The Anatomy of Partnership*; Thomas M. Franck, *Race and Nationalism* (New York: Fordham University Press, 1960); Philip Mason, *Year of Decision* (London: Oxford University Press, 1960); Harry Franklin, *Unholy Wedlock: The Failure of the Central African Federation* (London: George Allen and Unwin, 1963); Patrick Keatley, *The Politics of Partnership* (Penguin Books, 1963).

such benefits favored the white settler community to a highly disproportionate degree. William J. Barber's conclusion on the racial
bias of public expenditure within the federation is most relevant:

> Not only has the European community gained far out of
> proportion to its numbers, but even the *absolute* sums ex-
> pended have been much larger for Europeans than for Afri-
> cans. Federation did not create this situation. It has long been
> an established part of the institutional environment in the
> Rhodesias. But, under federation, this environment has been
> perpetuated.[36]

An example may be adduced from the field of education. Public
expenditures on African education did increase steadily during the
1950s; yet, in 1959, public expenditure on education for the non-
African population of 327,000 was greater than that for the African
population of 7,560,000.[37] Perhaps the most revealing indication of
the political character of "partnership" is given by the federal electoral system, as amended in 1958. This system provided that 44
members out of a total of 59 in the Federal Assembly would be
elected by persons who could qualify as "general" voters by meeting economic and educational requirements. Although the franchise was nonracial in principle, in practice those who qualified as
general voters were overwhelmingly European. In 1959 more than
86,000 Europeans were registered as general voters, compared
with some 1,700 Africans.[38] The figures on voter registration for
the territorial assemblies of Northern and Southern Rhodesia reveal similar degrees of European preponderance among registrants
for the regular or "ordinary" roll.[39] Not until 1962, with the future
of the federation gravely in doubt, did white leaders of the party in
power declare that Africans would form a majority of the electorate
within fifteen years.[40]

36. William J. Barber, "Federation and the Distribution of Economic Benefits," in
A New Deal in Central Africa, ed. Leys and Pratt, p. 92.

37. P. Mason, p. 265.

38. Ibid., p. 261.

39. Ibid. As in the case of the federal franchise, territorial franchise laws made
provision for the limited influence of "special" voters with lower economic and
educational qualifications, which were nonetheless beyond the reach of the vast
majority of adult Africans.

40. Sir Edgar Whitehead, the prime minister of Southern Rhodesia, made a
statement to this effect at the United Nations shortly before his party was defeated
by advocates of strict white supremacy. James Barber, *Rhodesia: The Road to Rebellion*
(London: Oxford University Press, 1967), p. 156.

In the northern territories, African opposition to the federation was widespread and intense. Africans deeply resented the imposition of federation without their consent and against their will. In their eyes, federation represented an extension of white power in Southern Rhodesia to the north; as such it was seen as a threat to African landholding and a retrograde step away from the goal of African independence towards permanent white domination and increased racial discrimination.[41] To be sure, the roots and manifestations of African nationalism in both Northern Rhodesia and Nyasaland extend back to the early years of European occupation. However, the culminating thrust of anticolonial nationalism in both countries, involving the formation of mass political organizations, came during and as a result of the campaign against federation.[42] In Northern Rhodesia, this campaign was sparked at first by the African National Congress, under the leadership of Harry Mwaanga Nkumbula. This movement split in 1958 on issues relating to both the quality of Nkumbula's leadership and his policy, in particular, his controversial decision to participate in elections under a new constitution that would ensure the perpetuation of a European majority in the territorial legislature. The more militant faction then formed the Zambia African National Congress, under the leadership of Kenneth David Kaunda, who had been secretary-general of the older movement.[43] In 1959 this organization was banned and its leaders were detained. Ten months later, Kaunda emerged from prison with the aura of "a national hero,"[44] to become president of the United National Independence party,

41. United Kingdom, *Report of the Advisory Commission on the Review of the Constitution of Rhodesia and Nyasaland,* Cmnd. 1148 (London, 1960), pp. 16–21. Logically, Africans in Southern Rhodesia were more inclined to hope that federation would mitigate the severity of repression in their country. Ibid., p. 21.

42. The basic study of African nationalism in both Nyasaland and Northern Rhodesia, from "the beginnings of indigenous protest" to "the battle over federation," is Robert I. Rotberg, *The Rise of Nationalism in Central Africa: The Making of Malawi and Zambia, 1873–1964* (Cambridge: Harvard University Press, 1965); see also Ian Henderson, "The Origins of Nationalism in East and Central Africa: The Zambian Case," *Journal of African History* 11 (1970): 591–603; and Henry S. Meebelo, *Reaction to Colonialism: A Prelude to the Politics of Independence in Northern Zambia, 1893–1939* (Manchester: Manchester University Press, 1971).

43. Kenneth D. Kaunda, *Zambia Shall Be Free: An Autobiography* (London: Heinemann, 1962), pp. 88–103. The name "Zambia" is derived "from a contraction of Zambezia, the earlier term for the general area of Northern Rhodesia" (Rotberg, p. 291).

44. Ibid., p. 310.

which had been formed in his absence by his supporters. Similarly, in Nyasaland, increasingly militant agitation led to disturbances and the detention of nationalist leaders, including Dr. H. Kamuzu Banda, in 1959.[45] Upon his release from detention in 1960, Dr. Banda assumed the leadership of the newly formed Malawi Congress party, which demonstrated its virtually unchallenged political supremacy in the territorial election of 1961.

The final stages of Northern Rhodesia's evolution as an African state were far more complicated than were those of Nyasaland. By 1960 Northern Rhodesia's European population had doubled over the preceding decade to total 73,000, which was eight times larger than the number of Europeans in Nyasaland. Moreover, the economic stakes in this territory were far greater than elsewhere in the federation, not only for the mining finance groups that controlled the Copperbelt, but also for the growing industrial sector of Southern Rhodesia's economy. It is generally thought that as a result of the redistribution of revenues following the establishment of the federation, Northern Rhodesia lost about £7 million per year to Southern Rhodesia—a total of £70 million during the federation's ten-year life span.[46] When Nyasaland's independence became inevitable, the leaders of white Rhodesia made a last ditch effort to save "the essence of the federation" by dusting off an old settler scheme to partition Northern Rhodesia in order to preserve the connection between its central strip—including the Copperbelt, the railway, and the main area of European settlement—with Southern Rhodesia.[47] These considerations were bound to compli-

45. United Kingdom, *Report of the Nyasaland Commission of Inquiry.* Cmnd. 814, Colonial Office (London, 1959). This report made a significant contribution to the substantiation of fundamental nationalist viewpoints.

46. Rotberg, p. 295. William J. Barber has commented, "In the last pre-federal year, Northern Rhodesia collected about 60 percent of Central African public revenue; by 1957–58, its share had fallen to less than 20 percent. . . . No one can say precisely what Northern Rhodesian revenues would have been in the absence of federation. But there can be no question that the Copperbelt has been the financial backbone of the federal fiscal structure" ("Federation and the Distribution of Economic Benefits," pp. 83–84). Confirmatory evidence is summarized by Arthur Hazlewood, "The Economics of Federation and Dissolution in Central Africa," in *African Integration and Disintegration: Case Studies in Economic and Political Union* (London: Oxford University Press, 1967), pp. 207–215.

47. Sir Roy Welensky, *Welensky's 4,000 Days: The Life and Death of the Federation of Rhodesia and Nyasaland* (London: Collins, 1964), pp. 317–323. Welensky, then prime minister of the federation, reports his argument to the British prime minister thus: "What I would not accept was secession for the central strip of Northern Rhodesia

cate the transfer of power to an African government. In addition, Northern Rhodesia, unlike Nyasaland, was faced with a serious threat of secession; this threat was posed by Barotseland, a separate "protectorate" within the far western part of Northern Rhodesia. The traditional rulers of Barotseland had special historic claims on the British government; they were also hostile to the main nationalist party and inclined to remain within a reconstituted federation comprising, in addition to their homeland, Southern Rhodesia and the central strip of Northern Rhodesia.[48] After some equivocation, the idea of partition was firmly rejected by the British government.[49]

During the course of constitutional negotiations in 1961–1962, Britain refused to permit an outright transfer of electoral power to the African majority.[50] With great reluctance, the African nationalists agreed to accept a highly restrictive franchise, which would permit African representatives to form a majority in the territorial legislature provided some of them were also supported by a minimum percentage of white voters. The outcome was an African majority in the legislature and the territory's first African government based on an awkward and obviously temporary coalition between the United National Independence party (UNIP) and the African National Congress (ANC). Within a year the constitution was revised once again, this time to provide for universal adult suffrage. This enabled UNIP to win a commanding majority in the general election of January 1964[51] and, as the government, to make preparations for independence in October.

---

or for Southern Rhodesia: if we gave in over this, the creditworthiness of the Federation would be affected and it would be impossible to seek any more capital investment" (Ibid., p. 322). See also Lord Alport, *The Sudden Assignment* (London: Hodder and Stoughton, 1965), pp. 165–169.

48. See Gerald L. Caplan, *The Elites of Barotseland, 1878–1969* (Berkeley, Los Angeles, London: University of California Press, 1970), pp. 196–197. According to Caplan, in its most ambitious version, the "new federation" scheme included the mineral rich and then secessionist Congolese province of Katanga.

49. On the British government's interest in this scheme, see Franklin, pp. 216–220. Britain's legal obligation to Barotseland was terminated in 1964 by the British government's formal endorsement of an agreement between the traditional rulers of Barotseland and the government of Northern Rhodesia, confirming that Barotseland would be an integral part of Zambia. Hall, pp. 241–242.

50. David C. Mulford, *Zambia: The Politics of Independence, 1957–1964* (London: Oxford University Press, 1967), pp. 184–210. This is an important and most enlightening study of both nationalist and colonialist political maneuverings during the last years of Northern Rhodesia.

51. UNIP won 55 out of 65 legislative seats elected by "main roll" voters; the

The fact that these final obstacles to African independence were
overcome expeditiously, peacefully (apart from violent protests in
1961), and without economic disruption was due in no small part
to the personal qualities of Kenneth Kaunda. Most notably, the
UNIP leader succeeded in projecting his own dedication to nonracial democracy as a public ideal for the new state.[52] His leadership
in this respect enabled many, black and white, to rise above their
ingrained racialistic attitudes during a tense period of political
transition. At the end of 1963, Britain dissolved the ill-starred Federation of Rhodesia and Nyasaland. In 1964 the two Central African protectorates were regenerated as independent states—Malawi
and Zambia.

Political Organization and Trends since Independence

Zambia achieved independence as a republic within the Commonwealth on October 24, 1964, six years to the day after Kaunda
and his associates had inaugurated the Zambia African National
Congress. Under the Constitution of the First Republic (1964–
1972), legislative power was vested in a Parliament of Zambia,
consisting of a president and a National Assembly.[53] From among
the members of the National Assembly, the president appointed
his cabinet, comprising a vice-president (responsible for the conduct of the government's business in the assembly), a secretary-
general to the government (in charge of the Cabinet Office as well
as the public service), and other ministers, most of whom were
responsible for the administration of government departments. All
members of the cabinet were (and are) subject to removal from
office by the president. Since 1969, a separate cabinet minister,
conceived as an "agent for development," has been responsible for

African National Congress won 10. The National Progress party won 10 seats in
constituencies reserved for European voters for the duration of the first National
Assembly. Ibid., pp. 327–328.

52. See *Black Government? A Discussion between Colin Morris and Kenneth Kaunda*
(Lusaka, 1960), esp. chap. 3: "We Want a Colour Blind Society," pp. 41–56; also
Colin Legum, ed., *Zambia: Independence and Beyond: The Speeches of Kenneth Kaunda*
(London: Nelson, 1966).

53. The Constitution of the First Republic as amended through 1970 appears in
Republic of Zambia, *Appendix 1 to the Laws of Zambia* (Lusaka: Government Printer,
n.d.).

governmental functions in each of the eight provinces that constitute Zambia.[54]

At all times, President Kaunda has possessed the constitutional and political authority to provide vigorous leadership. By any measure, the challenges to Zambian statecraft have been enormous. Despite the great prosperity of her copper industry, Zambia was born with exaggerated features of underdevelopment. Owing to the neglect of education under colonial rule, out of an African population of 3,400,000, there were, at independence, only some 1,200 Africans who had completed secondary school in the entire country; a mere 109 Zambian Africans had graduated from universities.[55] Insofar as benefits from the copper industry had trickled down to Africans, they were mainly enjoyed by employees of the mines, railways, and urban enterprises. The African rural sector, which comprised approximately three-fourths of the country's population, had suffered grievously from the effects of official policies. The latter were designed to promote the interests of European commercial farmers at the expense of Africans, who were intended by colonial planners to constitute an inexhaustible supply of cheap labor.[56] Over and above these endemic challenges to independent Zambia, external threats are implicit in the circumstance that Zambia borders on four countries that are subject to colonial and white minority rule—Angola, Mozambique, Namibia, and Southern Rhodesia. So long as the Zambian government remains deeply committed to the cause of African liberation, it must seek to reduce the extent of Zambia's inherited dependence upon neighboring and hostile white-ruled states without flagging in its determination to achieve basic developmental goals.

These challenges—to educate the people, to develop the country as a whole, to maintain national integrity and disengage from the economic clutches of hostile neighbors—tend to elicit responses that are revolutionary in their effects. They portend nothing less than the social reconstruction of Zambia. As in many another newly developing country, the leaders of Zambia have been inclined to equate the cause of reconstruction with the retention of

54. William Tordoff, "Provincial and Local Government in Zambia," *Journal of Administration* 9 (January 1970): 25.

55. Republic of Zambia, *Manpower Report* (Lusaka: Government Printer, 1966), pp. 1–2.

56. See the penetrating analysis of policies affecting African agriculture in Baldwin, pp. 144–162.

power by one political directorate, specifically, the leaders of UNIP. One-party tendencies in the Zambian system were evident for several years before President Kaunda's declaration of intent to create a one-party state in 1972. Thus, in 1967, the president pre-scribed an official "ideology" for both UNIP and Zambia, termed "humanism." The basic documents described a God-fearing but "man-centered" social philosophy, combining socialist and capitalist ideas within a context of concern for economic develop-ment and social justice.[57] "Humanism" is propagated in the schools, colleges, armed forces, and diverse public agencies. Be-sides the intrinsic appeal of its grounding in African traditional, especially rural, values, Kaunda's "humanism," presented as an indigenous African doctrine, is intended to counter the potentially dangerous effects of foreign ideological competition in Zambia. In fact, Kaunda has been inclined to castigate critics of his philosophy as if they were agents, conscious or otherwise, of "alien ideolo-gies."

Yet another one-party characteristic of the new state was the practice of senior civil servants and commanders of the armed forces to attend meetings of the UNIP National Council, the party's supreme deliberative body, in their official capacities. Indeed, UNIP's commitment to the creation of a one-party state was open and unequivocal. However, for several years, President Kaunda maintained that this objective should be accomplished gradually, by means of the ballot box at regular elections, and without the enactment of legislation to prohibit the existence of opposition par-ties.[58] Kaunda's position implied a practical distinction between the right of opposition, which would be respected, and the value of

57. The basic document, authored by Kaunda, is *Humanism in Zambia and a Guide to Its Implementation* (Lusaka: Zambia Information Services, n.d.). The economic implications of "humanism" were elaborated in Republic of Zambia, *Zambia Towards Economic Independence*, Address of His Excellency Dr. K. D. Kaunda, President of the Republic of Zambia, to the National Council of the United National Indepen-dence Party, at Mulungushi, April 19, 1968 (Lusaka: n.d.). See also Kenneth Kaun-da, *A Humanist in Africa: Letters to Colin Morris from Kenneth Kaunda, President of Zambia* (London: Longmans, Green, 1966). For an incisive, skeptical critique, see Fola Soremekun, "The Challenge of Nation-Building: Neo-Humanism and Politics in Zambia, 1967–1969," *Genève-Afrique 9* (1970): 1–39; and Fola Soremekun, "Ken-neth Kaunda's Cosmic Neo-Humanism," *Genève-Afrique 9*, 2 (1970): 1–28.

58. *Address by His Excellency Dr. Kenneth Kaunda, President of the Republic of Zambia to the Mulungushi Conference*, presented to the Annual General Conference of the United National Independence Party, August 15, 1967 (Lusaka: Government Print-er, n.d.), p. 13.

opposition, which would not be conceded. Inexorably, official intolerance toward the existence of organized opposition became pronounced.[59] But resilient opposition to the ruling party persisted on a sectional basis, most notably among Tonga-speaking people in the Southern and Central provinces, and among the Lozi in Barotseland. In the first general election since independence, held at the end of 1968, UNIP won 81 seats (30 of them unopposed) to 24 by the African National Congress, which nonetheless dominated the Southern and Barotseland (now Western) provinces.[60]

The tendency for political divisions in African countries to coincide with ethnosectional or "tribal" cleavages is frequently cited as a justification for the creation of one-party states. Even principled critics of the one-party state have acknowledged the saliency of this problem.[61] From the standpoint of those who are devoted to national development, it is difficult to see what is gained when Lozi- or Tonga-speaking people elect legislative representatives who are opposed to the predominant national party. What is more, the circumstances whereby particular ethnosectional groups become oppositionist are sometimes fortuitous: most Tonga-speaking voters have remained loyal to their favorite son, Harry M. Nkumbula, until recently president-general of the African National Congress, who is acknowledged by his opponents no less than his followers as the "father" of Zambian nationalism; Lozi voters abandoned UNIP partly as a result of ethnic tensions that had germinated within that party.[62] Heretofore, sectional opposition has been insufficient to threaten the overall political supremacy of UNIP. Consequently, competition between UNIP and its sectional rivals appears to be little more than a reflection or extension of more significant intergroup conflicts within the dominant party

59. In 1968, the United party, a small but significant party that drew its support mainly from among Lozis disaffected from UNIP, was banned following a violent incident.

60. Ian Scott and Robert Molteno, "The Zambian General Elections," *Africa Report* 14 (January 1969): 42–47; R. A. Young, "The 1968 General Elections," in *Zambia in Maps*, ed. Davies, pp. 52–55. When Parliament reconvened, the speaker of the National Assembly declined to recognize the ANC as the official opposition party on the ground that it could not muster a quorum of one-fourth of the members.

61. See, for example, W. Arthur Lewis, *Politics in West Africa* (London: George Allen and Unwin, 1965), pp. 64–74.

62. Robert I. Rotberg, "Tribalism and Politics in Zambia," *Africa Report* 12 (December 1967): 29–35.

itself.[63] These conflicts are frequently manifested in "tribalist" forms, although their root causes are really embedded in the dismal conditions of underdevelopment rather than ethnic diversity.[64] In any event, the intensification of this kind of conflict within UNIP has imposed an immense burden of mediation on the towering and conciliatory presence of President Kaunda.[65]

Between 1969 and 1971, Kaunda endeavored to minimize the divisive impact of sectional rivalries within UNIP by instituting reforms in party organization. These measures proved to be controversial; they were deeply resented by a number of Bemba-speaking politicians, who had been prominent in the party for many years.[66] At length, in August 1971, a former vice-president of Zambia, Simon Kapwepwe, resigned from UNIP to lead the newly formed United Progressive party (UPP). This development threatened to undermine UNIP's support among Bemba-speaking people in northeastern Zambia and in the crucial Copperbelt Province, where Bemba-speakers predominate.[67] After seven months of high political tension, during which time the potential for violence was often realized,[68] the government banned the UPP as a subversive organization and placed its leading members in detention. Kaunda then appointed a national commission to make recommendations for the establishment of a "one-party participatory

63. William Tordoff, ed., *Politics in Zambia* (Manchester: Manchester University Press, 1974; Berkeley, Los Angeles, London: University of California Press, 1974), esp. chap. 3.

64. See Thomas Rasmussen, "Political Competition and One-Party Dominance in Zambia," *The Journal of Modern African Studies* 7 (October 1969): 419–420; also Richard L. Sklar, "Political Science and National Integration—A Radical Approach," *The Journal of Modern African Studies* 5 (1967): 6–7; and Michael F. Lofchie, "Observations on Social and Institutional Change in Independent Africa," in *The State of the Nations: Constraints on Development in Independent Africa*, ed. Michael F. Lofchie (Berkeley, Los Angeles, London: University of California Press, 1971), pp. 274–276.

65. Although Kaunda was born and raised in the north of Zambia—among Bemba-speaking people—where his father served as a Presbyterian missionary, both of his parents come from Malawi. As Rotberg says, he is "atribal" in the Zambian context ("Tribalism and Politics in Zambia," pp. 31, 34). It has been reported that the task of selecting UNIP's candidates for the general election of 1968 was delegated to Kaunda personally by the party's National Council (Scott and Molteno, p. 43).

66. See Colin Legum, ed., *Africa Contemporary Record* (London: Rex Collings, 1970), 2:B230–B232; 3:B207–B211; 4:B253–B263.

67. See Robert Molteno, "Zambia and the One Party State," *East Africa Journal* 9 (February 1972): 6–18.

68. Highly contentious by-elections, involving coercive campaigning on the part

democracy" in Zambia.[69] Constitutional changes were effected in 1973: the president now appoints a prime minister (replacing the vice-president), who heads the government, and a secretary-general of the sole legal party—UNIP.[70] Presidential and parliamentary elections were held in December 1973; voters could choose between rival UNIP candidates in 125 constituencies. Although Kaunda, unopposed, was elected to a third five-year term as president, fewer than one-third of the registered electorate actually voted. Evidently, the search for durable means to mediate and resolve conflicts in this politically vibrant society will continue.

Features of the Economy

Preliminary Note on Currencies and Weights.—In January 1968, the Zambian pound was replaced by a new unit of currency, the Kwacha (which means "dawn" in Ci-nyanja and is understood to signify national freedom). Two Kwacha were worth one old pound, which was at par with sterling before the British devaluation of November 1967. As Zambia did not devalue at that time, the Kwacha was then worth approximately £0.58 (58p) sterling. In December 1971, the Kwacha was officially pegged to the U.S. dollar, reducing its sterling value to £0.54 (54p). The Kwacha was worth approximately U.S. $1.40 until the American devaluation of February 1973, at which time its value increased to $1.55.

Prior to Zambia's adoption of the metric system of weights and measurers in 1970, the avoirdupois units "short ton" (2,000 lbs.) and "long ton" (2,204 lbs.) were used. Now, the metric ton (2,204.6 lbs.), expressed "tonne" and "tonnes" (pl.), is the standard unit.

---

of the ruling party, were held at this juncture as a result of a constitutional provision that required any member of the Assembly who ceases to be a member of his party to vacate his seat. While Kapwepwe was reelected to Parliament in a Copperbelt constituency, the other candidates of his party were defeated. See Cherry Gertzel, Kasuka Mutukwa, Ian Scott, Malcolm Wallis, "Zambia's Final Experience of Inter-Party Elections: The By-Elections of December 1971," *Kroniek van Afrika* (June 1972), pp. 57–77.

69. The significance of the term "participatory democracy" in Zambia is discussed in chap. 6.

70. See Republic of Zambia, *Report of the National Commission on the Establishment of a One-Party Participatory Democracy in Zambia,* Government Paper No. 1 of 1972 (Lusaka, 1972).

In this book, the context should clearly indicate which unit of currency or weight is being used and, where relevant, the correct foreign currency equivalent.

The analysis presented in this study is based largely upon evidence relating to aspects of the Zambian economy. Each of the four following chapters will examine features of that economy in some detail. At this point, a few of the most prominent features will be noted for introductory purposes.

As Charles Elliott observes, "An appreciation of the structure of Zambia's economy inevitably begins with emphasis upon the dominant position occupied by the copper industry."[71] During the first six years after independence (1965–1970), the copper industry contributed, on the average, 45 percent of net domestic product (at factor cost), 60 percent of governmental revenues, and 95 percent of the value of exports.[72] The abundant revenues generated by this industry have been sufficient to pay for an uninterrupted supply of two essential but nonindigenous resources, namely, skilled labor and "organizational entrepreneurship," defined by Stephen Goodman as "the ability to organize, manage, and motivate complex organizations with delegated authority."[73] In 1966 there were some 29,000 non-Africans employed in Zambia, at an average wage of K4,090, compared with 307,000 African employees, for whom the average wage was K480. The total wage bill for non-Africans, the overwhelming majority of whom were expatriates of European origin,[74] stood at K120 million, which was but K25 million less than that for all African employees.[75] In brief, Zambia's enviable ability to meet the costs of rapid economic development was tied to her extreme dependence upon expatriate manpower.[76]

71. "Introduction," in *Constraints on the Economic Development of Zambia*, ed. Charles Elliott (Nairobi: Oxford University Press, 1971), p. 3.

72. Based on Copper Industry Service Bureau, *Mindeco Mining Year Book of Zambia 1971* (Kitwe), p. 24. Charles Elliott notes that "the proportion of total exports accounted for by the leading sector" in Zambia is exceeded in only four African countries: "Libya (petrol), Mauritania (iron ore), Mauritius (sugar), and Gambia (groundnuts)." In *Constraints on the Economic Development of Zambia*, ed. Elliott, p. 3n.

73. Stephen Goodman, "The Foreign Exchange Constraint," in ibid., pp. 234–237.

74. Here, as elsewhere in this work, the term "European" is used in a generic sense to include white Rhodesians and South Africans.

75. C. R. M. Harvey, "Financial Constraints on Zambian Development," *Constraints on the Economic Development of Zambia*, ed. Elliott, p. 142.

76. "In 1965–6, all but 4 percent of high-level manpower with degrees and all but

On the eve of independence, Zambia contained a technologically modern mining enclave with certain appendages, mainly along the line-of-rail, in the midst of a rural and traditional subsistence economy. This condition has been termed social and economic "dualism."[77] It implies the coexistence within a single country of two distinct spheres of economic activity, wherein the development of one need not promote, and may even retard, that of the other. Concerning Zambia, Charles Elliott has remarked that "no country in Africa faces such a contrast between, on the one hand, an urban industrial sector that is growing and developing very rapidly, and on the other, a semi-stagnant rural economy which seems to defy, often at very considerable expense, all attempts at restructuring it in the process of growth."[78] What is more, inflation, generated by the rising cost of imports and wage increases in the urban industrial sector, has undermined the economic position of small-scale farmers, giving impetus to the dangerous drift of job seekers into urban areas, where unemployment has become a serious social problem.[79]

Before independence, the dual economy was rooted in racial discrimination. The deliberate exclusion of African commercial farmers from fertile lands close to the railway has been noted above. In 1964 there were some 1,300 European expatriate farmers in Zambia; by 1971 their number had dwindled to about 412. But this remnant actually raised most of the country's marketed agricultural produce.[80] Similarly, the consequences of educational

---

12 percent with School Certificates were non-Africans. Very few of these non-Africans were citizens. Even at the lower secondary (Form 2) level, over two-fifths of those employed were expatriate. In spite of enormous expansion of education and training in the 1960s the number of educated Zambians at the end of the decade was still too small to reduce very significantly the chronic dependence on noncitizens over almost the whole range of the country's most skilled and influential occupations" (Richard Jolly, "The Skilled Manpower Constraint," in ibid., p. 27).

77. Leading studies of the Northern Rhodesian economy during the terminal phase of colonial rule adopt this standpoint. See William J. Barber, *The Economy of British Central Africa: A Case Study of Economic Development in a Dualistic Society* (London: Oxford University Press, 1961), pp. 1–43; and Baldwin, pp. 40–57.

78. Elliott, p. 9.

79. C. E. Young, "Rural-Urban Terms of Trade," *African Social Research,* no. 12 (December 1971), pp. 91–94.

80. C. Stephen Lombard, *The Growth of Cooperatives in Zambia, 1914–71,* Zambian Papers, no. 6, University of Zambia Institute for African Studies (Manchester: Manchester University Press, 1971), p. 6; see also R. A. J. Roberts and Charles Elliott, "Constraints in Agriculture," in *Constraints on the Economic Development of Zambia,* ed. Elliott, p. 270.

deprivation, some of which have been indicated above, would be difficult to exaggerate. With respect to technical training, it should be remarked that until 1959 it was illegal for an African to be engaged as an apprentice in Northern Rhodesia.[81] Furthermore, as we have seen, leaders of the Federation of Rhodesia and Nyasaland viewed the Copperbelt and line-of-rail as a white settlement region, which should be managed to promote the prosperity of other such regions in the federation and might even be detached from the rest of Northern Rhodesia. Little thought was given to the possibility of balanced development within Northern Rhodesia itself. Consequently, Zambia inherited a great mining industry that was poorly and minimally integrated with the national economy as a whole.[82]

A final feature that deserves comment is the great extent of Zambia's economic dependence upon the white-ruled states of Southern Africa. The leaders of Zambia have been determined to disengage their nation from the economic orbit of the minority regimes. Their resolve was strengthened as a result of the unlawful declaration of independence from Great Britain by Southern Rhodesia's white minority regime in 1965. The consequences of this resolution will be examined in chapter 5.[83] Here it will suffice to identify those transport and supply relationships with Southern Africa that Zambia would not be able to replace without massive expenditure on alternative facilities.

In 1965 Zambia's foreign trade was almost wholly dependent upon Rhodesia Railways, which has access to seaports via the Mozambique and South African railway systems. In that year, 34 percent of all Zambian imports (by value) were purchased from Rhodesian suppliers. Subsequently, a considerable portion of

81. Republic of Zambia, *Manpower Report* (Lusaka: Government Printer, 1966), p. 1.

82. An interindustry study by Norman Kessel shows that transactions between the copper companies and other Zambian enterprises in 1966 were "largely limited to only a few producing sectors" ("Mining and the Factors Constraining Economic Development," in *Constraints on the Economic Development of Zambia*, ed. Elliott, p. 261). For a concise summary of the characteristics of mineral export economies, derived from Latin American cases but resembling the economy of newly independent Zambia, see Norman Girvan, "Multinational Corporations and Dependent Underdevelopment in Mineral Export Economies," *Social and Economic Studies* 19 (December 1970): 512.

83. See also Richard L. Sklar, "Zambia's Response to the Rhodesian Unilateral Declaration of Independence," in *Politics in Zambia*, ed. Tordoff pp. 320–362.

Zambia's foreign trade, including some two-thirds of her copper exports, was shifted to alternative routes. Yet Zambia has been compelled to rely upon the Rhodesian route for something like 70 to 75 percent of the growing volume of imports required by her expanding economy. (In 1973, however, the Rhodesian rail route for exports and imports was abruptly severed.)[84] While the share of Zambian imports attributable to Rhodesia had been slashed to 7 percent of the total value of imports by 1969, South Africa's share had risen, both absolutely and proportionately (from 20 to 22 percent), between 1965 and 1969.[85] Zambia has also been dependent upon Rhodesia for certain essential supplies. Thus, Zambian industry could not do without Rhodesian coal until 1970, when Zambia herself developed the capacity to produce high-grade coal. Similarly, Zambia has been largely dependent upon electricity generated in Rhodesia, although the power station concerned is part of a hydroelectric project that is jointly owned by Rhodesia and Zambia. Until the completion of alternative facilities within Zambia, due in 1974, it would not be possible to sustain normal copper production without the importation of electricity in massive quantities from Rhodesia.

In sum, the economic problems of newly independent Zambia were intractable. Society was divided between a comparatively prosperous commercial/industrial sector and a retarded rural sector, which comprised most of the population. There were extremely severe shortages of both indigenous skilled labor and Zambian personnel with adequate education and training to occupy leading positions in the bureaucratic, managerial, technical, and professional spheres. The giant mining industry fed tax revenues to the state but contributed minimally and narrowly to the country's economic development. Furthermore, the new nation was burdened with a repugnant but clinging legacy of economic dependence upon Southern Africa. The first African government, established in 1964, groped for ways and means to cope with these problems, which were soon to be complicated by an international crisis over Rhodesia. Invariably, these problems

84. See chap. 5.

85. Republic of Zambia, Ministry of Finance, *Economic Report 1970* (Lusaka: Government Printer, 1971), pp. 61–63. Imports from Rhodesia, valued at K71,077,000 in 1965, were down to K21,772,000 (mainly for coal and electricity) in 1969; the corresponding figures for South Africa are K41,379,000 in 1965 and K69,946,000 in 1969.

involve the government's relationship with the country's dominant industry. Zambia's future—the substance of what will be
achieved by way of social reconstruction—may depend mainly
upon the nature and conduct of this relationship.

TWO

The Division of Wealth

Independent Zambia was richly endowed with a great source of wealth—a copper industry second to none among the copper exporting nations of the world. Under colonial rule, this industry had generated both handsome profits for its foreign owners and abundant public revenues that were mainly used to finance white-settler interests in both Northern and Southern Rhodesia. Meanwhile, as we have seen, relatively little was done to promote the material interests of the African people. Consequently, the government of independent Zambia was certain to be tested in the crucible of its policy on mining. Would it be able to regenerate this profitable industry as a foundation for national prosperity and development before the principal copper deposits have been exhausted or substantially depleted by the end of the century?

To cope purposefully and effectively with this challenge, the Zambian government would need to maximize the degree of consistency between its economic resources and its economic goals. If these goals were to be both ambitious and realistic, the government would need far more knowledge concerning the copper industry's potential output and much more control over its performance than it could expect to obtain so long as the pattern of ownership and control in that industry remained essentially as it had been during the colonial era. Without organizational reforms in the mining sector, the efforts of the government were likely to be undermined by a severe imbalance between its ends and means, or economic purposes and economic power.

The reforms of 1969–1970 represent a bold attempt by the government to remedy the imbalance between its purposes and its power. These measures involve both a new distribution of property rights in natural resources and the introduction of state participation in the ownership of the industry. The aims, methods, and proportionate financial results of these reforms will be assessed in this chapter. However, the actual, concrete financial results will depend upon the long-term operational effectiveness of the new system, involving such factors as the expansion of mine capacity, the stabilization of copper prices, the efficiency of marketing methods, and the establishment of copper-related industries. These matters will be considered in chapter 3.

THE CORPORATE STRUCTURE OF THE MINING INDUSTRY

Until 1970 the Zambian mining industry was controlled by two groups of foreign-owned companies, the Anglo American Corporation Group and the Roan Selection Trust Group. In 1969 the former group produced about 52 percent of Zambia's copper output, while the latter produced 48 percent.[1] On January 1, 1970, the Zambian government acquired a 51 percent share in the ownership of the mining companies. However, the existing pattern of dual organization was retained under the new arrangement for financial and management purposes. In the course of the brief description of the corporate structure of the industry that follows, the reader may wish to refer to map 3 and figure 1.

The Two Groups of Companies before Nationalization

The Anglo American Corporation Group.—The central unit of the group before nationalization was Zambian Anglo American Limited (ZAMANGLO), a finance and investment company incorporated in the Republic of Zambia. In addition to its paramount mining interests, ZAMANGLO had invested in various industrial and agricultural enterprises with a combined book value of approximately K3.7 million, or less than 1 percent of the book value of the mining and metallurgical assets of the AAC Group in Zambia.[2] ZAMANGLO's main subsidiary companies in the mining industry were the following:[3]

1. Copper Industry Service Bureau, *RST and Anglo American Corporation Mining Year Book of Zambia, 1969* (Kitwe), p. 5.
2. These interests included the following: breweries, cement production, clay product manufactures, copper fabrication, production of tires, welding electrodes, and potable spirits. Other interests of this group included commercial banking and the hotel business. *Anglo American Corporation of South Africa Limited 1970 Annual Report,* p. 34.
3. Sources for this information: *Zambian Anglo American Limited 1969 Annual Report;* Zambian Anglo American Limited, *Statement by the Chairman, Mr. H. F. Oppenheimer,* November 1967; December 1968; "Review by the President Mr. M. B. Hofmeyr, Zambia Copper Investments Limited," *African Development* (November 1970); pp. 20–21; *The Anglo American Corporation Group in Zambia* (Lusaka, n.d.).

MAP 3.

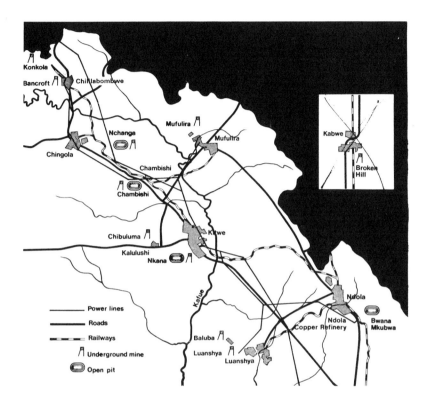

Mines and towns of the Copperbelt, based on the *Mindeco Mining Year Book of Zambia 1971* (Kitwe), p. 8. Reproduced by permission.

RHOKANA CORPORATION LIMITED, a copper mining company, located at Kitwe-Nkana. In 1969 ZAMANGLO held 53.7 percent of this company, which began production in 1932.

NCHANGA CONSOLIDATED COPPER MINES LIMITED, located at Chingola. Nchanga, which began to produce in 1939, is the second largest copper mine in the world, after the Chuquicamata mine in Chile. In 1969 ZAMANGLO and Rhokana Corporation together held 57.1 percent of this company, with Rhokana holding the larger share—34.7 percent.

BANCROFT MINES LIMITED, a copper company located at Chililabombwe. Nchanga held 99.4 percent of this company, which began production in 1957. To keep this mine in operation it is necessary to pump out an immense amount of water, up to 76 million gallons per day in 1970.

RHOKANA COPPER REFINERIES LIMITED, located at Kitwe-Nkana. This facility, opened in 1935, was jointly and evenly owned by Rhokana and Nchanga.

THE ZAMBIA BROKEN HILL DEVELOPMENT COMPANY LIMITED, a lead and zinc mine at Kabwe, 90 miles south of the Copperbelt. This mine, in production since 1906 and owned by diverse shareholders, has been managed by the Anglo American Corporation for many years.[4]

Lastly, KANSANSHI COPPER MINING COMPANY LIMITED, a small but historic mine, over 100 miles west of the Copperbelt. This mine had been worked by Africans considerably before the arrival of Europeans.[5] Owned by various interests (including the AAC Group, the RST Group, the Tanganyika Concessions Group, and the British South Africa Company), Kansanshi holds pride of place as "the first mine to produce copper under the regime of the British South Africa Company," apparently in 1908.[6] In 1957 the underground workings were flooded and all production ceased until the inauguration of a redevelopment program ten years later.

The Roan Selection Trust Group.—At the time of nationalization, the parent company of this group was an investment holding company, Roan Selection Trust Limited. Unlike its counterpart, ZAMANGLO, RST had few commercial interests outside of the mining field and services for the mining industry. Its mining and metallurgical interests were mainly vested in two principal subsidiaries, thus:[7]

    4. J. Austen Bancroft, *Mining in Northern Rhodesia* (London: The British South Africa Company, 1961), pp. 112–122.

    5. Ibid., pp. 37–38, 109; Richard Hall, *Zambia* (New York: Praeger, 1965), pp. 245–249, which also presents an account of traditional African methods of mining and smelting.

    6. Bancroft, p. 105.

    7. Sources: RST Group, *An Introduction to RST* (1964); F. Taylor Ostrander and Erasmus Kloman, "The Corporate Structure of Rhodesian Copperbelt Mining Enterprise," mimeographed for distribution by American Metal Climax, Inc., and dated August 31, 1962; RST Group of Companies, *Roan Selection Trust Limited 1969 Annual Report; Statement by the Chairman, Sir Ronald L. Prain,* November 1968 and October 1969.

LUANSHYA MINES LIMITED, a copper mining and processing company based at Luanshya. This is the site of the historic Roan Antelope Copper mine, which began production in 1931. As a result of its merger with Rhodesian Selection Trust Limited in 1962, Roan Antelope Copper Mines Limited became the Luanshya Division of the former company. With the emergence of independent Zambia in 1964, the name of this company was changed from "Rhodesian" to "Roan" Selection Trust. In 1968 the Luanshya Division became Luanshya Mines Limited, a wholly owned subsidiary of RST. Subsequently, Luanshya Mines became sole owner of an associated company, Ndola Copper Refineries Limited.

MUFULIRA COPPER MINES LIMITED, comprising three divisions. Mufulira Division, at Mufulira, includes the largest mine in the RST Group, second in production on the Copperbelt only to Nchanga. Indeed, the Mufulira mine, in production since 1933, is the second largest underground mine in the world, after El Teniente in Chile. A refinery was installed at Mufulira in 1952. Chibuluma Division, located at Kalulushi and developed with the aid of a £5 million U.S. government loan, began production in 1956. Formerly Chibuluma Mines Limited, it was taken over by Mufulira in 1967. At that time, Chambishi Mines Limited, at Chambishi, which began production in 1965, also became a division of the Mufulira company. RST Limited then held 65.6 percent of Mufulira Copper Mines Limited. The rest of the share capital, 34.4 percent, was held by ZAMANGLO and its subsidiaries.

Two other RST subsidiaries included mines that were not as yet in production:

BALUBA MINES LIMITED, a developing orebody near Luanshya, with ownership divided between the two groups thus: RST, 65 percent; ZAMANGLO and its subsidiaries, 30.3 percent.

MWINILUNGA MINES LIMITED (KALENGWA). The mining division of this mining and prospecting company was based on a small but high grade developing orebody at Kalengwa, more than 200 miles west of the Copperbelt. RST owned 53.5 percent; ZAMANGLO and other companies in the AAC Group were minority shareholders.

It should be noted that the Anglo American Corporation had significant minority shareholdings in several mining and prospecting companies administered by RST. This relationship was not reciprocal, since, with one insignificant exception, namely Kansanshi Copper Mining Company, RST did not hold shares in the Zambian mines controlled by the Anglo American Corporation.[8]

"Economic Independence" and the New Corporate Structure

In August 1969 President Kaunda announced his government's decision to acquire a 51 percent interest in the existing mines, and at least that much of the ownership of mines that would be opened in the future.[9] This announcement, coming after previous official disavowals of any intent to nationalize the mines, took many by surprise. Explaining the move, Kaunda emphasized his continuing dissatisfaction with the investment and development policies of the mining companies. Another, perhaps paramount reason, would be the profound commitment of many Zambian leaders to the goal of "economic independence." A third explanation turns on speculation about political maneuvering within the ruling party. By nationalizing the mines, Kaunda appeared to steal the thunder of radicals within UNIP. The timing of Kaunda's sensational announcement also forestalled a showdown between supporters and opponents of controversial Vice-President Simon Kapwepwe, who was destined to break with the party at a later stage.[10]

For this analysis, the latter explanation is the least relevant. One need not minimize the significance of factional conflict to feel that in this case it was at the very most a precipitating event. In other words, an examination of the factional struggle may be useful to

8. RST's interest in Kansanshi Copper Mining Company Limited was reported to be 10 percent. Ostrander and Kloman, p. 8.

9. *Towards Complete Independence*, Address by His Excellency the President, Dr. K. D. Kaunda, to the UNIP National Council held at Matero Hall, Lusaka, August 11, 1969 (Lusaka, n.d.).

10. It has been reported that seven out of eight provincial delegations to a conference of the UNIP National Council in August 1969 had planned to support a motion of no confidence in the vice-president. This would have alienated many Bemba-speaking members of the party. President Kaunda set forth the new economic policy in his opening address. He then adjourned the conference, instructing the delegates to return to their home areas to explain and defend "the economic revolution." See Martin Meredith, "Zambia: Kaunda on Top," *Africa Report* 15 (May 1970): 5–6; Colin Legum, ed., *Africa Contemporary Record* (London, 1970), 2:B231.

explain *how* the mines came to be nationalized in 1970, but not *why*. For the latter query, deeply held convictions about economic development and the meaning of independence seem most pertinent.[11] The reason given by Kaunda, bearing on the rate of mining investment and development, will be considered in the latter part of this chapter. The second reason, concerning the quest for economic independence, may be considered briefly at this point.

Mining and Mineral Rights—Aside from the obvious question of control over the industry, there were issues arising from controversial property rights in the natural resource itself. These included rights to the ownership of minerals, involving the receipt of royalties, as well as mining rights and prospecting rights. Throughout the colonial era, mineral rights in Northern Rhodesia had been held mainly by the British South Africa Company. This company, formed by Cecil Rhodes, was chartered by the British government in 1889 to administer territories in central Africa. From the outset, it engaged agents to obtain mineral and other concessions from traditional rulers. When the charter was terminated in 1924, an agreement with the British government confirmed the company's continued ownership of mineral rights in Rhodesia. In 1933 these rights were sold to the government in Southern Rhodesia for £2 million. In Northern Rhodesia, their validity was repeatedly challenged by various critics, including a paramount chief of Barotseland, a colonial governor, and spokesman for the European-settler community, most notably Roy Welensky. A truce, in the form of an agreement between the company, the government of Northern Rhodesia, and the British government, was called in 1950. This provided for an extension of the company's ownership of its mineral rights (free from special taxation) until 1986, in return

---

11. The well-informed economic journalist Antony Martin has suggested that strictly political considerations did affect the timing of Kaunda's announcement concerning 51 percent nationalization of the mining industry. He reports Kaunda to have discussed this matter in advance with a few trusted advisers only, whereas other matters covered in the same address had been carefully planned and thoroughly discussed. Yet Martin feels that "short-term political needs" happened to coincide with the bent of Kaunda's social philosophy, his perception of "long-range strategic considerations," his appreciation of economic realities, and the influence of certain advisers. He quotes with approval an assessment by *The Financial Times* (London) that in any explanation for the "'nature and timing'" of Zambia's action, "'the general political inspiration—the desire of the Zambians to become masters in their own house—should always be put first'" (*Minding Their Own Business* [London: Hutchinson, 1972], pp. 112, 153–164, 195).

for which the government of Northern Rhodesia would receive 20 percent of the royalty income.[12]

The concluding round of this contest was fought by African leaders shortly before they attained independence for Zambia. At first, the British South Africa Company was reported to require a payment of £50 million in return for the mineral rights. It has been disclosed that H. F. Oppenheimer, chairman of the Anglo American Corporation Group and a member of the board of the BSA Company, attempted, without success, to facilitate an agreement on the payment of compensation by installments that would have been favorable to the company.[13] It should be noted, however, that neither Oppenheimer nor the Anglo American Corporation raised any objection in principle to a compulsory transfer of the mineral rights to the state. In the RST camp, fewer criticisms were likely to be voiced, since that company was not closely related to the BSA Company. At the height of the controversy, the chairman of the American corporation that held the predominant interest in RST publicly expressed his support for the stand taken by the Zambian leaders.[14] Ultimately, on the eve of independence, Kaunda's government compelled the company to relinquish the mineral rights for £4 million—Britain and Zambia were each to pay one-half of

12. See L. H. Gann, *A History of Northern Rhodesia: Early Days to 1953* (London: Chatto & Windus, 1964), pp. 189–191, 392–395; Northern Rhodesia, *The British South Africa Company's Claims to Mineral Royalties in Northern Rhodesia* (Lusaka, 1964); Peter Slinn, "The Legacy of the British South Africa Company: The Historical Background," in *Economic Independence and Zambian Copper*, ed. Mark Bostock and Charles Harvey, Praeger Special Studies in International Economics and Development (New York: Praeger, 1972), pp. 23–52; and the brief summary in Lord Hailey, *An African Survey*, rev. ed. (London: Oxford University Press, 1957), p. 1521.

13. Hall, p. 231.

14. "As the Africans see it, the existence of a private company which has virtual sovereignty over the mineral rights of the country is an anachronism. . . . It is also quite apparent that there is a considerable difference in African eyes between productive capital and non-productive capital and in the treatment to be accorded each type. In this respect the position of the operating copper companies is entirely distinct. The latter have been assured many times by the responsible African leaders of Northern Rhodesia that their continued existence under private ownership will be respected. This is in keeping with a national policy which aims to attract new private investment to that country" (Walter Hochschild, "Chairman's Remarks at Annual Stockholders' Meeting—May 7, 1964," in American Metal Climax, Inc., "Statements Concerning African Developments—1960–1965" mimeo.) It will be seen that this distinction between productive and nonproductive companies has been relevant to the payment of compensation rather than immunity from nationalization.

that sum. Zambia's contribution was made as a "show of good-will," rather than a recognition of any legal or moral obligation.[15]

The elimination of these purely parasitical rights of ownership, which had been enjoyed by the BSA Company, did not dispel all Zambian objections to the inherited system of mineral control. In the first place, several other companies remained in possession of mineral rights in various parts of the country. Second, and most significant, the BSA Company had granted exclusive mining and prospecting rights, covering vast areas, to the major mining groups. The crucial decision to that effect, taken by the company in 1922, provided for the making of such grants to financially strong mining interests. It has been commended by one authority as "perhaps the most important single step which led to the opening up of the Copperbelt."[16] At the same time, these so-called special grants also had the effect of shielding monopolistic mineral rights in large areas where little or no prospecting or mining was done. Consequently, they were resented as infringements of the Zambian government's right to promote economic development through its control of natural resources. Moreover, the exclusive mining rights involved were held by the mining companies "in perpetuity, i.e., forever and ever."[17] As an added burden, these rights were thought to be protected by section 18 of the Zambian Constitution, relating to deprivation of property, one of numerous sections concerning fundamental rights, the judiciary, and other topics, that could only be amended by a national referendum in which a majority of the voters would give their assent. Kaunda himself declared that section 18 had been framed by the British

15. Quoted in Hall, p. 233, which presents a brief yet vivid account of this dramatic confrontation. See also Richard Hall, *The High Price of Principles: Kaunda and the White South* (London: Hodder and Stoughton, 1969), pp. 69–92; and M. L. O. Faber, "The Recovery of the Mineral Rights," in *Towards Economic Independence: Papers on the Nationalization of the Copper Industry in Zambia*, ed. M. L. O. Faber and J. G. Potter, University of Cambridge Department of Applied Economics, Occasional Paper 23 (Cambridge: Cambridge University Press, 1971), pp. 40–61.

16. R. L. Prain, *The Copperbelt of Northern Rhodesia*, The Henry Morley Lecture (London: Royal Society of Arts, 1955), pp. 7–8; see also Bancroft, p. 73; and Francis L. Coleman, *The Northern Rhodesia Copperbelt 1899–1962* (Manchester: Manchester University Press, 1971), pp. 32–35.

17. *Towards Complete Independence*, Address by . . . K. D. Kaunda, pp. 30–33. This phrase is attributed by President Kaunda to Cecil Rhodes. Cf. The Conscession of King Lewanika, Paramount Chief of the Barotse Nation, to the British South Africa Company, 1900, in L. H. Gann, *The Birth of a Plural Society* (Manchester: Manchester University Press, 1958), p. 216.

government for the "specific purpose" of protecting the interests of the mining companies.[18]

In June the special amending procedure was abolished by national referendum. This cleared the way for Parliament to amend section 18 so that the government of Zambia could expropriate without compensation both those mineral rights not previously acquired by the state and the extensive mining rights of the major mining groups. The new policy, outlined by the president in his address on nationalization and embodied in the 1969 Mines and Minerals Act[19] provided for the introduction of mining leases of twenty-five years duration for both the existing mines and new ones. Exclusive prospecting licenses of limited duration for designated areas would be confirmed or granted upon the condition that the state would be entitled to acquire a majority ownership interest in any new mine. Otherwise, all mining rights in areas where no prospecting had been done since independence would revert to the state. Subsequently, the two groups of companies were reported to have relinquished more than 65,000 square miles to the state and to have obtained licenses for the immediate exploration of less than 10,000 square miles of that territory, which had been their exclusive preserve.[20]

State Participation—With respect to the 51 percent takeover of existing mines, Kaunda had said that compensation would be based on "a fair value represented by book value." Furthermore, he insisted that payment for the shares would be made out of dividends that would accrue to the government after nationaliza-

18. *Towards Complete Independence*, Address by . . . K. D. Kaunda, p. 31. Hall also suggests that section 18 had been written to protect the mineral rights of the BSA Company. *Zambia*, p. 232; and see Faber, pp. 49–50.

19. Republic of Zambia, *The Laws of Zambia*, chap. 329; see A. R. Drysdall and E. J. Langevad, *The Mines and Minerals Act, 1969, and The Mineral Tax Act, 1970*, Economic Report No. 26, Republic of Zambia, Ministry of State Participation (Lusaka: 1970); and the succinct analysis by Alan Drysdall, "Prospecting and Mining Activity, 1895–1970," in *Economic Independence and Zambian Copper*, ed. Bostock and Harvey, pp. 77–81.

20. *Africa Research Bulletin*, Economic Financial and Technical Series 7, 1 (February 1970): 1593 (A). The special grant and prospecting areas held by RST were reported to total 44,502 square miles. W. G. Garlick, "How the Copperbelt Orebodies Were Formed," *Horizon* (August 1959), p. 10. Apparently the holdings of the Anglo American Corporation totalled between 25,000 and 30,000 square miles, indicating a grand total for both groups of between 70,000 to 75,000 square miles. The guarantee of first option to the existing mining and exploration companies was reported to cover 12.5 percent of the areas that they had formerly held. Drysdall and Langevad, p. 2.

tion, since other revenues were needed for development and could not be spared.

As anticipated, there were initial disagreements between the government and the companies over the method of payment, the basis of assessment, and the amount of compensation. The principle of state participation itself was not in question, nor did the acquisition of a majority share by the government become a question of principle for the companies. In the words of the chairman of RST, "it is a matter of record that the Zambian companies have in the past offered equity participation, but the Government has hitherto been unwilling to pursue such a suggestion."[21]

Furthermore, the RST chairman disclosed that proposals made by the companies were "based on the relatively simple proposition of a commutation of royalties and export tax into equity which would not be paid for."[22] In view of the government's contrary decision to collect taxes in full, amounting to about 73 percent of gross profits during the period of repayment, some company officials thought that part of the compensation should be paid in cash. Some objected to the basis of valuation, holding that the book value of the assets, which had been specified by President Kaunda as the basis of compensation, would not be a fair price.[23] Nonetheless, an agreement was reached in November 1969 in conformity with Kaunda's August address.

21. *Statement to Shareholders of Roan Selection Trust Limited by the Chairman, Sir Ronald L. Prain,* August 22, 1969. The influential *Report of the UN/ECA/FAO Economic Survey Mission on the Economic Development of Zambia* (Ndola, 1964) had recommended that the government of Zambia should become a shareholder in the mining industry (p. 169). In a public address in Lusaka, December 1964, R. L. Prain declared with reference to this proposal: "I would welcome this very much indeed. I know that this view is shared by the other group" (Sir Ronald L. Prain, *Selected Papers* [London: 1968], 4:11.

In 1968 the chairman of the Anglo American Corporation Group of Companies stated: "The desire of Zambians to play a larger part in the modern sector of their economy is understandable, and I would certainly favour a policy of partnership between private business and the Zambian State" (Anglo American Corporation of South Africa Limited, *Statement by the Chairman, Mr. H. F. Oppenheimer,* May 15, 1968).

The companies were reported to have offered the Zambian government a minority interest of between 30 percent and 50 percent at the time of independence. *The Wall Street Journal,* August 13, 1969, citing *The Times of Zambia.*

22. *Statement to shareholders of Roan Selection Trust Limited by the Chairman, Sir Ronald L. Prain,* August 22, 1969. This follows the recommendation of the UN Economic Survey Mission that the Zambian government might "receive equity shares in lieu of royalties and taxes" (*Report of the UN/ECA/FAO Economic Survey Mission,* p. 169).

In return for a 51 percent interest in the equity of the operating companies, a new state agency, Zambia Industrial and Mining Corporation Limited (ZIMCO), issued loan stock and bonds bearing interest at 6 percent per annum that were accepted by the former owners. Repayment was calculated on the basis of the book value of the mining and metallurgical assets of the companies concerned at the end of 1969. This was estimated to total K410 million ($574 million), divided between the two groups as follows: Anglo American Corporation, K245.2 million ($343.3 million); RST, K164.8 million ($230.7 million). Shareholders of the AAC Group received loan stock in return for assets worth K126 million ($178 million); those of the RST Group acquired bonds in return for assets worth K84 million ($117.8 million). The loan stock and bonds were freely negotiable, fully guaranteed by the Zambian government, exempt from Zambian taxation, and payable in United States dollars, in equal semiannual installments. Repayment periods of eight and twelve years were set for RST and AAC respectively. It was agreed that when installments due come to less than two-thirds of the dividend received by the Zambian government, payment to the creditors would be accelerated. This provision would come into effect for RST in 1971 and for AAC in 1972, depending upon the price of copper. It was also agreed that the mining companies would be permitted to externalize all of their nonoperating assets, including large sums of cash, reported to total over K45 million, which had been blocked since the imposition of exchange control restrictions in April 1968. In return, each group committed itself to hold a fixed percentage of these assets available

23. "Jean Vuillequez, an American who is vice chairman of Roan Selection Trust, said in an interview last week that 'there is no reason why Zambia cannot pay cash for some of this.' He cited an article in The Times of Zambia reporting that the country's balance of trade in the first six months of 1969 showed a surplus of more than $250 million.

" 'They always plead poverty, he said. 'It just isn't true.'

"Mr. Vuillequez, whose company is about 80 per cent owned by American shareholders, also challenged book value as a fair price. A far more just figure, he said, would be 10 times the company's annual earnings—which would more than double the price proposed by the Government" (R. W. Apple, Jr. in The New York Times, September 29, 1969).

The replacement value of RST mining properties has been estimated to be four to five times greater than the book value. Fortune (August 1970), p. 190. Cf. J. G. Potter, "The 51 Per Cent Nationalization of the Zambian Copper Mines," in Towards Economic Independence: Papers on the Nationalization of the Copper Industry in Zambia, ed. Faber and Potter, pp. 117–118.

for reinvestment in the development of its respective mining prop-erties. Finally, it was agreed that both groups would be given contracts to provide management, technical consultancy, and ex-clusive sales agency services along established lines for a minimum period of ten years.[24]

To facilitate the new arrangement, each group undertook to con-solidate the mining, smelting, and refining operations of the sev-eral companies affected into one new company for the group/state joint venture. Thus Bancroft Mines Limited, Nchanga Consoli-dated Copper Mines Limited, Rhokana Corporation Limited, and Rhokana Copper Refineries Limited were amalgamated into Ban-croft Mines Limited, which then changed its name to Nchanga Consolidated Copper Mines Limited (NCCM). Similarly, the Kalengwa Mine of Mwinilunga Mines Limited, Luanshya Mines Limited, and Mufulira Copper Mines Limited were amalgamated into the latter company, which changed its name to Roan Consoli-dated Mines Limited (RCM). On the governmental side, ZIMCO, with President Kaunda as chairman, and a board of directors that included trade unionists as well as cabinet ministers and other prominent citizens, acquired two wholly owned subsidiaries: The Industrial Development Corporation of Zambia Limited (INDECO), to administer diverse investments; and the Mining Development Corporation Limited (MINDECO), to hold both the government's share of the mining equity and its options under the 1969 Mines and Minerals Act to acquire 51 percent of all new mines.

Before nationalization, the two so-called group companies (in-vestment holding companies), namely, ZAMANGLO and RST Limited, had been domiciled in Zambia. These companies have been reincorporated abroad. ZAMANGLO transferred its place of domicile to Bermuda, where it created a new subsidiary, Zambia Copper Investments Limited (ZCI), in which it held approximately

---

24. For detailed, analytical summaries of the nationalization agreements, see R. M. Bostock, D. H. Murray, and C. Harvey, *Anatomy of the Zambia Copper Nationalisation,* An Occasional Paper by Maxwell Stamp (Africa) Limited (London, 1970), hereinafter cited as *Anatomy of the Zambia Copper Nationalisation;* Bostock and Harvey, *Economic Independence and Zambian Copper,* esp. chap. 7, app. A, B; and Potter, pp. 91–127. The negotiations have been vividly reconstructed by Martin, pp. 163–179, who records the leading role of Andrew Sardanis—"chief negotiator and architect of the Zambian strategy." Sardanis, a Zambian citizen of Greek Cypriot extraction, was then chairman of the Industrial Development Corporation of Zam-bia and Kaunda's principal adviser on the issues of nationalization.

50 percent of the shares. All of the assets of the operating mines of the former AAC Group that were not taken over by the government were vested in ZCI. As a result, this company acquired 49 percent of NCCM and a 12.3 percent interest in RCM. Those shares in ZCI that were not acquired by ZAMANGLO were assigned to diverse shareholders, some of whom are identified below as minority shareholders in the Zambian interests of the AAC Group. Apart from the mining sector, ZAMANGLO retained its interests in various properties, including Zamanglo Industrial Corporation Limited (ZAMIC), a wholly owned subsidiary, newly formed to hold the industrial and agricultural assets of the AAC Group in Zambia.

The successor to RST Limited, namely, RST International, Inc., is incorporated in the United States. This company acquired only 20 percent of RCM—the minimum shareholding required by the Zambian government for any company under contract with it to perform managerial and sales services.[25] The remaining shares in RCM—approximately 16.7 percent of the total—were distributed among some 44,000 investors, the vast majority of whom were Americans. RST International retained its holdings in various developing mines, exploration companies, and enterprises outside of Zambia.

Subsequently, the Baluba Mining Company was incorporated into RCM's Luanshya Division, while the Kansanshi Copper Mining Company and the Zambia Broken Hill Development Company became part of NCCM.[26] Figure 1 shows the basic structure of ownership and control of the Zambian mining industry both before and after nationalization.

THE PARENT COMPANIES

As indicated in figure 1, the foreign shareholders in Zambia's copper industry are controlled by parent companies in South Africa and the United States. These will be identified in turn.

The Anglo American Corporation of South Africa

The Anglo American Corporation of South Africa Limited is a multipurpose company, engaged in mining, manufacturing, com-

25. According to its agreement with the government of Zambia, RST's contracts to perform such services were subject to cancellation if its shareholding fell beneath this 20 percent minimum. Roan Selection Trust Limited, *Explanatory Statement for Meetings of Shareholders to be held on 6th August, 1970,* June 30, 1970, pp. 3–4.

merce, investment, and finance. It is self-described as "the head of a group that comprises a large number of companies which the Corporation administers, but which in most cases are not subsidiaries in the statutory sense."[27] This so-called group system has proved to be a singularly effective method of business organization. It serves to maximize the extent of corporate control through intermediate holding companies. Thus a listing of the interests of the group in a recent annual report includes no fewer than 292 companies, of which 196 were administered within the group.[28] In many of these companies, the Anglo American Corporation itself owns less than 50 percent of the equity capital, counting both direct and indirect shareholdings. Nonetheless, all companies administered within the group, and some of the others, are closely linked to the "parent house" through management and the provision of administrative and technical services.[29]

The corporation was founded in 1917 by the late Sir Ernest Oppenheimer. Consciously, but without bluster, Sir Ernest followed in the economic footsteps of Cecil Rhodes.[30] As Rhodes had endeavored to become the "king" of diamonds, Oppenheimer, who was equally though differently ambitious, sought with far greater success to become preeminent both in the diamond world and in the sphere of gold production. Sir Ernest led the corporation as its chairman for forty years, until his death in 1957, when his son, the present chairman, Harry F. Oppenheimer, succeeded him.

The corporation was named to acknowledge the national identities of its original shareholders—American, British and South African. At the time of its formation, 50 percent of the capital was subscribed by Americans associated with the House of Morgan and the Newmont Mining Corporation.[31] Subsequently, the proportion of American shareholding became relatively insignificant as

26. *Roan Consolidated Mines Limited 1971 Annual Report*, p. 4; *Nchanga Consolidated Copper Mines Limited 1971 Annual Report*, p. 4.
27. *Anglo American Corporation of South Africa Limited 1969 Annual Report*, p. 51.
28. Ibid., pp. 52–54.
29. Ibid., p. 5. On the origin and effects of the "group system," see Theodore Gregory, *Ernest Oppenheimer and the Economic Development of Southern Africa* (Cape Town: Oxford University Press, 1962), pp. 90–94. This massive and richly documented work, commissioned by the Anglo American Corporation itself, is an invaluable mine of information, despite the author's wholly uncritical identification with his subject.
30. Cf. Ibid., pp. 22, 106.
31. Ibid., pp. 84–89; H. F. Oppenheimer, "Sir Ernest Oppenheimer: A Portrait by His Son," *Optima* 17 (September 1967): 95–103.

Figure 1. *Major Holdings of the Two Groups of Mining Companies in Zambia before and after Nationalization*

Before Nationalization

Anglo American Corp. (South Africa)

Rand Selection Corp. (South Africa)

ZAMANGLO (Zambia)

22.4% → Kansan-shi / Broken Hill

34.7% → Nchanga

99.4% → Bancroft

53.7% → Rhokana Corp.

50% → Rhokana Refineries

50% Bancroft

54% → Kalengwa

65% → Baluba

30.3%

34.4%

AMAX (U.S.A.)

42.3% → RST (Zambia)

65.6% → Mufulira Copper Mines / Mufulira / Chibuluma / Chambishi

100% → Luanshya Mines

After Nationalization

Anglo American Corp. (South Africa)

Rand Selection Corp. (South Africa)

ZAMANGLO (Bermuda)

49.98% → ZCI (Bermuda)

49% / 51% → *NCCM* Chingola Konkola Rokana Broken Hill

Properties retained, including ZAMEX and ZAMIC

ZIMCO

100% → MINDECO

51% / 49%

51% / 20% → *RCM* Chibuluma Luanshya Mufulira N.C.R.

AMAX (U.S.A.)

100% → RST (U.S.A.)

Properties retained, including prospecting and explora-tion companies

Public

12.25% / 16.75%

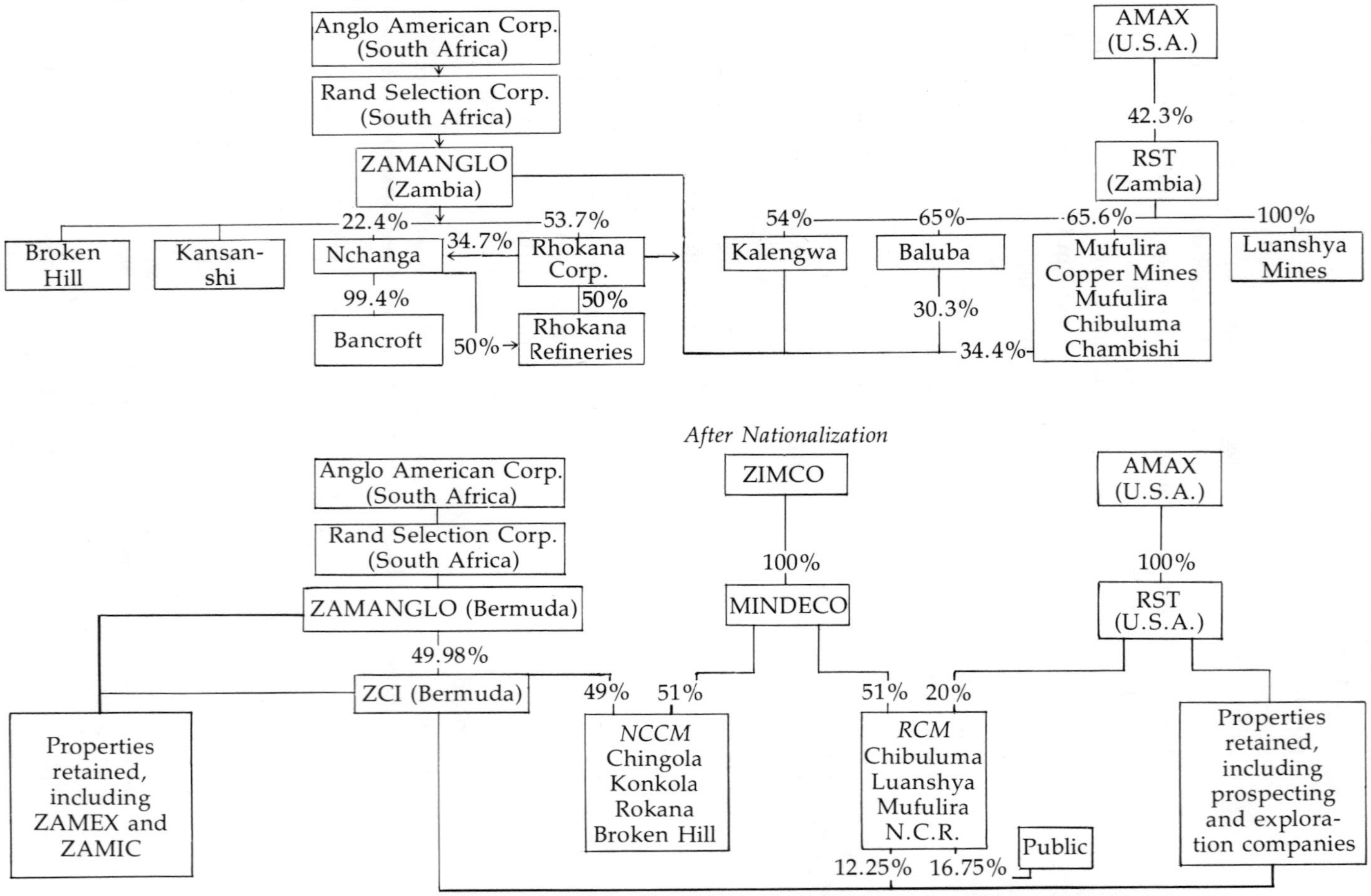

FIGURE 1

Key

SHORT FORM USED IN THE FIGURE	FULL NAME OF THE CORPORATE ENTITY OR SUBDIVISION
AMAX (U.S.A.)	American Metal Climax, Inc.
Anglo American Corp. (South Africa)	Anglo American Corporation of South Africa Limited
Baluba	Baluba Mines Limited
Bancroft	Bancroft Mines Limited
Broken Hill	The Zambia Broken Hill Development Company Limited; Broken Hill Division of NCCM
Chambishi	Chambishi Division of Mufulira Copper Mines
Chibuluma	Chibuluma Division of Mufulira Copper Mines; Chibuluma Division of RCM, comprising Chibuluma, Chambishi, and Kalengwa mines
Chingola	Chingola Division of NCCM; formerly Nchanga Consolidated Copper Mines Limited
Kalengwa	Mwinilunga Mines Limited (Kalengwa)
Kansanshi	Kansanshi Copper Mining Company Limited
Konkola	Konkola Division of NCCM: formerly Bancroft Mines Limited, incorporating Kansanshi Copper Mining Company
Luanshya	Luanshya Division of RCM incorporating Baluba Mines
Luanshya Mines	Luanshya Mines Limited
MINDECO	MINDECO Limited
Mufulira	Mufulira Division of Mufulira Copper Mines; Mufulira Division of RCM
Mufulira Copper Mines	Mufulira Copper Mines Limited
NCCM	Nchanga Consolidated Copper Mines Limited--NCCM
Nchanga	Nchanga Consolidated Copper Mines Limited
NCR	Ndola Copper Refinery Division of RCM
Rand Selection Corp. (South Africa)	Rand Selection Corporation Limited (South Africa)
RCM	Roan Consolidated Mines Limited
RST (U.S.A.)	RST International, Inc.
RST (Zambia)	Roan Selection Trust Limited
Rhokana Corp.	Rhokana Corporation Limited
Rhokana Refineries	Rhokana Copper Refineries Limited
Rokana	Rokana Division of NCCM; formerly Rhokana Corporation Limited and Rhokana Copper Refineries Limited; also incorporates the Bwana M'kubwa Mine
ZCI (Bermuda)	Zambia Copper Investments Limited
ZAMANGLO (Bermuda)	Zambian Anglo American Limited
ZAMANGLO (Zambia)	Zambian Anglo American Limited
ZAMEX	Zamanglo Exploration Limited
ZAMIC	Zamanglo Industrial Corporation Limited
ZIMCO	Zambia Industrial and Mining Corporation Limited

the corporation developed within a strictly British Imperial framework. In the latter 1920s, Oppenheimer's corporation stood as the main bulwark of Imperial capital that prevented American financial domination of the Rhodesian Copperbelt.[32] In 1971 it was officially reported that "more than half the share capital [of the corporation] is held in South Africa," while "the United Kingdom and other European countries" account "for about 42 per cent."[33] The directorate of the corporation, including the chairman (South African), joint deputy chairmen (British and South African), directors and alternate directors, comprised twenty-one South Africans and thirteen British.[34]

Today the holdings and operations of companies associated with the AAC Group span six continents. A representative sampling of interests outside of the group's primary sphere of activity in southern Africa might include the following: copper in Mauritania and Canada; potash in the United Kingdom; tin in Malaysia; diverse prospecting ventures in Canada, Mexico, Brazil, Fiji, Papua New Guinea, Australia, Thailand, Malagasy, and Zaire.

In recent years, mines of the Anglo American Corporation Group have accounted for 27 to 32 percent of gold production and 7 to 10 percent of copper production in the noncommunist part of the world. An associated company, De Beers Consolidated Mines Limited, has accounted for about 40 percent of world diamond production and has controlled the marketing of all diamonds, including Soviet diamonds in the West.[35] Heretofore, copper mining has ranked behind gold and diamonds as the third largest source of investment income for the Anglo American Corporation. In 1969, for example, copper accounted for 15 percent of the corporation's total income from investments, compared with 32 percent attributable to gold and 22 percent to diamonds.[36] While the exact percentage attributable to Zambian copper is not reported, this writer has

32. Gregory, pp. 29–32, 410–445. The "Rhodesian prospects" were crucial to efforts by Europeans to resist the operations of an American-controlled copper cartel. Alex Skelton, "Copper," in *International Control in the Non-Ferrous Metals*, William Yandell Elliott et al. (New York: Macmillan, 1937), p. 470.

33. *Anglo American Corporation of South Africa Limited 1970 Annual Report*, p. 5.

34. Ibid., p. 3. Until his death in 1971, an American, C. W. Engelhard, had been a member of the directorate.

35. While De Beers is administered outside of the AAC Group, it is intimately related to the group in shareholding and management. Thus H. F. Oppenheimer is chairman.

36. *Anglo American Corporation of South Africa Limited 1969 Annual Report*, p. 7. It should be noted that in addition to its income from investments (R33.9 million in

surmised that 12 percent would be near the mark, taking into account the increasingly significant operations in South Africa, Canada, and Mauritania.

The key company for Zambian copper investments, ZAMANG-LO, is shown by charts of the AAC Group to be a subsidiary of the Anglo American Corporation of South Africa itself, mediated in part by another large investment company, Rand Selection Corporation Limited.[37] A partial listing of shareholders in Nchanga Consolidated Copper Mines and Rhokana Corporation, obtained by this writer from corporation officials in 1967, reflected the controlling position of ZAMANGLO in both companies, as previously noted. This listing also revealed some French participation, 9 percent in Nchanga and 6.9 percent in Rhokana. Among other European shareholders, corporation sources specified Rio Tinto-Zinc Corporation Limited, a firm that has been identified with the Rothschild banking interest in Britain.[38] However, a substantial interest in Rio Tinto itself has been acquired by Charter Consolidated Limited, the principal company associated with the Anglo American Corporation in the United Kingdom.[39] It may be recalled that when the Zambian mines were nationalized, a new company, Zambia Copper Investments Limited (ZCI), was created to hold those assets of the companies affected that were not acquired by the state. It was noted that ZAMANGLO itself acquired only about 50 percent of ZCI. However, nothing here would suggest that any substantial portion of ZCI is held by owners outside of the Anglo American Corporation's web of control.

American Metal Climax

American capital has been paramount in Roan Selection Trust since 1927, when the American Metal Company Limited of New

---

1969), the corporation and its subsidiary companies earned R20.4 million from other sources, including interest payments and fees, before deductions. Ibid., p. 42. The South African Rand (R), like the Zambian Kwacha, was worth approximately U.S.$1.40.

37. Bostock and Harvey report that the Anglo American Corporation of South Africa holds 30 percent of ZAMANGLO, while Rand Selection Corporation holds 15 percent. Bostock and Harvey, *Economic Independence and Zambian Copper*, pp. 260–261.

38. Gregory, pp. 31, 422–430.

39. *Charter Consolidated Limited 1967 Annual Report and Accounts*, p. 23; in 1969, Charter Consolidated held 22.8 percent of ZAMANGLO. Bostock and Harvey, eds., p. 260.

York acquired a major interest in Roan Antelope Copper Mines Limited.[40] The American Metal Company itself had been formed in 1887 by a group of financiers associated with the German firm, Metallgesellschaft, and related firms in London and New York.[41] Its autonomy as an American company was firmly established as a consequence of World War I. However, the old ties to British mining finance proved durable, and the American Metal Company entered the Copperbelt mining field in partnership with a British company, Selection Trust Limited of London. Subsequently, in 1933, the latter company's direct investment was converted into a minority shareholding in its American partner.

In 1957 the American Metal Company and an associate of many years standing, Climax Molybdenum Company, merged to form American Metal Climax (AMAX), of New York. This company is the world's largest producer of molybdenum; recently, the Climax mine in Colorado has produced about one-half of all molybdenum consumed in the noncommunist part of the world.[42] In 1962 a highly successful American-based aluminum division was added, followed by ventures in agricultural chemicals, petroleum, and coal. Other ventures include iron mining in Australia, lead and zinc mining in Canada, nickel mining in New Caledonia, and oil exploration in the North Sea, in addition to numerous enterprises engaged in the processing and fabricating of minerals and metals in various parts of the world.

AMAX investments in base metal mining outside of the United States are mainly in Africa. In addition to its holding in RST, AMAX holds a substantial interest in Botswana RST (a copper and nickel property, as yet undeveloped),[43] a 29 percent interest in the highly lucrative Tsumeb Corporation Limited (a copper and lead producer) in Namibia, and an 18 percent interest in O'okiep Copper Company in South Africa. In 1969 dividend receipts from AMAX's investments in Africa totaled $21,820,000, derived as follows: RST Limited, $14,280,000; Tsumeb Corporation Limited,

40. Kenneth Bradley, *Copper Venture* (London: 1952), p. 92; see also RST Group, *An Introduction to RST*.

41. Seymour S. Bernfeld in collaboration with Harold K. Hochschild, "A Short History of American Metal Climax, Inc.," *1887–1962 American Metal Climax, Inc., World Atlas* (Chicago: Rand McNally and Company, 1962), pp. 1–16.

42. *American Metal Climax, Inc. (AMAX) 1966 Annual Report*, p. 13.

43. AMAX and a group headed by the Anglo American Corporation hold equal portions of the equity in Botswana RST, recently reported to be 30 percent each. *AMAX 1971 Annual Report*, p. 28.

$5,140,000; O'okiep Copper Company Limited, $2,400,000.[44] These African earnings amounted to about 21.5 percent of the company's total earnings before U.S. and foreign income taxes.[45] Earnings from investments in RST alone came to about 14.6 percent ($14.3 million out of $96.5 million).

The AMAX shareholding in RST Limited at the time of nationalization was 42.3 percent. The holdings of all American investors, including AMAX, amounted to some 80 percent of the issued shares.[46] Under the terms of the agreement on state participation reached with the Zambian government, all assets of RST that were not taken over by the government were vested in a new company, incorporated in the United States (Delaware), namely RST International, Inc. Such assets included exploration companies, sales companies, a 30.2 percent interest in Botswana RST Limited, and Zambian government bonds as well as the RST shareholding in Roan Consolidated Mines Limited. AMAX then acquired 100 percent of RST International by agreement of the boards of both companies. At the same time, it was decided that the former shareholders of RST, other than AMAX, would be compensated with a cash payment and a package of securities. This action was challenged by dissident American shareholders on the ground that the non-AMAX shareholders of RST had been falsely led to believe that the acquisition of RST by AMAX was an inescapable consequence of nationalization. Judicial proceedings in the United States established that disclosure provisions of the Securities and Exchange Act had been violated by AMAX and RST.[47] In fact, the board of RST, meeting without AMAX representatives, did canvass alternatives to merger with AMAX, in particular, the possible regeneration of RST as an independent international mining house, domiciled in either Luxembourg or the United States. This idea,

44. *AMAX 1969 Annual Report*, p. 39.

45. Ibid., p. 42.

46. In 1967 the shareholdings in RST were distributed as follows: AMAX, 45 percent; other U.S. investors, 39 percent; U.K. investors, 7 percent; others, 9 percent. Information obtained at the Executive Office of RST Limited in Lusaka.

47. The agreement between RST and AMAX provided that the non-AMAX shareholders of RST would receive in redemption of their shares a cash payment, a pro rata share of ZIMCO bonds, shareholdings in RCM up to 16.75 percent of the total, shares in Botswana RST Limited, and AMAX securities. RST shareholders, apart from AMAX, included approximately 40,000 U.S. citizens. The dissidents argued that the AMAX/RST agreement was unduly beneficial to AMAX at the expense of the non-AMAX shareholders of RST. Their suit did not object to the

favored in principle by the RST board, was abandoned with reluctance in view of the adverse financial and tax consequences that were foreseen by banking and legal consultants.[48] Evidently, the British directors of RST regretted the necessity of merger with AMAX.

AMAX itself is largely owned by Americans, although the largest single shareholding, 11.8 percent, belongs to the pioneer Copperbelt company, Selection Trust Limited of London.[49] A few British and Canadian members are included among the directors and officers of AMAX, the preponderant number of whom are Americans. Perhaps the best proof of the durability of this international relationship has been the distinctly British character of RST's management, exemplified by Sir Ronald Lindsay Prain, who was managing director of the RST Group from 1943 to 1968 and chairman from 1950 to 1970.

---

acquisition of RST shares by the government of Zambia; it was specifically limited to AMAX's acquisition of the entirety of RST.

In August 1970, the AMAX/RST agreement was affirmed by nearly two-thirds of the votes cast by RST shareholders other than AMAX. All shareholders, including AMAX, endorsed the agreement by more than the three-fourths majority required under Zambian law. The reorganization of RST, including the agreement with AMAX, was then upheld by the High Court of Zambia as being fair and equitable to all shareholders. Nonetheless, the United States Court of Appeals sustained a finding of inadequate disclosure, tantamount to the misrepresentation of material facts, against AMAX and RST. Initially, AMAX was ordered by the district court to offer the non-AMAX shareholders an opportunity to exchange what they had received by way of compensation for a proportionate share in the equity of RST International. However, a settlement, favorable to the shareholders concerned, finally resulted in the full consolidation of RST International with AMAX. A record of the initial proceedings in the U.S. District Court is contained in Roan Selection Trust Limited, *Explanatory Statement for Meetings of Shareholders to be held on 6th August, 1970,* app. R, June 30, 1970. Subsequent proceedings are recorded in *Kohn* v. *American Metal Climax, Inc.,* United States Court of Appeals for the Third Circuit, March 31, 1972, and noted in *AMAX 1973 Annual Report,* pp. 23, 25.

48. *Brief of Defendants-Appellants American Metal Climax, Inc., and Roan Selection Trust Limited* in *Kohn* v. *American Metal Climax, Inc., et al.,* United States Court of Appeals for the Third Circuit, Febraury 22, 1971, pp. 16–23, 45–55.

49. This is the only holding known to exceed 10 percent. Roan Selection Trust Limited, *Explanatory Statement for Meetings of Shareholders to be held on 6th August, 1970,* June 30, 1970, p. 5. It is of interest that Charter Consolidated Limited of London, a major company in the AAC Group, holds the largest single shareholding in Selection Trust Limited, reported to be 33 percent. *Botswana RST Limited,* Prospectus, April 21, 1972, p. 7; cf. RST Ltd., *Explanatory Statement,* p. 13. Thus, the Anglo American Corporation itself has at least one important corporate link with AMAX.

Comparisons

At this point, a brief comparison of the two main parent companies may be germane. By the criteria of ownership, management, operations, and diversity of domiciles, both companies qualify as multinational corporations. However, this designation applies more truly to the Anglo American Corporation, with its substantial minority of British shareholders and directors, and its close corporate relationship with Charter Consolidated Limited of London. While AMAX has a leavening of British participation, it does not have the quality of empire that so clearly distinguishes the Anglo American Corporation of South Africa. The latter, a growing monument to the entrepreneurial genius of Rhodes, no less than Oppenheimer, towers over the entire field of capitalist enterprise in Africa. Its size at the end of 1969 was reported thus:

> The estimated total value of the mining and industrial companies administered by the Corporation was about R1,500 million [$2,100 million]. This figure, when added to the participation of the Corporation and its finance companies in companies outside the Group of R1,400 million, gives an overall total of R2,900 million [$4,060 million] as the size of the Anglo American Corporation Group.[50]

This may well be "the largest mining finance group in the world."[51] Although its operations are far less diversified than those of the Anglo American Corporation, AMAX is nonetheless a very large corporation by American standards. At the end of 1969, its assets were valued at $940,920,000, ranking 110th among U.S. industrials.[52] With respect to rankings of net income, AMAX with $69,090,000, was even higher—77th among U.S. industrials.[53]

Both companies include statements of value and self-conception apart from commercial interest or significance in their annual re-

---

50. *Anglo American Corporation of South Africa Limited 1969 Annual Report*, p. 7.

51. *African Development* (July 1972), p. 66. The size of the Anglo American Corporation in relation to other world-class enterprises is difficult to determine. It is listed in *Moody's Bank and Finance Manual*, while other group companies, including De Beers Consolidated Mines, are listed in *Moody's Industrial Manual*. The latter company is also included in *The Fortune Directory: The 200 Largest Industrials Outside the U.S.*

52. A comparable company, Phelps Dodge Corporation, ranked 122nd. "The Fortune Directory of the 500 Largest Industrial Corporations," *Fortune* 81 (May 1970): 188.

53. Ibid. Phelps Dodge Corporation ranked 57th, with a net income of $89,435,000.

ports. These statements reflect their respective political orienta-
tions. The Anglo American Corporation affirms its belief in the
future of the African continent in the context of its primary commitment to South Africa.[54] AMAX conceives its business mission
in the context of America's increasing "need for access to foreign
mineral resources."[55] Its statement also acknowledges an "obligation to protect the environment in which we must work," which
reflects a widespread American preoccupation with this problem.
The express self-images of these companies suggest their limitations as international corporations. At bottom, they represent
South African capital and American capital respectively.

TAXES, DIVIDENDS, AND
THE PAYMENT OF COMPENSATION

Revenue Sharing before Nationalization

During the first five years of Zambian independence, the mining
industry contributed an average of about 60 percent of central government revenues.[56] This contribution was made up of royalties
and taxes. The mineral royalty was determined in accordance with
a formula that had been in effect for many years. The rate was
computed monthly at 13.5 percent of the average of London Metal
Exchange quotations for the month concerned, less £8 per long
ton.[57]

Despite its significance as a mechanism for the determination of
prices, the "free market" of the London Metal Exchange (LME)
actually handles only a small percentage of copper entering the
world market—probably less than 10 percent of export sales, including both newly mined copper and scrap. However, the Northern Rhodesian/Zambian companies have usually based their selling
prices on official LME quotations, which fluctuate constantly ac-

54. *Anglo American Corporation of South Africa Limited 1970 Annual Report*, p. 5.

55. *AMAX 1970 Annual Report*, p. 8. As might be expected, this emphasis ac-
companies the advocacy of legislation, including foreign investment guarantees,
desired by transnational companies.

56. Copper Industry Service Bureau, *Mindeco Mining Year Book of Zambia 1970*
(Kitwe), p. 31. In 1969 the revenues of the central government totalled K401 million;
the mining industry's contribution came to K237 million, or 59 percent.

57. *Report of the UN/ECA/FAO Economic Survey Mission on the Economic Development of Zambia*, p. 39.

cording to market conditions.[58] In January 1964, the Zambian companies, following the example and normal procedures of Belgian and American producers, switched from the LME quotations to a "producers' price" system, in which prices are set by the companies themselves. Such prices have been substantially lower than LME quotations, as they are mainly intended to counter the threat of substitution for copper by lower-priced metals. Thus at the beginning of 1966, Zambian, Chilean, and American producers were selling copper at £336 per long ton, while the LME price, inflated by a combination of Chilean strikes, Zambian export problems, and American demands resulting from the Vietnam war, had risen to unprecedented heights—occasionally above £700. In April 1966, following a substantial increase in the price of Chilean copper, to £496 per long ton, the Zambian companies decided to revert to pricing on the basis of LME quotations, which then declined to more normal levels, approximating £450 by the end of the year.[59]

In anticipation of the increased income that would result from this change in the basis of pricing, the Zambian government imposed a new tax on copper exports. The rate was set at 40 percent of the amount by which the average LME price for the month exceeds £300 per long ton. Income taxes, at a maximum rate of 45 percent, were levied on company profits after the payment of royalties and export taxes. In 1968 receipts from these sources amounted to 57.5 percent of central government revenues, derived as follows: income taxes paid by the mining companies, K42,197,000; mineral royalties, K65,833,000; copper export tax, K68,164,000.[60]

One careful estimate of profit distribution in the financial year 1968/1969 has indicated that the mining companies paid approximately 65 percent of their gross profits to the Zambian government in the form of royalties and taxes.[61] Assuming that 10 percent of

58. See Sir Ronald L. Prain, "Copper Pricing Systems," *Selected Papers*, Vol. II: 1958–60 (London, 1961), pp. 13–24.

59. *Copperbelt of Zambia Mining Industry Year Book 1966*, p. 15; "Royalties: Everyman's Guide," *Financial Mail* (Lusaka), February 1966, pp. 14–15; *Dealing on the London Metal Exchange 1966*, M. C. Brackenbury and Co. (London, 1966), pp. 19–24.

60. Republic of Zambia, *Statistical Year-Book 1969* (Lusaka, 1970), pp. 136, 138. During the previous eighteen months, from July 1966 to December 1967, governmental receipts from these sources amounted to 60 percent of all revenues. Republic of Zambia, *Statistical Year-Book 1968* (Lusaka, 1969), pp. 132, 136.

61. *Anatomy of the Zambia Copper Nationalisation*, p. 4, table 3.2. In 1969 the chairman of RST noted that "our contribution to Zambian Government revenues at

gross profits would be allocated for capital replacement expenditures, this estimate indicates an aggregate net profit that is about 25 percent of the gross profits. At this point, a crucial issue involves the division between that part of the profit that would be retained for new investments in Zambia and that part paid abroad in the form of dividends to the foreign shareholders.

The Investment Controversy

In 1968 President Kaunda sharply criticized the mining companies for having regularly remitted excessive portions of their profits abroad in the form of dividends. "Instead of re-investing," he alleged, "they have been distributing over 80% of their profits every year as dividends."[62] Henceforth, he declared, no foreign company would be allowed to pay as dividends outside of Zambia more than 50 percent of its net profit or 30 percent of its equity capital, whichever is the less. At the same time, Kaunda announced that his government would act to acquire the ownership of 51 percent of the shares of twenty-six large firms including one Zambian-owned business, a timber company owned jointly by the mining companies to service their needs, and a brewery in which ZAMANGLO had a 50 percent interest. However, nothing was said at that time about the possibility of state participation in the mining industry itself.

Shortly thereafter the chairmen of both mining groups retorted vigorously to President Kaunda's criticism. H.F. Oppenheimer declared that having paid 65 percent or more of their gross mining profits to the government by way of royalties and taxes, the com-

---

present copper prices represents over 70 percent of our gross profits" *(Speech by Sir Ronald Prain, OBE, Chairman of the RST Group of Companies to the Informal Meeting of Shareholders held in New York, 21 April 1969, p. 5).* For the Anglo American Corporation, H. F. Oppenheimer observed that "since independence the operating companies of our group have paid to the Government K285,000,000 or 62 per cent of gross mining profits by way of royalties and taxation" (Zambian Anglo American Limited, *Statement by the Chairman, Mr. H. F. Oppenheimer,* December 1968). This report adjusted the figure of 64.8 percent given seven months earlier, when the figure for the previous year was reported at 69.1 percent. Anglo American Corporation of South Africa Limited, *Statement by the Chairman Mr. H. F. Oppenheimer,* May 1968, p. 4.

62. Republic of Zambia, *Zambia Towards Economic Independence,* Address by His Excellency Dr. K. D. Kaunda, President of the Republic of Zambia, to the National Council of the United National Independence Party, at Mulungushi, April 19, 1968 (Lusaka, n.d.), p. 45.

panies "might have been forgiven if . . . they had, in fact, distributed to their shareholders 80 percent of what remained to them." In fact, he continued:

It has been our practice to charge to working costs each year the capital expenditure required to maintain production at established levels. In fact, massive investment has been required in recent years to make it possible to sustain the established rate of production from greater depths and lower-grade ores. We are concerned here not just with maintenance expenditure but with the financing of huge projects for the purpose of opening up new orebodies and treating the production from them. Since independence the mines of our Group have invested no less than K36.4 million in this way, a sum equal to 41 percent of the dividends paid during the same period. In addition, the sum of K12.6 million which was retained out of net profits was all used for capital expenditure purposes in Zambia so that since independence the mining companies of our Group have applied to capital purposes profits equal to 55.3 percent of the amount paid out in dividends during that period. For last year alone the figures are even more striking: capital expenditure of K21.2 million, a sum equal to 83.3 percent of the dividends for the year, was financed out of current profits.

It is also relevant to point out that dividends from Nchanga accrue to a substantial extent to Rhokana Corporation Limited, and dividends from both these companies flow largely to Zambian Anglo American Limited. Profit retentions thus take place at several levels, which in effect increases further the percentage of mining profits which are applied to reinvestment in Zambia.

Insofar as there has been any avoidable limitation in the rate of new mining development, this has been due to rapidly rising costs, to transport problems and to the difficulty of recruiting and retaining the necessary skilled labour force. These are not only the problems of the mining industry but of the economy as a whole. The shortage from which Zambia suffers is not of money but of men and materials.[63]

Speaking for the RST Group, R.L. Prain submitted that the rate of dividend payment had averaged 76 percent of net profits for the

63. Anglo American Corporation of South Africa Limited, *Statement by the Chairman, Mr. H. F. Oppenheimer*, May 1968, p. 4.

three preceding years.[64] This rate, admittedly high, "is a reflection of the high rates of taxation in Zambia, taking into account royalties, export tax and income tax. Because these rates of tax are high by world standards, it follows that the payout from the remaining profits must necessarily bear a fairly high ratio to those profits if the dividend is to represent the sort of return necessary to attract overseas investment." However, Prain categorically denied that the rate of dividend payout had either reduced the rate of development or inhibited expansion by RST. The group, he declared, "has never been without the ability to finance any development which has reached the viable stage."

In Prain's view, the chief impediments to mining development were the formulas in effect for computing royalties and export taxes. Both, as we have seen, were based on the price of copper rather than profits. The companies contended that the effect of this system was to discourage the development of low-grade or high-cost mines.[65] Various proponents of reform, including officials of the Ministry of Mines, believed that a royalty formula based on the profitability of individual mines would be equitable, conducive to development, and not less remunerative to government than the formula in effect. In their view, the government's refusal to revise the royalty formula was not only detrimental to mining development, but also unsound from a conservationist standpoint, since the high-cost mines were disinclined to treat low-grade ores that would be acceptable elsewhere. In this connection, a high government official told the present writer, "We throw away metal that would be mined in any other country."

Yet the government was slow to face up to its mistake in retaining the inherited royalty formula. Governmental leaders mistrusted the motives of the industry leaders who were suddenly so agitated by the alleged irrationality of a royalty formula that had been good enough for the British South Africa Company during the colonial era. As President Kaunda remarked, "I do not remember that they [the mining companies] complained about

64. RST Group of Companies, *Statement by the Chairman, Sir Ronald L. Prain,* November 1968, p. 7. An earlier statement to this effect was made to the annual informal meeting of shareholders in London, May 2, 1968 ("Report of Proceedings," mimeo.) His claim is corroborated by *RST Limited 1966 Annual Report,* pp. 24–25, and *RST Limited 1967 Annual Report,* pp. 28–29.

65. RST Group of Companies, *Statement by the Chairman, Sir Ronald L. Prain,* October 1965, p. 4; Zambian Anglo American Limited, *Statement by the Chairman, Mr. H. F. Oppenheimer,* November 1965.

it . . . . But after Independence we have been hearing nothing else."[66]

Prain has said that RST had been opposed to the formula for "many years."[67] Oppenheimer was less emphatic in pronouncing on this matter, since the Anglo American Corporation is intimately linked with the BSA Company itself, and may not have objected to the formula while that company was involved.[68] In any case, Kaunda chose to blame the inadequacy of mining development since independence on the investment policies of the companies and their greed for dividends. When, in 1968, he promised to change the royalty system in accordance with the "companies' point of view," he also took the occasion to declare that he did "not agree with the mining companies that royalties have been the obstacles to development of the industry."[69] It should be noted, however, that independent analysts, who were sympathetic to the Zambian government's policy of state participation in the industry, were unable to agree with the president on this point: "The 'royalty system,' and the Export Tax *did* inhibit development both because of their own direct disincentive effects, and because their unsuitability was so obvious, and so widely known and publicized, that a change was clearly indicated."[70]

Kaunda's announcement of the anticipated tax reform accompanied his unanticipated declaration on state participation. In place of both royalties and the export tax, the companies would thereafter be required to pay a mineral tax on copper equal to 51 percent of profits. In basing this tax on profits, he said, "I have met the mining companies' demands 100 percent."[71] Doubtless, a "particular uncertainty, so bad for investment," as well as the "direct disincentives" of the former tax system had been removed. Independent analysts thought that the new system would prove to be

66. Republic of Zambia, *Towards Complete Independence*, Address by . . . K. D. Kaunda, p. 35.

67. RST Group of Companies, *Statement by the Chairman*, October 1965; RST Limited, *Statement by the Chairman*, August 22, 1969; also Slinn, "The Legacy of the British South Africa Company," p. 37.

68. After the loss of its Zambian mineral rights, the BSA Company became a wholly owned subsidiary of Charter Consolidated Limited, a London-based associate of the Anglo American Corporation.

69. *Zambia Towards Economic Independence*, pp. 45–46.

70. *Anatomy of the Zambia Copper Nationalisation*, p. 5; see also Charles Harvey, "Tax Reform in the Mining Industry," in *Economic Independence and Zambian Copper*, ed. Bostock and Harvey, pp. 131–144; and Martin, pp. 130–132.

71. *Towards Complete Independence*, p. 35.

"a major incentive. If investment does increase," they wrote with philosophical detachment, "it does not really matter if the government claims that it is because of nationalisation, and the mine management claims that it is because of the changed tax system." So long as the rate of mining development is intensified, "both will benefit, as will the country at large."[72] However, the beneficial effects of reform might have been negated by the disruptive consequences of a struggle over nationalization. Hence it would be essential from either party's standpoint to negotiate a mutually acceptable agreement on the distribution of benefits.

Revenue Sharing after Nationalization

Under the new system of ownership and taxation, profit distribution would depend upon an intricate combination of factors, including taxes, dividends, fees, and the scheme of compensation for the nationalized shares. A succinct analysis of the agreed distribution has been presented by the aforementioned team of independent analysts under the auspices of Maxwell Stamp (Africa) Limited, a British firm of international economic consultants.[73] The first step is to determine the percentage of gross profit per ton that will be subject to taxation. Given the management fee of 1.25 percent of gross profit, and the provision of 10 percent of gross profit for capital replacement (this figure, which cannot be exact, includes both capital expenditures and depreciation), 88.75 percent of gross profit would remain subject to the 51 percent mineral tax. After the payment of that tax and an additional management fee, equal to 2 percent of gross profit less mineral tax, 42.36 percent of gross profit would remain subject to the company income tax, charged at a rate of 45 percent. This leaves a post-tax profit equal to 23.3 percent of gross profit or 25.9 percent of the taxable income. Under the new ownership and fiscal arrangements, 51 percent of the post-tax profit would accrue to the state, while the remainder would be distributed to other shareholders without restriction. In other words, the 1968 regulation prohibiting the payment of more than 50 percent of any company's net profit abroad was rescinded, with the result that an estimated 12.7 percent of the taxable income

72. *Anatomy of the Zambia Copper Nationalisation*, p. 5.
73. Ibid., pp. 3–4.

of the mining companies could be distributed to the foreign shareholders.

Under the old system, with the 50 percent limitation on remission of profits, the distribution abroad was but slightly higher— 13.3 to 14.2 percent of taxable income. Henceforth, in addition to dividends, the minority owners would receive compensation payments on the principal of their loan stock and bonds, bearing 6 percent interest, in annual amounts of not less than K14.8 million ($20.7 million) for NCCM and K13.5 million ($18.9 million) for RCM, with provision for the acceleration of payments when profits are high.[74] In addition, the Anglo American Corporation and RST would receive substantial fees for the provision of management and other services worth several million dollars per year.

Since 1970, Zambians and others have questioned the wisdom of those agreements that relate to the costly management contracts.[75] It has been suggested that these contracts may not have been needed, since MINDECO could have employed top-level managers directly. Such persons might even have been seconded to MINDECO by the minority owners, both to keep them employed and to ensure the continuance of efficient and profitable operations. From this viewpoint, the management contracts are seen as additional elements of compensation rather than remuneration for services rendered. However, as a Zambian mining official commented to me, the suddenness of Kaunda's decision to nationalize the mines might have unsettled the industry, in which case, the management contracts may have been "psychologically necessary" to create a climate of confidence during the critical period of transition to a new pattern of ownership and control. The continued exercise of executive authority by the former majority owners would also serve to reassure the apprehensive or startled members of the crucial expatriate work force, whose alienation could seriously damage the industry's performance.[76] Furthermore, a work-

74. The absence of a corresponding provision for the deceleration of compensation payments when profits decline was cited as a main disadvantage of the agreement from the government's standpoint. Bostock and Harvey, eds., *Economic Independence and Zambian Copper*, pp. 174, 176.

75. The management and consultancy contract with RST is summarized in ibid., pp. 229–232.

76. ''The majority of expatriate miners, in particular those who had served for a long time and were therefore in relatively key positions, not only identified themselves strongly with the company for which they had worked and might therefore have been averse to working for a Government controlled company but also often held substantial amounts of their savings in the shares of their company. Although

ing partnership between Zambia and the established companies would also reassure the consumers of Zambia's copper and favorably impress both potential private investors and the directors of international lending agencies.

In sum, the arrangements for majority participation by the state have provided for a transfer of ownership without disrupting an existing division of wealth that was satisfactory to the foreign shareholders and appeared to be adequate for the purposes of the government at the time of the agreement. The former majority shareholders lost a sizable portion of their total incomes and were required to accept compensation on a minimum basis of valuation—the book value of the assets. On the other hand, the authorized cash payments to foreign shareholders were indeed very generous: dividends would be paid to foreign owners without limitation; there would be no special taxation on such dividends for ten years, nor would they be subject to restrictive exchange controls; the interest on ZIMCO loan stock and bonds would be exempt from Zambian taxation; the repayment schedule provided for semiannual installments on both principal and interest (to be completed in only eight years in RST's case, while repayment to the Anglo American Corporation would take four additional years). Furthermore, the mining companies were permitted to externalize their liquid assets, which had been blocked by exchange control regulations. And the tax system had been adjusted to conform with their interests in various ways. As the Maxwell Stamp analysts observed, "in terms of remittable cash," the foreign shareholders "will now be able to increase their flow out of Zambia during the payment period, after which it will decline."[77]

---

this was of course a very small percentage of the overall shareholding, it was nevertheless extremely important. Poor compensation terms or any attempt to rearrange conditions of service might lead at best to labour unrest and, at worst, to a mass exodus. The attitude and position of these employees, numbering perhaps a thousand, played a major part in the Government's willingness to adopt, from the Mining Companies' point of view, reasonable settlement terms" (Potter, pp. 105–106).

77. *Anatomy of the Zambia Copper Nationalisation*, p. 7; Bostock and Harvey, pp. 171–173. A United States District Court judge found that AMAX, Inc., which now owns 100 percent of RST, would derive the following benefits as a result of the agreements: "AMAX's annual income will be increased by $7 million calculated at a $.50 per pound copper price"—K779 or £458 per ton; "AMAX's cash flow will be improved by $134 million over the period of 1970–1975; . . . AMAX's foreign balance of payments position will be improved by $91 million; . . . Although AMAX will increase its net exposure in Africa by about $24 million, 4½ years of incremental

In 1973 President Kaunda expressed his dissatisfaction with various aspects of Zambia's agreement with the minority shareholding and management companies. His list of specific objections included the lack of a provision to decelerate compensation payments "during lean years" when profits are low as a result of production losses or poor market conditions. In addition, he declared that certain concessions to the companies with respect to exchange control and taxation, some of which have been noted above, were excessively generous. Consequently, he announced that Zambia would immediately redeem the outstanding bonds and loan stock in order to allow for the rectification of these and other objectionable arrangements.[78]

The Zambian government financed this costly maneuver mainly by means of extensive borrowing from foreign banks.[79] Its success, like the financial success of nationalization itself, depends upon the maintenance of an efficient industry and a strong market. The following chapter assesses Zambia's attempt to develop, safeguard, and diversify the wealth-producing potential of her most lucrative natural resource.

---

earnings after the acquisition will recoup this; . . . AMAX will be acquiring high yielding assets." Roan Selection Trust Limited, *Explanatory Statement for Meetings of Shareholders To Be Held on 6th August, 1970,* June 30, 1970, app. R-5.

78. Republic of Zambia, *Address by His Excellency the President, Dr. K. D. Kaunda, at the Press Conference on the Redemption of ZIMCO Bonds,* State House, Lusaka, August 31, 1973.

79. Ruth Weiss, "Zambia Tightens the Grip," *The Financial Times* (London), October 10, 1973.

THREE

The Increase of Wealth

For newly developing nations the goal of economic independence implies at the minimum sufficient control over domestic resources to permit effective economic planning. In Zambia's case, measures were specifically designed to rationalize the exploitation of mineral resources and thereby to enhance the contribution of the mining industry to development. This chapter inquires into Zambia's ability to achieve ambitious production goals and to ensure the reliability of Zambian copper as a main source of national wealth for a reasonable period of time. It examines the mining development programs, pricing procedures, and marketing mechanisms of the industry; it also indicates some of the pitfalls of planning in this small country that virtually lives by the export of a single commodity.

Before the advent of state participation, Zambia's dependence upon foreign enterprise was obvious in all spheres of the copper industry. As a result of the fundamental reforms discussed in chapter 2, the question of dependence should be reappraised from time to time by students of this country's relationship to the industrial societies. A starting point may be suggested by the following question. To what extent does Zambia continue to depend upon the established groups of companies to conduct its mining, marketing, and newly launched venture into the field of copper fabrication? This question underlies the analysis that follows.

MINING DEVELOPMENT

The potential capacity of a country's mining industry depends upon may factors involving diverse areas of scientific knowledge and social organization, including geological knowledge, metallurgical technology, and the conditions of transportation and supply, as well as various economic and political considerations. To begin with, a sound estimation of the quantity and quality of mineralized ores is essential. In Zambia, the declared ore reserves of the Copperbelt are reported to total 745 million metric tons, grading 3.34

percent copper (compared with a world average grade of about 1.5 percent), or about 25 million tons of copper. This amounts to "some 13% of the world's known reserves of the metal."[1]

In rich mining areas, the published or "proved" reserves of ore tend to increase as mine development proceeds. However, the life span of a mining complex also depends upon the level and intensity of exploitation. In 1964 the UN Economic Survey Mission to Zambia surmised that the Copperbelt-based mining industry was likely to survive for forty to fifty years, although its annual output might begin to fall during the 1980s.[2] This cautionary observation, however speculative it might have been, points up the urgency for Zambia as a nation to put to productive use the wealth derived from her great but wasting asset.

As regards the level of production, in 1969 Zambian mines produced 720,000 metric tons (tonnes) of copper. From the government's standpoint, as we have seen, this performance did not represent a satisfactory rate of investment by the mining companies. Nonetheless, it did place Zambia third among all copper producing countries. Zambia's share of the total world production of primary or newly mined copper was slightly higher than 12 percent; its share of the total copper export trade outside of the communist sphere was over 20 percent. Comparative national production rates for the years 1969–72 are shown in table 1. In large measure, the prospects for significant increases in production depend upon the balance between mining costs on the one hand and incentives to invest on the other.

Mining Costs and Incentives To Invest

Commentaries on the financial costs of mining differentiate capital costs from production costs.[3] Capital costs include expenditures

1. Republic of Zambia, MINDECO Ltd., *Prospects for Zambia's Mining Industry*, (Lusaka, 1970), p. 20; Sir Ronald L. Prain has noted that between 1960 and 1969 "the average grade of ore mined [worldwide] has declined from 1½ percent to 1¼ percent copper" (*The Future Availability of Copper Supplies*, An Address to The Institute of Metals, Autumn Meeting, Amsterdam, 1970, p. 3). Prain's published papers are cited frequently in this chapter. As observed in a recent biographical note, the retired chairman of RST "is probably the world's leading authority on the [copper] industry in its broadest context" *Optima* 23 [March 1973]: 53).

2. *Report of the UN/ECA/FAO Economic Survey Mission on the Economic Development of Zambia* (Ndola, 1964), p. 45.

3. In preparing this section I have benefited from an anonymous paper presented by the Zambian mining companies to the Lusaka Inter-Governmental Cop-

TABLE 1

PRODUCTION OF PRIMARY COPPER
('000 metric tons)

	1969	1970	1971	1972
USA	1,401	1,560	1,391	1,499
USSR	875	925	990	1,050
Chile	688	686	708	721
Zambia	720	684	651	718
Canada	520	613	653	708
Zaire	364	387	406	436
Philippines	131	160	197	205
Australia	131	158	174	185
Peru	199	212	213	178
South Africa	127	144	148	155
China	110	120	130	132
Yugoslavia	91	98	107	124
Papua New Guinea	--	--	--	124
Japan	120	119	121	114
Poland	48	65	89	96
Mexico	66	61	63	64
Bulgaria	40	42	45	48
Spain	19	20	43	41
Other Countries	304	301	313	319
World Total	5,954	6,354	6,441	6,920

SOURCE: *Mindeco Mining Year Book of Zambia 1972,* Copper Industry Service Bureau (Kitwe), p. 19.

required to develop mines, install plants, build townships, and provide related facilities. Expenditures to expand and improve existing facilities also fall in this category. Recently, it has been estimated that a minimum of K1,000 ($1,400) capital investment is required for every one ton increase in the annual production of refined copper.[4] To finance mine expansion in the postnationalization period, the industry depends upon a combination of state and private investment at a presumed ratio of 51 percent state to 49 percent private. The viability of this combination in turn depends

per Conference, June 1967, entitled "Analysis of Comparative World Copper Production Costs" (LICC/WP(MC)/6).

4. R. M. Bostock, D. H. Murray, and C. Harvey, *Anatomy of the Zambian Copper Nationalisation,* An Occasional Paper by Maxwell Stamp (Africa) Limited (London, 1970), p. 8; see also Sir Ronald L. Prain, *Selected Papers* (London: 1968), 4:115.

upon both the profit that accrues to the state—which is a function of the price level—and the incentive for others to invest.

Production costs include all operating costs and other costs—for example, administrative costs, depreciation, royalties, export taxes, duties, and interest charges on loans—excluding taxes on profits. Production costs vary widely throughout the world depending upon the circumstances of mining. If copper is mined as either a co-product or by-product of other metals, as in the case of the Canadian nickel/copper mines, the cost of production is comparatively low. In general, but not invariably, large open-pit mines are less costly to operate than either small open-pit mines or underground mines. Other rules of thumb indicate that hill mining is advantageous, that wet mines entail costly pumping operations, and that the expenses of treating certain types of ore may offset a high grade in terms of copper content.[5]

In 1967 the Zambian mining companies prepared a comparative study of world costs for the production of copper to the electrolytic stage, at which point copper leaving the Zambian refineries is 99.98 percent pure. The study covered nine countries, which produced 97 percent of all so-called competitive copper.[6] It showed that among these major producing countries, Zaire and Zambia had the highest costs per ton—37 and 30 percent, respectively, above the world average.[7] For Zambia, this represented a drastic alteration of her competitive position since 1963, at which time her average cost of production had been very close to the world average outside of the Soviet sector.[8]

After 1963, mining costs in Zambia were boosted to a higher plateau by inflationary pressures from three principal sources. First, the industry was subject to rising labor costs, including increasing expenditures on training, which reflect the implementa-

5. D. R. DeVletter, "Mining Costs," memorandum by the Director of the Metals and Minerals Development Unit, Ministry of Lands and Mines, April 1968 (mimeo.)

6. "Competitive" copper is defined to exclude "by-product" copper as well as copper produced in countries that have comprehensively "planned economies" and/or "historic internal support prices" that protect mining profits by absorbing the costs of production. "Analysis of Comparative World Copper Production Costs." The countries surveyed were Australia, Canada, Chile, Peru, Philippines, South Africa, U.S.A., Zaire, and Zambia.

7. Ibid.

8. Prain, Selected Papers, 4:4. For many years, the Rhodesian mining companies were reckoned as "low cost producers." William J. Barber, The Economy of British Central Africa (London: Oxford University Press, 1961), p. 123.

tion of necessary and salutary social policies. [9] Second, Zambian mining, already burdened with high transportation costs owing to the country's geographical position, was saddled with a heavier expenditure as a result of the government's decision to develop new transport routes and other facilities in order to reduce the extent of dependence upon Rhodesia and the Portuguese territories. Reacting to Zambia's policy of withdrawal from traditional routes, Rhodesia Railways imposed higher rates on Zambian traffic. In 1968 ZAMANGLO and RST reported that as a result of these events their transportation costs had increased by 50 and 30 percent respectively. [10] Third, the costs of materials have risen substantially, largely as a result of spiraling transport costs, increased port handling charges at the overburdened port of Dar es Salaam, and other supply problems. Furthermore, unit costs have increased as a result of a decline in the grade of ore mined at Nchanga (now the Chingola Division of NCCM), which has accounted for about 40 percent of the total output of the Copperbelt. In 1967 only Zaire, among the major producing countries, exceeded Zambia both in the grade of its ores and in the cost of production. [11] In Chile and Peru, the costs of production were only about 60 percent of the Zambian cost. By 1971, however, production costs in both Chile and the United States had risen well above those in Zambia and Zaire. These variations were largely attributable to steep wage increases in Chile, where unit costs rose by 65 percent between 1969 and 1971, and the incidence of high pollution control costs in the United States. [12]

In countries like Zambia, that rely upon large-scale private investments in high-cost mineral industries, fiscal incentives are es-

9. This subject is discussed in chap.4.

10. DeVletter, "Mining Costs." Also R. M. Bostock, "The Transport Sector," in *Constraints on the Economic Development of Zambia,* ed. Charles Elliott (Nairobi: Oxford University Press, 1971), pp. 358–360. The efforts required to develop alternative routes will be discussed in chap. 5.

11. "The grade of ore milled in 1963 ranged from a copper content of 1.7 per cent on Roan Antelope mine to 5.2 per cent on Nchanga. The Copperbelt average is just under 3 per cent, and the only major producing country with a higher average grade is the Congo. In the United States, which mines a quarter of all the world's primary copper, the average grade is well under 1 per cent" (Prain, *Selected Papers,* 4:4-5). Average grades of ore mined in the major producing countries during 1970 have been reported as follows: Zaire, 4.2 percent; Zambia, 3.38 percent; Chile, 1.53 percent; Peru, 1.14 percent; Canada, 1.04 percent; U.S.A., 0.79 percent. D. R. De-Vletter, "Zambia's Mineral Industry and Its Position Amongst World's Major Copper Producers," *Geologie en Mijnbouw* 51 (May-June 1972): 253.

12. Ibid., p. 254.

sential to attract investors. At present, as Ronald L. Prain has said, "there is tremendous international competition" for capital resources.[13] It should also be noted that "in both absolute and percentage terms" copper production increased more in the industrial countries than in the developing countries—42 to 25 percent— during the decade 1960–1969.[14] Rising costs in the industrial countries may stimulate the less developed countries to compete more vigorously for the investment funds that may be attracted.

The Mineral Tax Act of 1970 was conceived in this spirit. It eliminated the regressive royalty formula, which would have been detrimental to new mining development, in favor of a mineral tax at 51 percent of gross taxable profits.[15] In addition, a new and liberalized system of capital allowances was introduced: all capital expenditures, as well as prospecting expenditures, would be deductible for both mineral and income tax purposes.[16] Yet, spokesmen for the companies have said that the rate of taxation in Zambia (at 73 percent of gross taxable profits, given the combined mineral and income taxes) is high and may therefore discourage new investments.[17] Nevertheless, both major groups have embarked upon significant programs to expand production in keeping with the national goal of 900,000 tonnes by 1976.[18]

13. Prain, *The Future Availability of Copper Supplies,* p. 10.

14. Ibid.

15. See chap. 2.

16. P. Bottelier, "Taxation," in *The Mines and Minerals Act, 1969, and The Mineral Tax Act, 1970,* by A. R. Drysdall and E. J. Langevad, Economic Report No. 26, Republic of Zambia, Ministry of State Participation (1970), pp. 22–23.

17. "The changeover to a taxation system based entirely on profits is a development which I very much welcome, though the new combined rate of mineral and income tax at 73 per cent is very high indeed; too high, I would judge, to give adequate encouragement to the development of new low-grade mining projects" (Anglo American Corporation of South Africa Limited, *Statement by the Chairman, Mr. H. F. Oppenheimer,* May 1970, p. 6). It should be noted that The Mineral Tax Act of 1970 allowed the established companies to deduct their expenditures on new projects from their tax liabilities for current profits. This advantage would not have been available to new entrants. See the critique and proposal by Andrew Gordon, "The Prospects for New Mine Investment," in *Economic Independence and Zambian Copper: A Case Study of Foreign Investment,* ed. Mark Bostock and Charles Harvey, Praeger Special Studies in International Economics and Development (New York: Praeger, 1972), pp. 189–209. The 100 percent capital allowance provision for income tax purposes was revoked by the Zambian government in 1973, upon payment in full of its compensation debt to the minority shareholders.

18. Republic of Zambia, Ministry of Development Planning and National Guidance, *Second National Development Plan, January, 1972-December, 1976* (Lusaka, December 1971), p.85.

Programs

In 1969 the operating mines of the two major groups produced a record 754,000 metric tons (tonnes) of copper,[19] derived as follows:

AAC Group

Nchanga	242,444
Rhokana	100,123
Bancroft	50,361
Group Total	392,928

RST Group

Mufulira	188,562
Luanshya	116,822
Chibuluma	29,315
Chambishi	26,585
Group Total	361,284

Grand Total	754,212

SOURCE: Alan Drysdall, "Prospecting and Mining Activity 1895–1970," in *Economic Independence and Zambian Copper*, ed. Mark Bostock and Charles Harvey (New York: Praeger, 1972), p. 67.

Anglo American Corporation-NCCM.—In the decade prior to 1966, the copper mines of the Anglo American Corporation Group in Zambia increased their total annual production from 175,000 to nearly 400,000 long tons at a cost of some £70 million.[20] Subsequently, this group inaugurated an investment program that aimed to reach a production goal of 500,000 metric tons per year by 1974. The capital expenditure required to finance the anticipated new projects in addition to sustaining improvements of the exist-

19. The total production for 1969 shown at this point is some 34,000 tonnes higher than that shown for Zambia in table 1, which does not include sales of concentrates (before smelting and refining). See Copper Industry Service Bureau, *Mindeco Mining Year Book of Zambia 1970* (Kitwe), p. 36.

20. Zambian Anglo American Limited, *Statement by the Chairman, Mr. H. F. Oppenheimer*, November 1965.

MAP 4.

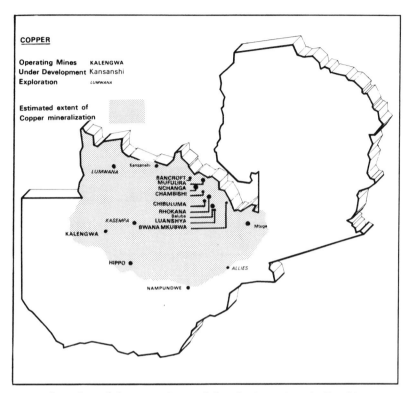

COPPER

Operating Mines   KALENGWA
Under Development Kansanshi
Exploration   LUMWANA

Estimated extent of
Copper mineralization

Location of the operating and developing mines in Zambia
and the estimated extent of copper mineralization. From
Prospects for Zambia's Mining Industry, Republic of Zambia,
MINDECO Limited (Lusaka, 1970), p. 21. Reproduced by
permission.

ing facilities was estimated at K175 million.[21] At the Chingola Division alone, the level of production would climb to more than 300,000
tonnes per year.[22] New ventures elsewhere include the reopening
of two historic mines, namely, Bwana Mkubwa, under the Rokana
Division, and Kansanshi, over 100 miles west of the Copperbelt, in
addition to the pyrite mine at Nampundwe, near Lusaka, where a
small amount of copper is also mined. The operations at Bwana

21. "Review by the President, Mr. M. B. Hofmeyr," Zambia Copper Investments
Limited, May 1970, in *African Development* (November 1970): 20–21.
22. The Chingola Division of NCCM would hold its position of second place in
world production, since the Chuquicamata mine together with the Exotica mine in
Chile is reported to have aimed at an annual production goal of 460,000 long tons.
DeVletter, "Mining Costs."

Mkubwa, Kansanshi, and other mines have been facilitated by the development of a new process called Torco ("treatment of refractory copper ores") whereby copper may be extracted from ores that are not susceptible to treatment by conventional methods. This technological breakthrough, accomplished by the AAC Group, is thought to have great "potential value in the treatment of hundreds of millions of tons of refractory ores in Africa, South America and elsewhere."[23]

As a rule, mining ventures depend heavily upon loans and capital market transactions. The measure of a mining group's effectiveness is largely determined by its ability to borrow money. An instructive example is the arrangement concluded in 1968 between Nchanga Consolidated Copper Mines Limited and the two largest customers of the Anglo American Corporation in Japan, namely, Mitsubishi Shoji Kaisha Limited and Mitsui and Company Limited. It was agreed that the Japanese companies would raise $42 million to loan to Nchanga in return for 100,000 tons of copper a year for ten years, part of which would be applied in servicing the loan. In addition, Nchanga was given "a credit facility up to the value of $28,000,000 for purchases of Japanese plant and equipment."[24] The significance of this loan was explained by the chairman of the AAC Group thus:

This is the largest loan raised for Zambia since independence and by any standards is a major commodity deal, reflecting the continued prosperity and growth of the Japanese economy and the increasing demand for copper in that country. The willingness of the two Japanese companies to assist the development of Zambia so substantially is propitious and I believe that both countries will benefit from the strengthened business relations. [25]

23. E. T. Pinkney, "Torco: The key to 'unyielding' copper ores," *Optima* 17 (June 1972): 83–87. The Torco process is being applied in the newly created copper mining industry of Mauritania, which is managed and partly owned by Charter Consolidated Limited of London, a member of the AAC Group. K. C. G. Heath, "Making a Desert Give up Its Treasures," *Optima* 17 (June 1967): 75–82.

24. Zambian Anglo American Limited, *Statement by the Chairman, Mr. H. F. Oppenheimer*, December 1968. It was also reported that the Japanese firms would raise $32 million of the $42 million loan in London with the Standard Bank; the remaining $10 million would be raised in Europe or with banks in Zambia. *The Times of Zambia*, April 18, 1968.

25. Zambian Anglo American Limited, *Statement by the Chairman, Mr. H. F. Oppenheimer*, December 1968. Clearly this statement does not refer to loans raised by the government itself.

RST-RCM.—In the decade ending 1968, the copper mines of the RST Group increased their total annual production from 188,000 long tons to more than 300,000 long tons at a capital expenditure cost of about K130 million.[26] The greatest achievement was recorded at Mufulira—the world's second largest underground copper mine—where annual production rose from 88,000 to 162,000 long tons. A subsequent expansion program, intended to reach the level of 190,000 metric tons per year, was nearly completed in September 1970, when production was suddenly disrupted by a massive cave-in that claimed eighty-nine lives and will have resulted in a prolonged, drastic loss of output—more than 150,000 tonnes—before previous production levels have been recovered, probably in 1974. It was estimated that this disaster would deprive the government of as much as one-quarter of its expected income from the mining industry for one year, since RCM, burdened with the expenses of rehabilitation and operating at a loss, would not be liable to pay income taxes for the time being. Furthermore, the company undertook to retain its employees at the disabled mine despite the collapse of production.[27]

Meanwhile, development has been intensified in other divisions of the RST-RCM Group, notably at Chambishi, where underground workings have been added to the open-pit operations, at Baluba mine, which entered production as a part of Luanshya Division in 1973, and at Kalengwa, a small but high-grade (17.25 percent copper content) mine about 250 miles west of the Copperbelt. Were it not for the cave-in at Mufulira, the RCM development program would have increased production to an annual rate of 375,000 tonnes by 1973.

Prospects: The Changing Structure of Production.—In order to stimulate development, the UN Economic Survey Mission of 1964 recommended the termination of those exclusive mining and prospecting rights, extending over vast areas, which were held "in perpetuity" by the major mining groups.[28] As we have seen in chapter 2, this step was taken with the Mines and Minerals Act of 1969, which abolished the exclusive concessions, vesting all min-

26. RST Group of Companies, *Statement by the Chairman, Sir Ronald L. Prain,* October 1959, November 1968.

27. "Zambia after the Mufulira mine disaster," *African Development* (December 1970), p. 8.

28. *Report of the UN/ECA/FAO Economic Survey Mission on the Economic Development of Zambia,* p. 48.

eral rights in the President of the Republic of Zambia. This act also
provides for the granting of prospecting licenses of four years duration for specified minerals in designated areas to be followed by
the issuance of three-year and renewable exploration licenses if
mineral deposits are discovered. Minimum expenditure programs
are among the conditions stipulated for these licenses. Finally,
approved mining operators will be granted mining licenses for
twenty-five-year periods.

As a result of this act, the established mining groups relinquished their rights to all but 12.5 percent of the 65,000 square mile
area in which exclusive concessions had been obtained (see chapter 2). Henceforth the government would be able to exercise initiative in the issuance of prospecting and exploration licenses. The
UN Economic Survey Mission explicitly suggested that mining opportunities should be extended to new foreign companies "with
fresh sources of capital. There is in any case," their report declared,
"something to be said for ceasing to rely on the same pair of giant
companies."[29] Furthermore, under the terms of the act, the government would have the option to acquire up to 51 percent of the
equity in any company to which a mining license is issued. Thus
MINDECO acquired 51 percent of Bwana Mkubwa and Kansanshi
in the NCCM Group, and 51 percent of Baluba and Kalengwa in
the RCM Group, after the new pattern of state participation was
established.

Despite these far-reaching legal changes, the new pattern of
ownership is not expected to result in any substantial alteration of
the predominance of the two established groups of mining companies in the foreseeable future. Yet the efforts of new entrants are
not without significance, since they test the realism of Zambia's
attempt to diversify foreign participation in this industry by means
of mixed (state-private) enterprise. One of the more promising
new ventures involved a Japanese-American company, Suico Limited, founded by Mitsui Mining Company and Continental Ore
Corporation in 1970. Suico was awarded prospecting licenses for
two allegedly rich concessions, one in the vicinity of the Copperbelt, the other 100 miles from the Copperbelt in the Northwestern
Province. The leading American architect of this venture envisaged
the eventual construction of a refinery in Zambia to treat ores pro-

29. *Report of the UN/ECA/FAO Economic Survey Mission*, p. 46.

duced by Japanese concessionaires in both Zambia and Zaire.[30]

Subsequently, Japanese enthusiasm for this project appeared to diminish. Japanese mining consultants reported that the capital costs would be considerably greater than indicated in early estimates, while the grading, thus far established at 2 to 2.5 percent copper, was about half that of ores open to Japanese firms in Zaire. The Americans concerned were quick to speculate about the possible influence of the established mining companies on Japanese investors. As we have seen, a trading company in the Mitsui group is involved in a major financial arrangement with the Anglo American Corporation Group mines in Zambia. This same company is also closely associated with AMAX.[31] If the Mitsui Mining Company decides to withdraw from competitive operations in Zambia, their American partners in Continental Ore Corporation may see the hand of influence at play.

PRICING AND MARKETING

In the copper industry, profitability largely depends upon two related but separate and distinct determinants—the production cost and the price level. (Other determinants include fiscal conditions and the adequacy of the infrastructure.) We have seen that production costs vary widely—indeed the extent of variation is tremendous—throughout the world, depending upon the social and technical conditions of mining. Major changes in the cost of production in significant mining regions may affect the supply of copper, which in turn would affect the prevailing world market price. However, in the short run international market prices do not normally fluctuate according to changes in the cost of production. By contrast, the price of copper is extremely sensitive to fluctuations in demand and supply.[32] This section is particularly concerned with problems that arise from instability in the market price of copper.

30. Hans Ries, former vice-president, Continental Ore Corporation, to whom I am indebted for this information.

31. In 1973, Mitsui and Company acquired 50 percent of the AMAX aluminum business. AMAX and Mitsui are also partners in an Australian mining enterprise. *Business Week*, August 25, 1973, p. 18.

32. S. D. Strauss, "Marketing of Nonferrous Metals and Ores," in *Economics of the Mineral Industries*, ed., Edward H. Robie (New York: The American Institute of Mining, Metallurgical, and Petroleum Engineers, Inc., 1959), pp. 281–282.

In countries that depend upon the production and export of primary products, such as copper, a healthy price level is the ruling economic passion, shared by the producing companies, their employees, and the governmental leaders. Increasingly in recent years it has been appreciated that a healthy price level should be differentiated from one that is excessively high. Responsible mining men speak of their quest for the "right price"—one that is high enough to yield moderate profits in the costlier mining enterprises but not so high that manufacturers will be provoked to abandon copper in favor of lower-priced substitutes, such as aluminum or plastics. Thus R. L. Prain, the former chairman of RST, insists that there is "a new discipline" in the copper industry, specifically "a deterrent to higher prices."[33]

However, the application of this deterrent is more precarious in underindustrialized mining countries than in the United States and Japan, where mining enterprises are extensively integrated with the fabricators and end-users of copper products. As a result of such vertical integration, the markets for copper mined within the system are relatively secure. Thus, it has been estimated that copper companies in the United States sell about 70 percent of their output to subsidiary fabricators.[34] Furthermore, copper produced for sale within the United States is generally sold at prices that are set by the major domestic producers themselves. Such prices are controlled to serve the interests of a vertically integrated industry; they are relatively stable and frequently (but not necessarily) much lower than prices quoted by the commodity exchanges.[35] By contrast, producers for foreign markets are liable to the vicissitudes of an unstable pricing mechanism, while their customers may be tempted to switch away from accustomed lines of supply to new suppliers or substitute materials. This temptation is greatest in Europe, where patterns of vertical integration normally involve the

33. Prain, *Selected Papers*, 2:15; 3:7.
34. Orris C. Herfindahl, *Copper Costs and Prices: 1870–1957* (Baltimore: The Johns Hopkins Press, 1959), p. 184.
35. For example, between 1965 and 1969, the United States domestic price for copper averaged 39.6 cents per pound, while the LME cash price averaged 60.4 cents per pound. Prain, *The Future Availability of Copper Supplies*, p. 5. Michael West has summarized the relationship between LME quotations and U.S. producer prices thus: "During periods of shortage, real or anticipated, the LME quotations have been well above the U.S. producer price, . . . during periods of surplus the quotations tend to converge at the lower levels" ("Price Stability for Copper: The Prospects and Problems," *Optima* 23 [September 1973]: 152).

postmining stages of fabrication and manufacture. In the absence of a primary producer (mining) component, it is alleged that European industry, notably in Britain, is "becoming less copper oriented" and more inclined to use substitute materials.[36] This tendency could endanger the economic well-being of countries that live by the export of copper.

Furthermore, it is widely understood that severe fluctuations in the price of copper are likely to discourage investments in the development of new mines. High prices usually entail higher costs in the form of tax and wage increases that weigh heavily after prices have fallen. Nowadays investment decisions are linked to systematic market research and scientific predictions of profitability. A constantly and severely fluctuating copper market compels the institutional investor to accept an excessive element of risk. As Prain has said, the copper industry resembles the shipbuilding industry "since the time taken to build an ocean liner [5 years] is about the same as that taken to construct a mine."[37] Permanently chaotic market conditions diminish the probability that low-grade or marginally viable orebodies will be developed. The governments of countries that depend upon copper exports have a specific interest in the economical development of such orebodies. To the extent that they rely upon private capital investment, wise governmental leaders, like the major mining executives, will desire stable prices.

Inevitably, students of the Zambian economy are preoccupied with the price of copper. It is a standard procedure for analysts to estimate critical copper price levels below which governmental expenditures will exceed receipts. Under the original agreement on state participation, the government was obligated to pay about K28.7 million per year until 1978 as compensation to the mining groups. The government planned to meet these payments out of its copper dividend earnings, for which purpose the critical aver-

36. "Marketing of Primary and Secondary Copper" (LICC/WP(MC)/2), and "The Substitution of Copper by Other Metals and Plastics and the Development of Other Copper Uses" (LICC/WP(MC)/5), papers presented by the Zambian mining companies to the Lusaka Inter-Governmental Copper Conference, June 1967; also Prain, Selected Papers, 4:120; and Martin S. Brown and John Butler, The Production, Marketing, and Consumption of Copper and Aluminum, Praeger Special Studies in International Economics and Development (New York: Praeger, 1968), pp. 103–104, 164–169.

37. Prain, Selected Papers, 2:150–151; 4:125.

age price level was initially estimated at K750 (£437.50) per tonne.[38] In August 1969, when President Kaunda announced his government's intention to acquire 51 percent ownership of the mines, the price of copper on the London Metal Exchange had risen to approximately K1,200 (£700) per long ton. This boom in price has been explained thus: "The unexpected strength of the copper market in 1969 was basically due to strong demand, some production difficulties including strikes, the fact that stocks have not yet recovered from the long American strike, and the emergence of China as a substantial buyer since its dispute with Russia cut off its major source of supply."[39]

The price of copper continued to rise during the early part of 1970, reaching a peak of K1,284 (£735) per tonne at the end of March. Thereafter, the demand for copper suddenly slackened and the LME price collapsed to K732 (£432) per tonne at the end of 1970. The average price for 1971 was K767 (£444) per tonne. This steep decline, coinciding with the great loss of production at Mufulira, resulted in a substantial decrease in the value of Zambia's total copper production—from K718 million in 1969 to K441 million in 1971—and a similarly severe setback to the balance of payments. In order to finance its expenditures, the government drew heavily upon its reserves of foreign exchange, which were thereby depleted by about 50 percent during 1971.[40] Zambia can ill afford so great a loss of its vaunted export earnings before the gains of independence have been consolidated in the economic sphere.[41]

The Quest for a Stable Price

The continuous fluctuation of copper prices—their extreme sensitivity to short-term changes in demand and supply—reflects on

38. "Should prices fall below this level then the government will be forced either to use previously accumulated earnings, or obtain funds from other sources. In the final analysis, of course, the bonds are guaranteed by the Government of the Republic of Zambia" (Bostock, Murray, Harvey, *Anatomy of the Zambia Copper Nationalisation*, p. 6); Bostock and Harvey, *Economic Independence and Zambian Copper*, p. 214.

39. Republic of Zambia, *Economic Report, 1969* (Lusaka, 1970), p. 27. There were no major strikes in Zambia during this period. The strike of copper industry workers in the United States had lasted for nine months during 1967–1968. Shortly before it ended, the cash price for wirebars on the LME reached an all time high of £817 (K1,401) per long ton. *Copperbelt of Zambia Mining Industry Year Book 1968*, p. 16.

40. Bank of Zambia, *Report and Statement of Accounts for the Year Ended December 31st 1971*, pp. 8, 13, 31.

41. The average LME price in 1972 declined to £428 per tonne. This undoubtedly influenced Kaunda's decision to pay off the loan and renegotiate the terms of

the system of price determination that depends upon the London Metal Exchange (LME). Briefly, prices are quoted daily on the LME for both immediate ("spot") payment and future ("forward") payment to be made at a specified time in return for delivery of the copper three months from the date of sale.[42] As noted in chapter 2, only a small percentage of the international trade in copper is actually transacted via the LME, which maintains warehouses at a number of British and Continental ports. These facilities are used mainly by metal merchants who are not engaged in production and seek to profit from fluctuations in the market price.[43] Major producers, including the Zambian companies, who base their prices on official LME quotations (either "spot" or "forward") normally ship their product directly to their customers. The role of the LME in such transactions is aptly explained thus: "These producers and fabricators adopt the official London Metal Exchange quotations as their pricing basis in the same way as one might use the official Stock Exchange quotations for a private share deal."[44]

---

agreement with the minority shareholders. (See chap. 2.) However, spectacular increases were recorded in 1973 and 1974 (resulting partly from production problems in Chile and circumstances noted in chap. 5), when monthly averages of more than £800 per tonne were recorded. Planners in the copper exporting countries do not believe that such windfall profits make up for lean years and the constantly rising costs of industrial imports. Michael West has noted that between 1966 and 1972, "the purchasing power of Zambia's (or any other producing nation's) copper exports has fallen by 30 per cent." ("Price Stability for Copper," p. 152).

42. Separate prices are quoted for electrolytic copper wirebars (the preponderant form of Zambia's export product) and two other common forms—blister (an unrefined product) and cathodes (a highly refined product that has not been cast into a commercial shape).

43. A paper prepared by the Zambian mining companies for the Lusaka Inter-Governmental Copper Conference of 1967 states that copper merchants, like the owners of independent copper refineries, are not concerned with promoting price stability. But this source also states that the merchants and refineries themselves are not particularly to blame for instability in the market. Furthermore, it is noted, "merchants and refineries have a proper role to play in the rational deployment of supplies given that such a large proportion of copper consumption is accounted for by scrap and that a significant tonnage of copper is produced from small mines widely scattered geographically and without refineries of their own" ("Marketing of Primary and Secondary Copper"). The sale of copper scrap is indeed a very important factor in the overall supply situation. Copper is easily recycled for use and scrap is reported to account for some 42 percent of annual consumption. However, many countries restrict the export of scrap copper, and its sale does not bulk large in international trade. Ibid.; also "Copper Scrap: A Study of Scrap and Its Influence on the Copper Market," an interim report by the International Wrought Copper Council, April 1967; and Prain, Selected Papers, 4:107, 134.

44. R. L. Prain, "Copper Pricing Systems" (1958) in Selected Papers, 2:16. This article, which is also a source for what follows, is especially recommended. For a

Although Zambian copper has usually been sold on the basis of LME quotations, this historic relationship has not been without interruptions. In 1939 copper was designated a strategic raw material by the British government and trading on the LME was suspended. Price controls and bulk purchase agreements with the British government remained in effect for fourteen years until transactions on the LME were finally permitted to resume in 1953.[45] Since then the companies have periodically attempted to regulate and stabilize the selling price of copper with limited success. In 1955 world production was disrupted by strikes in the Chilean, Northern Rhodesian, and United States mines. To counteract rising prices, both RST and the Congo producer, Union Minière du Haut-Katanga (UMHK), decided to sell on the basis of monthly "announced" prices that were lower than the prevailing market prices.[46] When price levels declined again during 1956–1957, the Rhodesian and Katangan producers, including the Anglo American Corporation as well as RST and UMHK, decided to cut back production by 10 percent. In 1962 all three producing groups made cutbacks of 15 percent; RST and the Congo company reduced production, while the AAC Group cut its sales and stockpiled the surplus to be sold at a later time. These actions, supplemented by selective market support operations on the LME, helped maintain the price at satisfactory levels.

In 1964, with prices on the upswing, the Zambian and Congo mining companies decided to abandon the LME basis in favor of a producers' price, initially set at £236 per long ton. The Chilean producers' decision to line up with this pricing basis solidified a potentially powerful deterrent to spiraling prices that would endanger the long-term interests of the industry. Nonetheless, prices on the LME continued to rise, strongly stimulated by demands that were generated in part by the Vietnam war. The producer price itself was gradually hiked to £336 per long ton, while the LME spot price climbed to a peak of £790 per long ton. In April 1966, the Chilean producers unilaterally decided to increase their price to

historical account of copper marketing with particular reference to the London Metal Exchange, see Brown and Butler, pp. 113–140; also Peter Bohm, *Pricing of Copper in International Trade: A Case Study of the Price Stabilization Problem* (Stockholm: The Economic Research Institute, 1968).

45. "During those 14 years Roan delivered more than 98 percent of its production to the British Government" (RST Group, *An Introduction to RST* [1964]).

46. "Marketing of Primary and Secondary Copper," pp. 17–18.

£496 per ton. The Zambian producers then reverted to LME quotations, which then declined to a more normal level. Meanwhile the Zambian government imposed an export tax on copper to skim off part of the surplus profits.[47]

The producer price experiment of 1964–1966 is noteworthy as a concerted effort by major producers to stabilize rising prices at a healthy level. Although a united front of major producers in the principal exporting countries could not be indefinitely maintained, a moderate if temporary success was nonetheless achieved. The companies themselves drew a modest and sober conclusion to the effect that the basic causes of price fluctuations "are intimately related to trade cycles and wars. Attempts to stabilize the copper price through improved marketing methods alone are not going to be wholly successful."[48] This statement did not imply that the companies had come to accept the LME as the best possible pricing basis. Prain, a leading critic of pricing by reference to exchange quotations, has clearly stated the principal drawback of this method: "The much-sought-after stability for copper does not appear to be attainable so long as copper is quoted on a commodity exchange."[49]

However firm may be the attachment of industry leaders to the goal of price stability, it is far more fervently desired by the national governments of the major mining countries. The fundamental importance of price stabilization for the primary products of less-developed countries has been emphasized by authoritative studies and reports for many years. Even the soundest economic planning for such countries is liable to disorientation as a result of extreme fluctuations in the prices and export proceeds of crucial products.[50] Given the flagrant instability of copper prices and the inadequacy of attempts by industry leaders to devise reliable and effective remedies, governmental action appears necessary.

Shortly before Zambian independence, a UN economic mission recommended that copper producing countries hold a conference at the governmental level in order to reconcile their diverse interests with their common need for price stabilization.[51] In

47. See chap. 2.

48. "Marketing of Primary and Second Copper," p. 27.

49. Prain, *Selected Papers*, 4:106–107, 119.

50. See Gunnar Myrdal, *An International Economy* (New York: Harper & Bros., 1956), pp. 250–253, for a cogent analysis of this problem.

51. *Report of the UN/ECA/FAO Economic Survey Mission on the Economic Development of Zambia*, p. 49.

November 1966, the presidents of Zambia and Chile jointly announced their decision to convene a conference of four countries that are foremost in the production of newly mined copper for export, namely, Zambia, Chile, the Congo, and Peru. Together, they noted, these countries are responsible for three-fourths of the export trade in copper throughout the world.[52] In June 1967 these four countries participated in an Inter-Governmental Copper Conference at Lusaka. They agreed to establish a permanent organization—the Inter-Governmental Council of Copper Exporting Countries (CIPEC) with headquarters in Paris. The council would operate through a Conference of Ministers, a Governing Board of governmental representatives, and a Copper Information Bureau that would perform the functions of data gathering, analysis, and research.[53]

Despite this organizational achievement, the conference made little if any progress toward the elusive goal of price stabilization. Few original ideas appear to have blossomed on this thorny subject.[54] The final communique implicitly endorsed an industry view, which had been advocated by Prain, to the effect that an attempt should be made to arrange for a permanent option to sell copper at a fixed minimum price to the United States government strategic stockpile. Prain had suggested that this stockpile, which was originally intended to promote military security, might be rededicated to the purpose of world development.

> It does seem to me . . . that the existence of the U.S. stockpile concept may prove to be complementary in the next few years to the developing countries' concept of a guaranteed market for their raw material at a floor price, which will prevent distress in such countries at times when production exceeds consumption; a situation which would otherwise leave such developing countries with no alternatives but to accept prices which cannot cover their development ambi-

52. "The Santiago Declaration," November 30, 1966. For background, from the Chilean standpoint, see Raymond F. Mikesell, "Conflict and Accommodation in Chilean Copper," in *Foreign Investment in the Petroleum and Mineral Industries: Case Studies of Investor–Host Country Relations* (Baltimore: The Johns Hopkins Press, 1971), pp. 369–386.

53. "Inter-Governmental Copper Conference: Draft Communique," June 7, 1967 (mimeo).

54. This was noted immediately by astute observers in Zambia. "How Safe Is Zambia's Copper?" *Business and Economy of Central and East Africa* (July 1967), pp. 8-10.

tions or to create unemployment and social distress through heavy curtailment.[55]

Other suggestions by the Zambian industry involved the use of agreements to curtail either sales or production, where necessary to support prices by restricting supply. Prain specifically proposed the deliberate creation of reserve mine capacities, which would be a new departure in the mining industry. Heretofore, he observed, copper producers have held to the ideal of production at 100 percent of capacity. In practice, 93 percent has been the normal average utilization of capacity. In his view, the percentage of utilization should be cut to 85 or 90 percent of capacity while total production and mine capacity continues to rise. This kind of planning would enable the industry to "meet surges in demand without the expensive alternative of carrying excessive amounts of copper in stocks."[56]

Five years after the expression of these ideas it was painfully apparent that the architects of intergovernmental cooperation had failed to protect the price of copper from destabilizing forces. Their ability to attain this elusive goal is widely doubted. Since the industry has been substantially nationalized in three of the leading copper-export countries—Chile, Zambia, and Zaire—international corporations may lack the incentive to take initiatives in this field. Moreover, these nationalizations appear to have diminished a previously existing capacity in the world of copper for industrial leadership on an international scale. This result is attributed to excessive bureaucratization as well as possibly divergent national viewpoints. These causes may detract from the effectiveness of CIPEC, which in other respects provides an adequate framework for the exercise of leadership by the governments of the producing countries. At the very least, it seems clear that ample scope for potential

55. Prain, Selected Papers, 4:110, 121. Also, "The Problems of Establishing a Stable Price for Copper" (LICC/WP(MC)/10, Part II), paper presented by the Zambian mining companies to the Lusaka Inter-Governmental Copper Conference, June 1967, pp. 13–14. The precedent for stockpile operations of this nature was set in 1954 when the U.S. government purchased 100,000 tons of surplus metal from Chile to support the market for Chilean copper. Strauss, pp. 281–282.

56. Prain, Selected Papers, 4:132. The cost of financing a stockpile equivalent to 15 percent of the Zambian mine capacity—about 100,000 tons—was estimated to be about £20 million. "The Problems of Balancing the World Supply and Demand for Copper" (LICC/WP(MC)10, Part I), paper presented by the Zambian mining companies to the Lusaka Inter-Governmental Copper Conference, June 1967, p. 12. This was deemed "a very considerable sum to be locked up."

leadership exists within the flexible framework created by CIPEC.[57]

The Organization of Sales

Under the agreements on state participation, each of the two new Zambian holding companies entered into a sales and marketing contract with its former majority owner—NCCM with the Anglo American Corporation; RCM with Roan Selection Trust. These contracts provided for remuneration amounting to .75 percent of gross sales proceeds (turnover). Sales organization and procedure is a specialized and complicated aspect of the international copper trade. The principal sales agencies are located in consumer-country capitals, like London and Paris, rather than producer-country capitals, like Lusaka and Kinshasa. These agencies with their multiple business relationships are indispensable to the primary producers, but they cannot be nationalized like the mines themselves, nor can they be replaced overnight without disastrous consequences. With preparation, however, it would be possible for the Zambian government to operate a marketing company of its own, which would effect a saving of the large fees that have been paid in satisfaction of the sales contracts. Presumably a Zambian marketing company would decide to engage certain established companies to act as its sales representatives in various national markets.[58] Necessarily, governments that expropriate producing facilities must come to terms with those who control adequate marketing facilities.[59]

57. Comparisons between CIPEC and the far more effective Organization of Petroleum Exporting Countries (OPEC) are inevitable. One distinguishing feature of the copper market, which limits the potential effectiveness of joint action by the exporting countries, is the great importance of scrap, which accounts for more than 40 percent of all copper sales. In a sense, Europe produces a large percentage of its copper requirement—in the form of scrap.

58. Chile's state copper corporation (CODELCO) has operated in this manner since 1967, shortly after the introduction of state participation in joint ventures with American companies, according to information from CODELCO, New York. In 1973 the Zambian government created a wholly owned Metal Marketing Corporation. A new marketing system was being negotiated when this study went to press.

59. The Zaire experience is instructive. Following the expropriation of all mining properties belonging to the Union Minière de Haut-Katanga in 1967, the government of the Congo Democratic Republic entered into an agreement with the former owners whereby the latter would provide both processing and marketing services for the new Congolese company—GECOMIN. In 1969 the parties reached agreement on compensation based on sales. Under the terms of this agreement, a sub-

In recent years, Zambian copper has been exported to three principal destinations, namely, Britain, other countries of the European Economic Community, and Japan.[60] The marketing arrangements for these areas are often based on long-standing relationships between established firms. In 1968 the Ministry of Lands and Mines sent questionnaires to the mining groups that were intended to penetrate the mysteries of marketing. Detailed replies were forthcoming, but these shed far more light on the structure of this activity than its inner dynamics.

It emerges that each of the Zambian mining groups has vested primary responsibility for the conduct of sales in a recently formed company that is registered in London. In 1966 the Anglo American Corporation Group created Anmercosa Sales Limited of London to take over marketing functions previously performed by British and French agents. The shares of this company were held by several member-companies of the AAC Group, including Anglo American Corporation (Central Africa) Limited (a Zambian-based management company), Charter Consolidated Limited (of London), and Rand Selection Corporation Limited (of Johannesburg). In certain important markets Anmercosa Sales is represented by other leading firms; for example, R. Aumas et Cie. in France, and Metallgesellschaft A. G., the historic progenitor of the American Metal Company, in Germany. In Japan, Anmercosa Sales works through the giant Mitsubishi corporation.

The evolution of RST's marketing system includes a curious circumstance. The RST Group transferred its head office from London to Lusaka when the Federation of Rhodesia and Nyasaland was formed in 1953. For the next ten years, while the federation existed, this group's marketing activities were directed from Lusaka. In 1963 a wholly owned subsidiary sales organization—RST International Metals Limited—was formed in London. The RST management has explained this move as the result of a decade of growing intimacy between producers and consumers:

---

sidiary of Union Minière—Société Générale des Minerais—will receive 6 percent of the total value of sales in return for services for a period of fifteen years. An excellent account of the dispute leading to nationalization of the mines is contained in Richard Gott, *Mobutu's Congo*, Fabian Research Series No. 266 (London, 1968), pp. 16–28. The subsequent arrangements are reported in Colin Legum and John Drysdale, ed., *Africa Contemporary Record, Annual Survey and Documents 1969-1970* (Exeter, 1970), p. B411.

60. Republic of Zambia, *Economic Report, 1970* (Lusaka, 1971), pp. 66–68.

Between 1953 and 1963 the character of the copper industry in Europe became much more intimate as between producers and consumers. In 1957 producers were invited for the first time to attend as guests at periodical meetings of the International Wrought Non-Ferrous Metals Council (IWNFMC), an association of European copper fabricators. It became apparent at these meetings that producers had to pay more attention to and spend more money on research and development work and at the 1960 meeting of the Council in Salisbury the idea of forming an international organization of producers to support and direct this work was first mooted and resulted in the formation of the Copper Promotion Producers Committee (CPPC) in April 1961. This greater emphasis on promotional work and the more intimate relationship between producers and consumers necessitated the head of the Sales Department spending a great deal of his time travelling abroad as consumers were no longer satisfied with a remote contact with producers through the producers' agents.[61]

The declared object of this change—"to bring the sales staff into the centre of the international copper trade and enable them to keep in close contact with consumers and become directly involved in promotional work"—is entirely plausible. But its coincidence with the demise of European rule in Northern Rhodesia was at least symbolic of an underlying mistrust that would condition future relations between the new African government and the mining companies. In any case, the general reorganization resulted in a three-tiered structure. RST International Metals Limited (of London) acquired a wholly owned subsidiary, namely, Ametalco Limited (London), which was newly formed by the amalgamation of existing sales agencies of American Metal Climax. Ametalco Limited, in turn, acquired several wholly owned regional subsidiaries of its own: Ametalco Inc. (New York), Ametalco S.A. (Geneva), Ametalco GmbH (Frankfurt), Ametalco (Toronto) Limited, and Ametalco (Vancouver) Limited. A fourth tier of this organization is represented by Ametco Shipping Inc., a wholly owned subsidiary of Ametalco Inc. (of New York).

In response to the 1968 governmental questionnaires, each mining group declared that the sole responsibility for determination of its sales policy was vested in its respective executive office in Lu-

61. Roan Selection Trust, "Reply to Questionnaire Submitted to RST by the Ministry of Lands and Mines," January 1968 (mimeo).

saka.[62] The questionnaires also attempted to elicit information about the existence of business relationships involving the sales companies that might be inconsistent with their commitments to market Zambian metals in the most effective manner. For example, an involvement in the marketing of competitive materials, such as scrap copper, aluminum, stainless steel, or engineering plastics, would be questionable from the standpoint of Zambian interests. On this question, each group reported that its respective sales organization eschewed business relationships with companies that were engaged in producing or marketing these materials. On another matter, it was disclosed that the Ametalco Group markets copper, lead, and zinc produced in countries other than Zambia (South Africa, Namibia, Cyprus, Canada, and the United States), deriving the greater proportion of its sales agency revenues from non-Zambian companies.[63] (By contrast, Anmercosa Sales Limited is geared almost exclusively to the sale of Zambian copper, as it had been created for that specific purpose.) Since copper is normally sold at uniform prices for all producers in a given market, an efficient and well-established sales agency may be able to represent the interests of several producers without prejudice to any of them. This follows from the common interest of producers generally in market and price stability. By contrast, as we have noted, metal merchants, who are not producers, do not seek price stability and may gladly accept speculative profits at the expense of the long-term interests of the industry. In reply to a specific question, each group acknowledged that the representatives of its principal sales company may and do act on their own as metal merchants. Specifically mentioned in this connection were Metallgesellschaft A. G.,

62. At the top executive level, the affairs of the AAC Group in Zambia are conducted by Anglo American Corporation (Central Africa) Limited (ACA), a Lusaka-based firm of technical consultants and managers. Since the advent of state participation, ACA has administered the management, consultancy, marketing and other services for NCCM. These services have been contracted to a Swiss subsidiary of the Anglo American Corporation, namely, Anglo American Corporation Management Services A.G.

In 1970, RST Limited (of Zambia), which maintained an executive office in Lusaka in addition to a central office in Ndola, was succeeded by RST International, Inc. (of Delaware). The latter firm was appointed to perform management, consultancy, and marketing services for RCM. Its wholly owned Zambian agency, RST Management Services Limited, was succeeded by AMAX Zambia, Inc. (of Delaware) in 1973.

63. RST Limited, *Explanatory Statement for Meetings of Shareholders To Be Held on 6th August, 1970*, June 1970, Appendix F.

which is reputed to be a particularly effective sales company, and
the several companies in the Ametalco Group. Indeed, Ametalco
Limited is a "ring dealing member" (i.e., certified to participate in
transactions) of the London Metal Exchange, as is the Anglo Chem-
ical and Ore Company (of London), a significant metal trading
company in the AAC Group.

The 1968 questionnaire was designed both to elicit information
about the dual marketing organization and permit an assessment
of its performance and suitability from a Zambian standpoint. It
did not reach the question of the hold that the marketing organization itself might have over the Zambian producing companies. This
form of power may not be apparent because the conflict of interest
in question lies dormant within an established order of conduct.[64]
So long as experienced and influential sales companies identify
their interests with those of the producers, they would be disposed
to refrain from speculative activities that could undermine the
long-term interests of the producers. Conversely, the outbreak of
economic warfare between the African-based producers and their
overseas marketing agents would be costly to each side and unlikely to attract partisans in either camp. Thus market relationships
that transcend nationalism and survive the nationalization of productive enterprises may prove to be the most enduring commercial
ties between the capitalist powers and their erstwhile colonies.[65]
These ties will remain tainted with imperialism until the world
economic order of industrial rich and nonindustrial poor regions
has been fundamentally transformed.

The Problem Pursued

Thus far we have discussed factors that affect the increase of
wealth derived from the copper industry, or the size of the pie that

64. The importance of nonevents or "nondecision-making" as a "face" of power
has been emphasized in an influential article coauthored by a political scientist and
an economist. Peter Bachrach and Morton Baratz, "The Two Faces of Power,"
American Political Science Review 56 (1962): 947–952.

65. The current Marxist view that trading relations have superseded capital ex-
port relations among the bases of imperialism is cogently presented in Pierre Jalée,
The Pillage of the Third World (New York: Monthly Review Press, 1968), pp. 97–115.
Jalée cites Hamza Alavi, "Le Nouvel Imperialisme," *Les Temps Modernes* (August-
September 1964). A comparable analysis of African economic dependence as a
consequence of "balkanization" and an excessive reliance upon raw material ex-
ports is provided in Reginald H. Green and Ann Seidman, *Unity or Poverty: The
Economics of Pan-Africanism* (Baltimore: Penguin Books, 1968).

is divided between Zambia and its non-Zambian partners in mining. The realization of wealth from mining depends upon the development and effective economic use of mineral resources. Such resources are created out of raw materials by scientific and technological means under suitable economic and political conditions.[66] Resource creation in the copper industry consists in the discovery and development of orebodies. According to Prain, the following nontechnological factors are fundamental in determining whether or not orebodies will be developed in areas of mineralization: the potential market for the product; the estimated viability of potential mines, based on anticipated costs and selling prices; the adequacy of the infrastructure, including fuel, power, and transportation facilities; political conditions; finally, if all other conditions are satisfactory, the ability to raise capital for the required investment.[67]

Two of these factors—political conditions and infrastructure—normally lie beyond the span of effective control by mining companies. In avidly nationalistic but underdeveloped countries like Zambia, big companies may be content to reach satisfactory partnership agreements with populistic governments. As shown in chapter 2, the companies were unable to win a strongly desired and economically rational reform of the fiscal system until the advent of state participation in the industry. To be sure, indirectly and in the long run, big business may shape the political environment of any society. The extent to which it does so in Zambia is a basic question in the present study.

The adequacy of the infrastructure is also substantially outside of the sphere of company control, more clearly so since Zambian independence than during the colonial era. Formerly, the companies could decide on economic grounds to use convenient facilities and supplies. Since the Rhodesian crisis, a new and relatively costly logistical pattern has been imposed upon the industry for political reasons.[68] In the past, proposals to improve the infra-

66. This conception of resource as a human creation from raw materials is used imaginatively by Thomas R. De Gregori, *Technology and the Economic Development of the Tropical African Frontier* (Cleveland: The Press of Case Western Reserve University, 1969), pp. 1-33, citing Erich Zimmermann, *World Resources and Industries* (New York: Harper & Bros. 1951).

67. Interview with R.L. Prain, Lusaka, June 7, 1967. Prain has since defined the term "ore" most succinctly as "mineralisation capable of being worked economically" (*The Future Availability of Copper Supplies*, p. 12).

68. See chap. 5.

structure for mining that were favored by the companies were likely to receive sympathetic consideration from relevant governmental agencies in central Africa and abroad. A case in point is the Rhodesia Congo Border Power Corporation, organized in 1953 on the basis of an £8 million loan from the U.S. government (Export-Import Bank). This company, a wholly owned subsidiary of the two mining groups, provided for the transmission of electrical power from installations in the neighboring Katanga province of the Congo.[69] Since Zambian independence, industry leaders have cooperated with the governments of Zambia and various Western powers to resolve emergency logistical problems. For the most part they have adapted to governmental planning and initiatives. The most significant new development in transportation—construction of the Tan-Zam Railway by the People's Republic of China—was well beyond the span of company influence or control.

Two of the five determinants noted by Prain—the ability to raise capital for investment purposes and the perceived potential market for the product—depend in good part upon the capabilities of the mining interests themselves. Big mining groups with established competence in the various phases of discovery, production, and supply, are usually able to borrow large sums of money ("Chiefly," it is argued, "on the security of their high reputation.")[70] from governments and public lending institutions. For instance, in 1951 the U.S. government extended a loan of £5 million to develop the RST mine at Chibuluma in return for the delivery of metal to the United States strategic stockpile.[71] As mentioned earlier, in 1968 the government of Japan gave its approval to a multimillion-dollar loan by large Japanese companies to the Anglo American Corporation in Zambia. In their new seminationalized forms, the two groups have been able to raise large loans from British banks and governmental sources in West Germany and the United States.[72]

69. James Mitchell, general manager, Copperbelt Power Company, "Electricity Supply in Zambia," 1968 (mimeo). Also Barber, pp. 125–126. Between 1951 and 1954 the U.S. government also made loans totalling $24 million to the Rhodesia Railways. Ibid., p. 126, n. 1.

70. K. C. G. Heath, "New Patterns of World Mining," Optima 19 (March 1969): 30.

71. Chibuluma Mines Limited, Statement by the Chairman, Sir Ronald L. Prain, October 1956; also Barber, pp. 125–126, where a U.S. government grant of £200,000 to the AAC Group's Rhokana Corporation for the construction of its cobalt refinery in return for "an option on its output" is also noted.

72. Nchanga Consolidated Copper Mines Limited 1972 Annual Report, p. 6; Roan Consolidated Mines Limited 1972 Annual Report, pp. 6–7.

As regards the perceived potential market for new products, we may remark that the major mining groups have access to unparalleled expertise in the fields of forecasting and research[73] in addition to their intimate relationships with the most experienced marketing agencies.

Prain's fifth factor—the estimated viability of any potential mine—depends upon cost calculations, including the question of taxation, and expectations about the selling price of copper. Costs may be regarded as being relatively predictable and stable in Zambia now that certain fiscal issues (including the royalty question) have been resolved and labor relations have been reestablished on a nonracial foundation. The market price for copper, however, continues to be an unruly element, subject to unpredictable fluctuations that could threaten the well-being of the industry and the welfare of the country.

The mining groups, which still control marketing, have been unable to translate that power into a solution to the problem of chronic instability in prices. As noted previously, their spokesmen attribute the persistence of such instability to forces beyond their control, particularly "trade cycles and wars." While they are wary of governmental encroachments on their marketing functions, they are not averse to the principle of governmental action in support of price stabilization.[74]

For its part, the Zambian government may be inclined to perceive a relation between price instability and its own lack of control

73. Research and development organizations established by copper producers on an international basis include The International Copper Development Council (CIDEC) and The International Copper Research Association, Inc. (INCRA). "The Substitution of Copper by Other Metals and Plastics and the Development of Other Copper Uses."

74. As noted previously, the Zambian mining companies have favored an option to sell at minimum prices to the U.S. government stockpile. However, they dislike the idea of national government stockpiles in various countries since such stockpiles would tend to depress prices at all times and might be used to thwart price increases to the detriment of the producers. Prain's version of this objection is succinct: "On the question of stocks, not only does this require very large sums of finance, but here copper is at a disadvantage compared with certain competitors who produce substitute materials, because the latter are able to build up considerable stocks without any effect on price, since none of these competitive materials are quoted on commodity exchanges whose level of price is greatly influenced by the level of stocks" (Selected Papers, 4:120). Yet the mining companies would favor consideration of governmental stockpiling schemes provided they allow for "a substantial measure of producer control" ("The Problems of Balancing the World Supply and Demand for Copper," pp. 18-19).

over the mysterious organization of marketing. In 1968 the government decided to create a Metal Marketing Company of Zambia, in which it would own 51 percent while the two mining groups would hold equal shares of the balance. In this way the government meant to assert its right to control the formulation of marketing policies. The mining companies did not object since the proposed arrangement was adapted to their existing channels and procedures.[75] Although the governmental marketing company lapsed temporarily with the advent of state participation in the industry, the principles of state control over general marketing policies and participation by Zambian trainees in marketing procedures was incorporated into the marketing contracts that were negotiated with the former majority owners.

From the standpoint of this analysis, neither of the foregoing explanations penetrate to the core of the problem. Prain is foremost among those who have identified the most relevant explanation. It consists in the virtual absence of vertical integration "from the mine to the ultimate consumer" in Europe as compared with the extensive degree of such integration in the United States.[76] The American producers sell copper at prices which they themselves establish in accordance with business requirements. By contrast, the price of Zambian copper is difficult to insulate from destabilizing market forces because it is produced in one economic and political jurisdiction for sale in another. The condition of a country that produces basic industrial resources that are not usable in the domestic economy is termed underdevelopment. This is the root of the problem.

The implied solution involves industrial development—the construction of industries that would process raw materials to successively higher levels of manufacture. Clearly the immediate prospects for industrial growth in Zambia by itself are severely limited. As Reginald H. Green and Ann Seidman have demonstrated, pan-African unity in the form of effective continental planning and the creation of multiterritorial markets is a precondition for industrialization on a major scale in Africa.[77] But the impulse toward such unity at present is feeble in comparison with the grip of postcolonial parochial nationalism. For the time being, therefore, Zam-

75. RST Group of Companies, *Statement by the Chairman, Sir Ronald L. Prain*, November 1968, p. 5.
76. Prain, *Selected Papers*, 4:121–122.
77. Green and Seidman, *Unity or Poverty*.

bia's program for vertical integration beyond the stage of copper production must be modest. Nonetheless, efforts to this end are important from the standpoint of technical education as well as economics. Furthermore, the lessons of an early achievement in this field are not without significance for the wider concerns of this study.

ON THE FABRICATION OF COPPER IN ZAMBIA

The newly developing countries are expected to consume increasing quantities and percentages of the world supply of primary copper. However, the statistics on present consumption are sobering. Briefly, it has been observed that nonindustrial countries, comprising some two-thirds of the world's population outside of the communist sector, account for a mere 6 percent of primary copper consumption.[78] In 1967 the consumption of primary copper outside of the Soviet-supplied sector was estimated as follows:[79]

	Consumption of Refined Copper in short tons
U.S.A.	2,510,000
Canada	240,000
Japan	600,000
Europe (including Turkey)	2,010,000
Elsewhere	400,000
Total Refined Copper	5,760,000
Less the amount refined from secondary copper (recycled in the form of scrap, etc.)	950,000
Total Primary Consumption	4,810,000

78. *Report of the UN/ECA/FAO Economic Survey Mission on the Economic Development of Zambia*, p. 41. A figure of 10 percent has also been suggested, allowing for the copper content of goods imported from the industrial countries. Ibid.

79. "Summary of the Known Expansion Plans for All Copper Producing and Treating Countries of the World" (LICC/WP(MC)/1), a paper presented by the Zambian mining companies to the Lusaka Inter-Governmental Copper Conference, June 1967. Cf. Brown and Butler, pp. 75–89.

Prain has estimated that the total annual copper consumption for the entire world during the mid-1960s, including primary copper, secondary copper, and the copper content of remelted alloy scrap, was nearly 9 million short tons.[80] The industrialized regions of North America, Europe, the USSR, and Japan consumed 90 percent of it. In this sector of the world average per capita annual consumption was 16 pounds, compared with .75 pounds, per head in the rest of the world. In the United States consumption had reached an average of 26 pounds per head, which appeared "to represent a saturation point, that is, a point where increases in income per head are not matched by growth in copper consumption per head." Prain anticipated that for the balance of this century the greatest absolute and percentile increases in copper consumption will occur in the industrialized sectors outside of the United States:

> As infrastructure nears completion less copper is needed for capital goods. The industrial countries in one way or another enjoy the copper consumption of the last fifty years which went into railways, telephones, electricity generation and so on whilst consumer durables, cars, refrigerators, etc., become relatively more important. It does not seem unreasonable to suppose that, provided copper be available at reasonable prices, the richer group may by the year 2000 be approaching copper saturation at 24 lb. per head, making total consumption of 18 million tons, 10 million more than now.[81]

In the poorer, underindustrialized countries, consumption levels would also rise, but at a more modest rate:

> If the growth pattern outlined under the United Nations Development Decade were in fact to take place, we might expect 4 lb. a head by the year 2000; however, this is very ambitious and more likely to be reached in say two generations rather than by the end of the century, when we might reasonably expect to see at least 2 lb. a head. Even 2 lb. a head for 5½ billion people amounts to 5½ million tons, an increase of over 4 million tons on the present.
>
> Taking richer and poorer countries together we can very

80. Prain, *Selected Papers*, 4:52. Elsewhere Prain has defined primary copper as "copper produced directly from a mining operation," and secondary copper as "copper supplies arising as a result of re-melting copper in the form of scrap, etc." (Ibid., 3:10).

81. Ibid., 4:53.

tentatively guess at a world consumption in the year 2000 of over 20 million short tons; this includes primary copper, refined from scrap, and also copper in scrap that does not become refined again as pure copper. These figures are of course based on assumptions of continued availability and reasonable price.[82]

These statistics may be interpreted to demonstrate both the feasibility of, and the necessity for, copper fabricating industries in the less-developed countries. However, the comparative advantage of production for home use rather than export may be debatable. Thus, the UN Economic Survey Mission to Zambia of 1964 cautiously recommended the study of a limited project involving the installation of machinery to produce wire rods for local and regional markets.[83] In a similar vein, Prain argued that for the time being Zambia would gain more from investments in the expansion of its mining output than from the commitment of resources to construct a fabricating plant.[84] This argument did not persuade those Zambian leaders and planners who were dissatisfied with the rate of mining investment in proportion to the flow of dividends. Furthermore, the mining companies were believed to lack enthusiasm for local fabrication for reasons that were not truly disinterested. In particular, it was noted that fabricated products might be competitive with goods produced by the mining companies' own customers. In any case, a number of governmental ministers and key civil servants were strongly attached to the idea of making a start in domestic fabrication, both as an economic proposition and as a symbolic commitment to the industrial future of Zambia. This goal was accomplished by 1971 with the assistance of a consortium of outside interests.

The original feasibility study was performed by Maxwell Stamp (Africa) Limited, a British firm of international economic consultants that is highly regarded by the Zambian government, under the auspices of Continental Ore Corporation, an American metal trading firm with small mining interests in Zambia. Upon completion of this study, Continental Ore approached the Swedish company, Svenska Metallverken, which had formed a joint company

82. Ibid., pp. 53–54.
83. *Report of the UN/ECA/FAO Economic Survey Mission on the Economic Development of Zambia*, p. 78.
84. Prain, *Selected Papers*, 4:45.

with the American copper giant, Phelps Dodge Corporation, in New York. Soon it became apparent that whatever reservations the Zambian mining companies might have, they were not about to abandon this significant cognate field to outside interests.

In general, the Anglo American Corporation was more inclined to diversify its Zambian interests than was RST. Their respective attitudes were consistent with Anglo American's self-conception as an African continental company in contrast to RST's self-image as a specialized mining company. Accordingly, RST raised a few broad objections to the proposal for fabrication, arguing that an overseas export trade in semimanufactured products would be costly to Zambia (tariffs, shipping, competition with the Zambian companies' own customers, the high cost of financing supply stocks, etc.), while the domestic and African regional markets did not as yet justify the required expenditures on economic grounds.[85] For their part, officials of the Anglo American Corporation seemed mainly concerned to head off any uneconomic operation that might be used as a device to undermine the price of copper.

Faced with an external challenge in the form of other, potentially rival corporate interests, the Zambian mining groups offered a proposal (initiated by RST) to build a plant to produce high quality copper rods, a premium product that might be sold both abroad and in Africa to manufacturers of cable and wire. Desirable in itself, this proposal did not fully satisfy the Zambian government, which also wanted a plant that would produce more conventional semimanufactured products as well as cable and wire for Zambia and the eastern African market. At length a compromise was reached providing for the formation of two separate companies: one to produce high-quality rods as proposed by the mining companies; the second to manufacture cable and wire from rods produced by the first company. Initially it appeared that the first company would be owned by the two Zambian mining groups in partnership with the Industrial Development Corporation of Zambia (INDECO), while the second company would include all of the aforementioned participants in negotiations as well as the state agency. In 1968 the government decided to create a single company, Metal Fabricators of Zambia Limited (ZAMEFA), in which

85. Most of these arguments appear in Prain, "Prospects for Fabricating Copper in East and Central Africa," ibid., pp. 39-49.

INDECO would hold a controlling interest of 51 percent. The remaining 49 percent of this enterprise was shared as follows: Phelps Dodge Svenska Metallverken, 19.6 percent; Continental Ore Corporation, 9.8 percent; Anglo American Corporation, 9.8 percent; RST, 9.8 percent.

The opening of ZAMEFA's K2.5 million plant at Luanshya in 1971 marked a signal achievement for the Zambian government. It was particularly gratifying to those who believe that Zambia should develop as an industrial country. ZAMEFA's early performance was highly successful.[86] Clearly the consortium organized by Continental Ore Corporation made a crucial contribution. However, RST officials insist that Phelps Dodge Corporation would not have acted contrary to the wishes of their own company. An understanding of sorts between these companies may well have existed; indeed Phelps Dodge is reported to have corporate links with RST's parent company, AMAX, Inc.

The government achieved its purpose by using the consortium as a means of leverage to move the mining groups from an obstructive to an accommodative position. In the end, potential conflicts of interest had been removed through negotiations. A lasting pattern of action may have been revealed. So long as Zambia relies upon capitalist enterprise for development, it will be necessary to cooperate with the established international companies. This finding repeats the lesson of recent attempts (cited earlier in this chapter) to introduce capitalist competition into the field of mining itself. The established mining groups may be cajoled and maneuvered into new positions, but they are too big and influential to be beaten at their own game.

86. Zambia prohibits the importation of items that are manufactured by ZAMEFA. Meanwhile, a ZAMEFA subsidiary has acquired (from British Insulated Callender's Cables Limited—one of the largest customers for Zambian copper) exclusive rights to import and sell, within Zambia, cable and wire products that ZAMEFA itself does not produce. During its first year of operations, ZAMEFA produced a wide variety of high quality cable products for sale in Zambia at prices that were lower than those that had been charged for imports. ZAMEFA has purchased refined copper from NCCM at the prevailing LME price, so that the mining companies do not incur any loss in sales revenue. The Zambian mining industry constitutes ZAMEFA's main market; but other domestic markets, as well as an export trade, are being vigorously developed.

FOUR

The Claims of Society:

LABOR AND SOCIAL RELATIONS

The first care of a commercial company is the security of its investment; the second is the realization of profits for the owners. These
aims are normally reconciled with the public moralities of an enlightened age. In newly developing societies, enlightenment has
often come with the blinding flashes of political change. The
pent-up claims of society, long muted, are then asserted with re-
lentless energy. Those commercial organizations that seek to survive and prosper under the new order contrive to satisfy the new
ensemble of social expectations. Their success or failure may hinge
on the alacrity, or lack of it, with which they adapt to the forces of
social and political change.

This chapter deals with the mining industry's response to the
demands of its host society in two broadly defined spheres. First,
labor relations in the mining industry have been transformed by
the emergence of a skilled and cohesive African working class.
With the formation of the African Mineworkers' Union in 1948, this
section of the working class assumed a leading role in the national
struggle against white domination.[1] The nature and experience of
this labor force, including its social environment and political significance, has been studied with particular distinction by a number
of social scientists. The present account is indebted to previous
work and strictly limited to the consideration of a few issues that
have tested the adaptability of the mining companies to new condi-

---

1. This is phrased to allow for the fact of considerable dissonance between the
perceptions of the African Mineworkers' Union on the one hand and those of the
nationalist political party leaders on the other. See Robert H. Bates, *Unions, Parties,
and Political Development: A Study of Mineworkers in Zambia* (New Haven: Yale University Press, 1971), pp. 128–136; Elliot J. Berg and Jeffrey Butler, "Trade Unions," in
Political Parties and National Integration in Tropical Africa, ed. James S. Coleman and
Carl G. Rosberg, Jr. (Berkeley and Los Angeles: University of California Press,
1964), pp. 353–356; and Shimshon Zelniker, "Changing Patterns of Trade Unionism: The Zambian Case, 1948–1964" (Ph.D. diss., University of California, Los
Angeles, 1970).

tions. Second, the mining industry has been responsible for the rise of a conurban region—the multitown Copperbelt—and related demographic phenomena, such as the ribbon-like pattern of settlement along the 500-mile line-of-rail. Inevitably, the mining companies have become involved in activities other than mining. Paramount among such activities are their continuing commitments to build and develop mining townships, including the obligation to provide health and social services. The implications of these and other nonmining commitments will be considered in the latter part of this chapter.

LABOR RELATIONS

In 1922 the British South Africa Company adopted a new policy to the effect that henceforth mining concessions in Northern Rhodesia would be granted to financially potent enterprises only (see chapter 2). Thereafter the forerunners of the Copperbelt mining companies—in particular, the Bwana Mkubwa Company (a subsidiary of the Anglo American Corporation) and Selection Trust Limited—undertook to make systematic explorations of the territory. Between 1925 and 1927, vast deposits of easily treated sulphide ores were discovered beneath the surface of the Copperbelt. This gave rise to a period of construction and intensive mine development. By 1931, some 21,000 Africans were employed by the Northern Rhodesian mines.[2]

Formation of the Proletariat

Previously, Northern Rhodesian Africans had been employed by a few mines in Northern Rhodesia—Kansanshi, Broken Hill, and Bwana Mkubwa—as well as the mines of neighboring countries, namely South Africa (until 1913), Southern Rhodesia, and the Congo. In 1921 there were some 6,000 Northern Rhodesians employed by the Union Minière du Haut-Katanga, comprising 56 percent of that Belgian company's African work force.[3] It has been estimated that by 1930 some 100,000 Northern Rhodesians were

2. Charles W. Coulter, "The Sociological Problem," in *Modern Industry and the African*, 2nd ed., ed. J. Merle Davis (London: Frank Cass, 1967), p. 35.
3. Ibid., p. 53. This proportion declined sharply during the next decade as Union Minière undertook to recruit its labor force locally.

working for wages either within the country or across its borders.[4] Fewer than 10 percent of this work force had settled permanently at their places of employment. The others were migrant workers whose lives have been described as follows: "The vast majority of these workers keep their roots in the country. They regard a distant village as their home. In many cases their wives and families remain there. They work for short periods of time, often as little as a few months, seldom more than a couple of years."[5]

The most powerful stimulus for Africans to seek employment away from home was the introduction of a poll tax throughout both North-eastern and North-western Rhodesia between 1900 and 1904. The tax was specifically intended by the administrators of these two territories to produce a steady flow of labor without resort to legal compulsion.[6] In 1914, three years after the amalgamation of these territories to form Northern Rhodesia, a uniform rate of ten shillings per annum was adopted for the entire country. As L.H. Gann has observed, "Taxation gave an enormous impetus to migration. It created a regular instead of a seasonal demand for cash, and extended that demand over the whole of the Territory, not just areas near to labour centres."[7]

African labor was obtained by means of recruitment procedures that were regularized over a period of years. In 1903 a Native Labour Bureau was created and granted the exclusive right to recruit labor north of the Zambezi River for employment in Southern Rhodesia. Other agents recruited workmen for employment in Northern Rhodesia and the Congo. Their methods were dubiously legal and coercive.[8] During the Copperbelt boom of the latter 1920s, the various mining companies engaged in competitive recruitment. In 1930, under pressure from the government, the companies merged their recruitment programs to form a new Native Labour Association. At this time, the period of service for recruited laborers was extended from six months to just over a year (twelve "tickets" of thirty days of labor each), while workers who presented themselves independently were employed on a monthly

4. E. A. G. Robinson, "The Economic Problem," in *Modern Industry and the African,* ed. Davis, p. 136.

5. Ibid., pp. 136–137.

6. L. H. Gann, *The Birth of a Plural Society* (Manchester: Manchester University Press, 1958), pp. 76–81.

7. Ibid., pp. 84–85.

8. Michael Gelfand, *Northern Rhodesia in the Days of the Charter* (Oxford: Basil Blackwell, 1961), pp. 100–102.

THE CLAIMS OF SOCIETY

basis. By now, however, the pull of employment at the mines was strong enough to produce an abundant supply of low-wage labor without organized recruitment. Consequently, such recruitment for the Copperbelt mines was terminated in 1931, after which all African workers were engaged on a monthly basis at wage rates that were high by comparison with local pay scales, although they were decidedly low by world mining standards. (Underground workers were paid at a rate of thirty shillings for a "ticket" of thirty working days, while surface workers were paid seventeen shillings sixpence.) In addition to wages, mine employees were provided with rations, housing, and medical care; they were also repatriated to their homes at the end of their contracts.[9]

The regular repatriation of migrant laborers to their home villages following fixed periods of service was a crucial part of the recruitment system. In an illuminating essay on the formation of the Zambian proletariat, Helmuth Heisler contends that this practice gave rise to a transitional class of proletarianized peasants that he terms a class of "target-proletarians."[10] This class of working people depended upon a combination of wages and farm incomes for their livelihoods.[11] Low wages, the lack of job security for Africans and, consequently, the perpetuation of migrant labor delayed the inevitable formation of a true proletariat—a class of persons who are primarily if not exclusively dependent upon wage labor—on the Copperbelt. However, the termination of organized recruitment in 1931 prompted many African men to make themselves available for employment in urban mining areas.

At this time, governmental policy was designed to strengthen the traditional authority of tribal chiefs and prevent the emergence of urban African communities.[12] This viewpoint was consistent with the desire of white settlers to maintain racial segregation and prevent African advancement within the modern economic sector.

9. Robinson, pp. 155–177.

10. Helmuth Heisler, "A Class of Target-Proletarians," *Journal of Asian and African Studies* 5 (July 1970): 161–175.

11. See also Robert E. Baldwin, *Economic Development and Export Growth: A Study of Northern Rhodesia, 1920–1960* (Berkeley and Los Angeles: University of California Press, 1966), pp. 114–121; William Watson, *Tribal Cohesion in a Money Economy* (Manchester: Manchester University Press, 1958); Walter Elkan, *Migrants and Proletarians* (London: Oxford University Press, 1960), pp. 129–140; E. J. Berg, "Backward-Sloping Labor Supply Functions in Dual Economies: The Africa Case," *Quarterly Journal of Economics* 75 (August 1961): 468–492.

12. Richard Gray, *The Two Nations: Aspects of the Development of Race Relations in the Rhodesias and Nyasaland* (London: Oxford University Press, 1960), pp. 110–112.

The mining magnates too had reason to appreciate "the unity between town and country" as a form of social insurance in the event of sudden cutbacks in production and employment. With a large pool of migrant labor at their disposal, they could expand or contract the African work force as required at will.[13] On the other hand, the companies also desired to retain the services of their experienced African workmen. As Robert E. Baldwin shows, they were eager to employ married workers, who would remain on the job for long periods, and built housing facilities for that purpose.[14] Realistically, the white mineworkers anticipated that the companies would become increasingly inclined to employ low-cost African labor for semiskilled jobs. In 1936, white miners organized the Northern Rhodesia Mine Workers' Union, mainly to guard against the growing threat, as they saw it, of economic competition from the African work force.[15]

From Tribal to Industrial Organization—On the Copperbelt, as elsewhere in southern Africa, white capital undertook to create a black proletariat but refused to acknowledge the right of black workers to enjoy rudimentary rights of labor on the ground that these workers were first and foremost tribesmen rather than members of an industrial working class. This contemptuous attitude pandered to the self-serving racial biases of white settlers, including privileged white workingmen. It also supplied a rationalization for white resistance to the introduction of trade unionism for African workers. Such attitudes colored the labor policies of the Copperbelt mining companies until the early 1950s, when the industrial strength of an African mineworkers' union was decisively established. Since then, sociologists have demonstrated that the diverse tribal identities of the Copperbelt miners do not detract from their desire to unite as workers for the conduct of normal industrial relations.[16]

13. Ibid., pp. 113–114.
14. Baldwin, pp. 86–89, 130–131.
15. Gray, pp. 104–106.
16. The works of J. Clyde Mitchell and A. L. Epstein shrewdly appraise the extent to which tribal identities are significant in Copperbelt communities. Mitchell found that although tribal identity is "the primary category of social interaction" within the African community, it is scarcely relevant to "Black-White relations," particularly those involving African workers and European managers. *The Kalela Dance,* The Rhodes-Livingstone Papers, No. 27 (Manchester: Manchester University Press, 1956), pp. 31–34. Similarly, Epstein's study of politics and administration in

The first form of representation for African miners—a Council of Tribal Elders—was introduced at the Roan Antelope mine in 1931. Under this sytem, "elders," chosen by and from the various ethnic groups, were recognized by the mine management as official spokesmen for the African workers; they were also empowered to perform judicial functions in petty cases, mainly domestic disputes involving African customary law.[17] During the first major Copperbelt strike in 1935, the tribal elders proved to be singularly ineffective as workmen's representatives.[18] Yet the tribally based system of representation was favored by company management and extended from the Roan Antelope mine to Mufulira. In 1940, a second Copperbelt-wide African strike, involving serious bloodshed at the Nkana mine,[19] resulted in the appointment of an official commission of inquiry; this commission considered a recommendation for the creation of an African trade union. While it rejected this proposal as being premature for the African work force, the commission did envisage the eventual emergence of a mineworkers' union from a revitalized system of tribal elders. In accordance with the commission's report, tribal elders were redesignated more precisely as tribal representatives and introduced at all mines throughout the Copperbelt.[20] A. L. Epstein has noted that the new tribal representatives were viewed by the Northern Rhodesian government as "an embryonic organization for collective bargaining, under the guidance of the Labour Department."[21]

During the 1940s other forms of representation, including boss boys' committees (consisting of representatives of the leaders of

---

Luanshya between 1930–1954 concludes with this observation: "The evidence of the present study shows that in situations involving the total field of Black-White relations the tribal factor tends to be overborne" (*Politics in an Urban African Community* [Manchester: Manchester University Press, 1958], p. 240).

17. Mitchell, pp. 31–32; Epstein, pp. 27–28.

18. Epstein, pp. 29–32.

19. See Robert I. Rotberg, *The Rise of Nationalism in Central Africa* (Cambridge: Harvard University Press, 1965), pp. 156–178, for graphic accounts of the miners' protests in both 1935 and 1940.

20. Epstein, pp. 61–62.

21. Ibid., p. 62. Shimshon Zelniker has described the "renovated system" of tribal representatives thus: "Each tribal group was entitled to representation if its membership on the mine exceeded twenty-five people and by 1941 there were about 105 Tribal Representatives on all of the mines. The status and scope of power permitted the Tribal Representatives were set in a 1942 agreement between the Chamber of Mines—representing the companies—and the Northern Rhodesian Government" ("Changing Patterns of Trade Unionism," pp. 86–87).

labor "gangs") and Works Committees (consisting of representatives of the various mine departments) were devised by the companies to supplement the tribal-representative system. While these innovations were based on industrial rather than ethnic principles, they were introduced by the grace of management and were entirely dependent upon company support.[22] Contrary to the official expectation, trade unionism for the Copperbelt mineworkers was not destined to arise out of the paternalistic and tribalistic agencies that had been created by the companies. Yet the crucial importance of one external European element should be marked: the British Labor government had decided to promote trade unionism in British colonies, "guiding it into a reformist rather than revolutionary channels."[23] Consequently, in 1947, the Colonial Office dispatched William M. Cǫmrie, a trade unionist, to assist in organizing Northern Rhodesian unions.

Comrie's contribution to the formation of an industry-wide African mineworkers' union between 1947 and 1949 has been narrated elsewhere.[24] As Robert H. Bates has observed, both the mining companies and the Northern Rhodesian government were wary of a possible attempt by the Northern Rhodesia Mine Workers' Union (whose membership was composed of Europeans) to organize African workers and favored the alternative proposal for a separate African union.[25] Nonetheless, the companies were disinclined to dispense with the existing agency of tribal representation, even after they had agreed to recognize the new African union's exclusive right to represent African interests in the mines. Shimshon Zelniker has shown that the mining companies were fearful of the African union's potential ability to exert political influence in the mining communities. Consequently, the companies tried to exclude all nonmining matters relating to conditions in the company-owned mine townships from the ambit of union jurisdiction.[26] To this end, the companies, supported by government officials, attempted to strengthen the tribal-representative system as a parallel agency for African interests. But the union's star was ris-

    22. Ibid., pp. 104–112.
    23. L. H. Gann, *A History of Northern Rhodesia: Early Days to 1953* (London: Chatto and Windus, 1964), pp. 367–368.
    24. Epstein, pp. 91–93; Gann, *A History of Northern Rhodesia*, pp. 367–369; Zelniker, pp. 124–135.
    25. Bates, p. 20.
    26. Zelniker, pp. 152–162.

ing, and its membership was growing by leaps and bounds. In the wake of an effective strike in 1952, followed by a favorable arbitration award, the union resolved to eliminate tribal representation in every sector of company jurisdiction. This objective was attained by means of a referendum in 1953, when an overwhelming majority of the 35,000 African mineworkers voted to do away with a system of industrial relations that had become anachronistic in their eyes.[27]

Toward Equal Opportunity: Division of the African Workers

The African mineworkers' union[28] was born into a society rent by the paramount division between privileged Europeans and subordinated Africans. Other social cleavages were minor by comparison with this great racial divide. With regard to the disparity between black and white incomes during the early days of the union, Baldwin has observed that in 1952 "the average real earnings of Europeans (even neglecting their subsidized housing and other facilities) were about 20 times greater than those for Africans."[29]

Yet it would be misleading to perceive the black work force of the 1950s as a single interest group. Inevitably, the growing number of African supervisors and senior clerical employees coalesced to form a relatively privileged interest group apart from the main body of African workers.[30] During the ten-year life span of the racially inspired Federation of Rhodesia and Nyasaland (1954-1963), the mining companies were inclined to foster the diversification of African interests on an incipient class basis. This aspect of company policy is revealed by the record of events relating to the

27. Epstein, pp. 98–101.
28. The official name of this union until January 1965 was Northern Rhodesia African Mineworkers' Trade Union. The name was then changed to Zambia Mineworkers' Union. In 1967, the name Mineworkers' Union of Zambia was adopted.
29. Baldwin, p. 98. According to Baldwin, the official arbitrator who granted a substantial wage award to African mineworkers in 1953 "pointed out that the average basic wage for European surface workers was £89 per month, and that for African employees only £4 2s. 7d. per month. The latter group received free rations, housing, and water valued at £3 2s. 7d. per month, but Europeans, in addition to their basic wage, were getting a copper bonus that amounted to 75% of their basic rate."
30. See the perceptive discussion of social differentiation within the African mining community of this period by Epstein, pp. 148–149.

most emotive issue on the Copperbelt during the 1950s, the great question of "African advancement."

"African Advancement"—In colonial Zambia, this term connoted the admission of Africans to skilled and supervisory categories of employment that had been monopolized by Europeans. African aspirations for skilled employment in the mines were stimulated by opportunities created during World War II, when many European employees left temporarily to enlist in the armed services. It was agreed that for the duration of the war various jobs would be split up among more numerous, less-skilled, and much lower-paid African workmen. In return for this concession, which "proved to be negligible" in practice, the (European) Northern Rhodesia Mine Workers' Union exacted a "closed shop" agreement from the companies, which were told to grant it by the British government for the sake of uninterrupted production.[31]

Immediately after the war, the European union reiterated its opposition to any continued "dilution of labor." This principle was embodied in a new and racially exclusive agreement with the companies. To be sure, the union had offered to represent all employees, including Africans, but the companies "were unwilling to let their African labour force come under the European Union's control."[32] Probably, the companies did not object to the idea of a racially integrated union per se, but they did object to its logical corollary, which was the union's leading principle, that is, "equal pay for equal work and responsibility" or "the rate for the job." European rates of pay, intended to attract and retain skilled workers from abroad, were far higher than prevailing rates for the best-qualified African workers. As a condition of African advancement, the European pay scale would block progress. Furthermore, the companies also concluded that a substantial advancement program would require an extensive revision of the job structure of the industry, involving the creation of many more jobs at low rates of pay, since the industrial skills of African workers generally were not as yet comparable to those of European workers.

For its part, the European union opposed the "fragmentation" of existing jobs and alleged that the mining companies were mainly motivated by a desire to exploit cheap labor. Here was a situation

---

31. Northern Rhodesia, *Report of the Board of Inquiry appointed to inquire into the Advancement of Africans in the Copper Mining Industry of Northern Rhodesia* (Lusaka: Government Printer, 1954), p. 7.

32. Ibid.

that illustrates perfectly the paradox of a colonial society. The legitimate stand of a trade union in defense of high working standards and the dignity of labor ran counter to the immediate requirements of racial justice, defined in terms of a substantial African advancement into the ranks of skilled labor.[33] As a practical matter, European workers, represented by a strong union, monopolized all of the skilled jobs, while African workers were held back by a *de facto* color bar.

In 1953 the time was ripe for action against the industrial color bar. "By this time," as Baldwin has observed, "it was perfectly obvious that African advancement was in the best interests of the mining companies."[34] Furthermore, the color bar would be inconsistent with the meritocratic premise of the emergent Central African Federation. At the behest of the companies, discussions were initiated with both the African and European unions on the issues of advancement.

Predictably, the European union reasserted its stand against both fragmentation and differential wages. However, a governmental board of inquiry found in favor of both devices in order to facilitate African advancement.[35] When the European union rejected this recommendation, the RST Group acted to break the impasse. It gave the European union six months' notice, as required, that the existing labor contract would be terminated and should therefore be renegotiated. Spokesmen for RST have cited this action as a high point of company statesmanship. In the words of a former chairman of AMAX, Inc., this step was taken "at the end of 1954, a time of high copper prices and high profits. RST's readiness to risk a strike under such conditions came to the European Mineworkers' Union as a great shock and brought them to their senses."[36]

In 1955 the European union agreed to the elimination of all racial restrictions in theory and to the transference of twenty-four specific job categories to Africans at lower rates of pay and differential

33. Even the African union endorsed the theoretically sound but from its standpoint impractical European doctrine of "equal pay for equal work." Ibid., pp. 9–10.

34. Baldwin, p. 102.

35. *Report of the Board of Inquiry* (1954), p. 28.

36. Harold K. Hochschild, "The Copper Mining Industry of Northern Rhodesia" (Paper presented at the 50th Anniversary Conference of the Harvard Business School Association, September 5, 1958), p. 15 (mimeo).

conditions of employment. This initial breach in the color bar was expected to benefit only a small number of Africans. Yet it was a significant step toward racial justice in the mining industry for which the RST Group should be credited. Apparently, the Anglo American Corporation Group followed RST's lead "haltingly and reluctantly" throughout these negotiations, which threatened to engender hostile reactions against the corporation by white trade unionists in South Africa.[37]

Dual Unionism—From the African union's standpoint, the advancement scheme posed a threat as well as an opportunity. In 1953 a Mines' African Staff Association had been organized to represent the interests of senior clerical employees and certain supervisors. The formation of this group, which paralleled an existing European organization—the Mine Officials and Salaried Staff Association—was bitterly resented by the African union, which perceived it as a deliberate attempt on the part of the companies to separate the union from "the most influential segment" of the working class.[38] In fact, most of the advanced jobs created in 1955 were allocated to the African staff association rather than the union.[39] The companies favored the formation of the African staff association as a matter of "sound management," on the ground that staff and supervisory employees should not belong to the rank and file union. Candidly, company spokesmen also contemplated with satisfaction the presumed political effects of social differentiation: "The Companies considered that an organization such as the African Staff Association would facilitate the growth of a strong and responsible African middle class, and a stable and level-headed body of African opinion."[40]

Given the African union's adamant opposition to dual unionism, a severe jurisdictional conflict became inevitable. The outcome was a period of intense industrial unrest, spanning several months in

37. Ibid.; and see Nan S. Waldstein, "The Struggle for African Advancement within the Copper Industry of Northern Rhodesia" (Center for International Studies of the Massachusetts Institute of Technology, 1957), pp. 52–88 (mimeo). The Anglo American Corporation's position is set forth in Theodore Gregory, *Ernest Oppenheimer and the Economic Development of Southern Africa* (Cape Town: Oxford University Press, 1962), pp. 476–484, 488–489.

38. Zelniker, pp. 254–255.

39. Northern Rhodesia, *Report of the Commission Appointed to Inquire into the Unrest in the Mining Industry in Northern Rhodesia in Recent Months* (Lusaka: Government Printer, 1956), p. 19.

40. From a summary of submissions by the mining companies to the commission of inquiry. Ibid., p. 31.

1956 and culminating in the detention of more than forty top leaders of the African union on the dubious ground that they had
fomented strikes in order to promote ulterior political objectives.[41]
Thereafter, the African union, reflecting the strong personal conviction of its first president, Lawrence Katilungu, scrupulously
avoided entanglements with political parties.[42] In 1957, the union
agreed to prohibit the use of its funds or facilities by political parties in return for a long-desired dues check-off agreement with the
companies. Bates perceives the union's policy of categorical
abstention from political activity as a response to pressures exerted
by the mining companies: "The companies' efforts appear to have
created in the Mineworkers' Union a pronounced and persistent
suspicion of overtly political activities. Indeed, it would almost
appear that built into their conception of a trade unionist is the
attribute of being uninvolved in party affairs."[43]

In a Marxist vein, the nonpolitical approach of the African
Mineworkers' Union may be termed "economism," or the primary, if not exclusive, reliance upon economic means of struggle (for
better wages, hours, and conditions) on the part of the working
class.[44] Political leaders in Zambia, before and after independence,
have been frustrated by their inability to control either the policies
or the leadership-selection processes of the African Mineworkers'
Union. After examining several illustrative cases, R. H. Bates concludes that the mineworkers effectively distinguish between their
political and industrial interests. Since the emergence of the United
National Independence party (UNIP) as the leading nationalist
party in 1960, nearly all union leaders have been UNIP members

41. This allegation was not substantiated by a subsequent commission of inquiry, which attributed the unrest to the African union's "irresponsible opposition"
to the African staff association. Ibid., pp. 49–52. See also Bates, pp. 251–253.

42. For Katilungu's "conviction that the union should not become embroiled in
political controversy," see ibid., pp. 129 and 251, n. 6. Katilungu was removed from
the union presidency in 1960, after he had changed course and become deeply
involved in party politics. Ibid., pp. 141–146.

43. Ibid., p. 163.

44. See V. I. Lenin, *What Is To Be Done?* (New York: International Publishers,
1943), chap. 3. For a comprehensive documentation of this thesis from a non-
Marxist standpoint, see the work of S. Zelniker, who shows how the African
mineworkers' union has been "able to withstand great political pressure and escape
the danger of becoming a labor appendage of a political party. The struggle for
autonomy," he writes, "illustrates how different a labor ideology can be from that
of a party in search of political independence" ("Changing Patterns of Trade Unionism," p. 7).

as a matter of course. But the basic condition of viable leadership in the African Mineworkers' Union is dedication to the union's separate, nonpolitical identity and to its autonomy as an industrial organization.[45]

During the year preceding independence, UNIP, acting through the United Trade Union Congress, attempted to wrest control of the mine labor force from the African Mineworkers' Trade Union. Briefly, the politically motivated congress, from which the African union had recently withdrawn, encouraged like-minded leaders of the Mines' African Staff Association to adopt a new name and attempt to organize African workers at all levels of the industry in opposition to the established union. Under distinctly left-wing leadership, the previously moderate staff association transformed itself into an aggressively militant general union, called the United Mineworkers' Union. The explanation for this turnabout may reveal a crucial difference between the interests of the most privileged African workers and those of the mining companies as they endeavored to adapt to changing conditions.

It will be recalled that the Mines' African Staff Association had been organized in 1953 by the most highly qualified African employees with the warm approval of the companies. During the "advancement" debate of 1954, the African staff association had characterized the existing employment structure in the mines as "a ladder with only bottom and top steps, with all the middle steps taken away."[46] African advancement by means of job fragmentation and differential pay was intended to provide "some missing rungs in the African industrial ladder."[47] Initially, the rate of advancement was relatively modest, affecting some 1,000 Africans, less than 3 percent of the African work force, between 1955 and 1960.[48] As a result of negotiations during 1960–1962, the African ladder was extended to reach the lowest level of European wages. This provision of greater opportunity for a qualified minority of workers did not satisfy the main African union, which had always been wary of the elitist implications of the "ladder" concept. Reflecting the attitudes and interests of most rank and file African mineworkers, who would not qualify for advancement into the

45. Bates, pp. 126–165.
46. *Report of the Board of Inquiry* (1954), p. 26.
47. Ibid., p. 28.
48. Baldwin, p. 103.

new jobs, the African union pressed for substantial increases in general wages. The union's idea of advancement was very aptly characterized as "the conception of the escalator," in contradistinction to the "ladder" conception of the companies *and* the African staff Association.[49]

By 1963, when Zambian independence had become inevitable, the companies were prepared to do away with all of the remaining obstacles to full Zambianization of the work force.[50] First, it would be necessary to reorganize the "manning structure" of the industry, that is, the description and content of most jobs. Second, the idea of a unified or integrated wage structure, underlying the ladder conception of advancement, would have to be abandoned. In its place, the companies decided to introduce a dual wage structure: one wage rate for "local" workers, based on "local economic factors"; another, higher rate for expatriate workers, to induce them to remain in the industry for as long as they were needed. In keeping with these objectives, the old European workers' union was persuaded to relinquish its closed shop and change its name to the Mine Workers' Society, a frankly expatriate staff association. A monetary compensation scheme was devised for the European workers, who would be asked to relinquish their long-term career expectations in this industry. At the same time, it was also necessary to provide compensation for slightly over one hundred Africans who had advanced into jobs previously held by Europeans at European rates of pay. Henceforth they would be required to work at reduced "local" rates of pay.[51]

At a stroke, the ladder of advancement into the European economic stratosphere had been taken away from African supervisors and other members of the staff association. Henceforth, their interests would be linked more closely with those of the main body of African workers. Consequently, from their point of view, the *raison d'être* for a separate staff association disappeared. Hence, the leaders of the staff association embraced the insurgent United

49. Northern Rhodesia, *Report of the Commission Appointed to Inquire into the Mining Industry in Northern Rhodesia* (Lusaka: Government Printer, 1962), p. 11. It was noted that sixty-one of the proposed new jobs would fall within the jurisdiction of the African staff association while thirty-one would fall to the union. Ibid., p. 7.

50. See Republic of Zambia, *The Report of the Commission of Inquiry into the Mining Industry of Zambia, 1966* (Lusaka: Government Printer, 1966), pp. 10–11.

51. Ibid., pp. 21–22.

Mineworkers' Union (UMU), hoping thereby to reunite the African mineworkers' movement under their own leadership.[52]

Despite governmental recognition and the strenuous efforts of UNIP officials on the Copperbelt in its behalf, UMU "failed to make significant inroads into the [established] union's membership."[53] A contributing cause of the failure was the steadfast refusal of the mining companies to extend recognition or negotiate with the new union. UMU's aim to unite all employees, including those of staff grade, within a single union was contrary to the company doctrine that supervisors should not be represented by the same union as other workers. This viewpoint, based upon a concern to prevent the erosion of industrial discipline, prevailed with the demise of UMU and subsequent formation of the Mines' Local Staff Association in 1965.

Company officials were also wary of leftist political tendencies in UMU; certain of its leaders appear to have been associated with the communist-controlled World Federation of Trade Unions, while the main African union was firmly in the camp of the Western-oriented International Confederation of Free Trade Unions.[54] In the event of an anticipated governmental decision to the effect that there would be one union only in any given industry, the companies resolved to support the established, hard-bargaining, bread and butter African union in preference to one that would be motivated by political and ideological values.[55] Revising their earlier outlook, the mining magnates now perceived that, in newly developing countries, a nascent bourgeoisie is more revolutionary than the working class.

Toward a Nonracial System of Industrial Relations

After independence, two issues were central to the conduct of industrial relations in the mining industry. These were the dual wage structure, devised by the companies in 1963, and the pace of

52. This interpretation of the United Mineworkers' Union is developed by Zelniker, pp. 475–481.

53. Bates, p. 151.

54. Copper Industry Service Bureau (C.I.S.B.) File No. 100.20, Vol. 28; Zelniker, pp. 437–439.

55. Copper Industry Service Bureau, "Future Dealings with UMU," September 19, 1964, C.I.S.B. File No. 100.20, Vol. 28. Alice H. Amsden has described a similar strategy for labor relations on the part of international companies in Kenya. *International Firms and Labour in Kenya: 1945–70* (London: Frank Cass, 1971).

Zambianization—the replacement of expatriates by Zambian nationals. In company planning, these questions were closely related, inasmuch as the high expatriate pay scale was justified in part as a bonus to temporary employees for services that they would be expected to render in training Zambians to replace themselves.

The dual wage system was implemented through complicated and protracted negotiations between the companies and the various employee organizations over a two-year period, commencing in February 1964.[56] At length, the expatriate (in practice, European) organizations, the Mine Workers' Society and the Mine Officials and Salaried Staff Association, agreed to accept fixed-period (three-year) contracts for all of their members. The final settlements included various payments and allowances that were designed both to compensate those expatriates who would be displaced by Zambians and to attract or retain the services of those who would be needed for the conduct of operations and training.[57] Negotiations with the local (in practice, African) organizations, the Zambia Mineworkers' Union (formerly, African Mineworkers' Trade Union) and the Mines' Local Staff Association, were less successful. Both groups had been induced to accept the principle of a dual wage structure and specific wage settlements under some duress, owing to the fratricidal jurisdictional conflict of 1964 and the continuing insecurity of union leaders. Evidently, these settlements were not acceptable to the rank and file of African workmen.[58] In March 1966 African workers began a series of crippling strikes that appear to have been spontaneous and to have taken both the companies and the union leaders by surprise. President Kaunda then appointed a commission of inquiry to make recommendations on conditions of employment in the industry.

Ending the Dual Wage System—The companies defended their dual wage policy on the ground that expatriate and local wage scales were determined in accordance with essentially different considerations. For the time being, they submitted, it was imperative to retain the services of non-Zambian skilled workers. Their

56. *Report of the Commission of Inquiry* (1966), pp. 15–29.

57. See K. Quinn, S. J., "Industrial Relations in Zambia, 1935–69," in *Constraints on the Economic Development of Zambia,* ed. Charles Elliott (Nairobi: Oxford University Press, 1971), pp. 72–73.

58. "While Europeans constituted only 13 percent of the labor force in 1966, they earned over half of the wages paid by the mining companies" (Bates, p. 82).

"salaries and conditions of service have to be such as to compete on a world market for scarce skills."[59] Several objections were raised by company spokesmen against general and continuing increases in the level of wages for local workers: that they would deter expenditures on labor-intensive mine development; that mine wages were already much higher than wages paid in other Zambian industries; that a general wage spiral would be detrimental to the developing economy; that an excessive spread between incomes in the industrial sector and those in the rest of the country would accelerate the exodus of persons from rural areas to the major towns, contrary to the government's policy for national development.[60]

Spokesmen for the Zambian workers, rebutting the company case, insisted upon abolition of the dual wage structure, which they regarded as a degrading legacy of colonialism, and called for substantial wage increases to local workers. Their submissions were supported in principle by the United National Independence Party, which did, however, acknowledge the need for reasonable inducement payments to expatriate workers. The party submitted that if just wage increases in the mining industry happened to create other economic problems outside that industry, this was a matter for the government and should not be cited by the industry as an excuse for its existing "low wage policy."[61]

On the whole, the commission of inquiry found in favor of the unions; it condemned the dual wage structure as being inescapably tainted with racialism and essentially inconsistent with good labor relations. It recommended the adoption of a single wage scale, with inducement allowances for expatriate workers, subject to governmental approval. To establish a new unified wage scale, the commission recommended "a uniform increase in the existing local scale of 22 per cent."[62] This recommendation was endorsed by the government;[63] its subsequent implementation by the industry was

59. *Report of the Commission of Inquiry* (1966), p. 34. Between 1966 and 1968, the turnover rate for expatriate employees was about 30 percent.

60. Ibid., pp. 35–38, where the companies quote at length from the *Report of the UN/ECA/FAO Economic Survey Mission on the Economic Development of Zambia* (Ndola, 1964), pp. 31–33.

61. *Report of the Commission of Inquiry* (1966), pp. 38–42.

62. Ibid., p. 46.

63. Republic of Zambia, *Government Paper on the Report of the Commission of Inquiry into the Mining Industry (Brown Report, 1966)* (Lusaka: Government Printer, 1966), p. 4.

reported to cost some £5 to £6 million in wage increases. However, it was still not accepted by the Zambia Mineworkers' Union as a final determination of the local scale for basic pay.

Other recommendations by the commission of inquiry were as follows: the elimination of unfair distinctions between local and expatriate workers in the provision of allowances and other benefits; the improvement of housing conditions in mine townships; the extension of modern forms of local government to such townships; the eliminations of residual forms of racial discrimination in social, medical, and other public facilities; the creation of a governmental committee to supervise Zambianization and related training programs in the industry; the discontinuance of expatriate recruitment in South Africa under conditions that discriminate against Africans; the establishment of a single union for all regular employees in the industry, and a single association to represent the interests of expatriate employees.[64]

A few of these matters will be considered below. In the matter of employee representation, mergers advocated by the commission of inquiry soon occurred. Thus in 1966, the two expatriate miners' organizations merged to form the Zambia Expatriate Mineworkers Association. This was an interim arrangement, since collective bargaining by expatriates on fixed-term contracts would not be permitted. Yet the mere existence of a separate labor organization for expatriate employees was contrary to Zambian beliefs and a source of great irritation. Eventually, in 1969, the expatriates' association was dissolved.

In 1967 the Zambia Mineworkers' Union, the Mines' Local Staff Association, and the Mines' Police Association merged to create the Mineworkers' Union of Zambia. The new union, which would represent some 44,000 employees, persevered in the long quest of the African mineworkers for a satisfactory determination of basic wages. In 1970 following a comprehensive evaluation of more than 7,000 jobs by an independent firm of industrial consultants, the union and the recently nationalized companies negotiated a basic pay scale for the entire industry. The new agreement, good for three years, involved a 10 percent increase in basic wages plus "annual pay increments for all employees in the union's field of representation, the great majority of whom had previously been on

64. *Report of the Commission of Inquiry* (1966), pp. 50–79.

fixed rates."[65] This agreement eliminated the dual wage system as an issue of industrial conflict in the mining industry. However, the expectations of many mineworkers, especially those in the higher pay grades were disappointed; some of their jobs were actually downgraded to lower pay levels as a result of the evaluation exercise.[66] Aside from the issue of basic pay, African mineworkers would continue to coexist with a large and apparently privileged expatriate work force, whose members receive various incentive payments and other benefits to which local workers are not entitled.

Zambianization—Systematic training to facilitate the advancement of African workers within the copper industry has been provided on a comprehensive basis since the latter 1950s.[67] Between January 1965 and December 1966, expatriate employment in the mines was reduced by more than 1,500 to the approximate level of 6,000, while African employment was increased by over 3,000 to an approximate total of 44,300. By 1966 the vast majority of junior supervisors (section bosses) were Zambians. Above this level, however, among senior supervisors (shift bosses and mine captains), there were only 9 Zambians, while the expatriate total was 714.[68]

A critical appraisal of labor relations in the mining industry in 1966 found "no reason to doubt the sincerity or good faith of the companies" with respect to their programs for the training and promotion of Zambians. But the authors of this assessment also concluded that the Zambian African workers generally did not trust the companies to promote rapid Zambianization at the expense of their expatriate employees.[69] Consequently, a governmental committee on Zambianization in the mining industry was established, including representatives of the companies and unions in addition to civil servants, under the chairmanship of a minister of state. As a result of its own inquiries and consultations,

65. Copper Industry Service Bureau, *Mindeco Mining Year Book of Zambia 1970* (Kitwe), p. 14.

66. R. H. Bates, personal communication.

67. Northern Rhodesia, *Report of the Commission Appointed to Inquire into the Mining Industry in Northern Rhodesia* (Lusaka: Government Printer, 1962), pp. 14–15, 43–58.

68. Republic of Zambia, *The Progress of Zambianisation in the Mining Industry* (Lusaka: Government Printer, 1968), pp. 1–3; *Report of the Commission of Inquiry* (1966), p. 70.

69. *Report of the Commission of Inquiry* (1966), pp. 73–74.

this committee forecast that by the end of 1972, over two-thirds of the senior supervisory positions of shift boss and mine captain would be held by Zambians. Similar achievements were anticipated in other spheres of technical and senior administrative work, as in the personnel departments, where Zambians were expected to hold all of the most senior positions, including those responsible for industrial relations. By 1972 the entire expatriate work force would decline to an estimated 3,200, or 40 percent of what it had been at independence.[70]

Despite these projections, it was clear that skilled expatriate employees would be needed for an indefinite period to come. In certain crafts and technical trades, to which access had been regulated by apprenticeship, there were no Zambian employees at the time of independence, since federal legislation excluded Africans from positions of apprenticeship before 1959. This was expected to be the sole significant sphere of work, apart from professional and senior management positions, in which expatriates would continue to outnumber Zambians. In September 1972 the operating departments of the mines employed some 1,065 graduates with degrees in mining, metallurgy, chemistry, or engineering. Zambian graduates in all fields, then employed in the mining industry, numbered approximately 40.[71] Advancement into the ranks of senior management normally requires professional training in ad-

70. Republic of Zambia, *The Progress of Zambianisation*, pp. 3–7. In September 1972 officials responsible for Zambianization recorded that the expatriate work force had been reduced to 3,200 and that 80 percent of all jobs at the shift boss level had been Zambianized. However, only a small number of Zambians had been advanced to the position of mine captain. As anticipated, the personnel departments had been almost entirely Zambianized. In a critical vein, Michael Burawoy suggests that mere numerical evidence of Zambianization is misleading in that it obscures the persistence of a racially tinged bureaucratic paternalism in the work situation. He suggests further that the manipulation of figures by officials may "militate against effective Zambianization. When Zambianization is imposed from above, wholehearted co-operation is unlikely to prevail. When there is compulsion to satisfy forecasts, then there is a danger that Zambians will be promoted to positions for which they are obviously unprepared, with the result that new posts may be created for expatriates to oversee the new Zambian successor" (*The Colour of Class on the Copper Mines*, Zambian Papers, no. 7, University of Zambia Institute for African Studies [Manchester: Manchester University Press, 1972], pp. 27–29). Similarly, the present writer was informed that in order to facilitate Zambianization, the companies have "thickened up on supervision" by expatriates at senior levels. Burawoy shows statistically that this has been the case; he vividly records the resentment of Zambians to the overbearing expatriate presence. Ibid., pp. 30–41.

71. Information obtained at the Copper Industry Service Bureau, Kitwe, September 1972.

dition to many years of practical experience. Since independence, the mining companies have supported numerous students at universities and technical institutes in Zambia and abroad. As yet, however, few Zambians outside of the personnel departments have attained high managerial office in the mining industry.

A particularly difficult aspect of the Zambianization issue involves the treatment of those non-Zambian Africans who are not recruited on expatriate terms. The vast majority of them are either unskilled or semiskilled workers. At the end of 1966, they comprised 19 percent of the African work force—more than 8,000 employees. Over half of them were Malawians; 28 percent were Tanzanians; the remainder included Congolese, Mozambiquans, Rhodesians, and South Africans.[72]

During the colonial period, Northern Rhodesian Africans suffered, as we have seen, from extreme educational deprivation. Often recruits from Malawi and Rhodesia were better educated than most local workers; a disproportionate number of them were able to take advantage of opportunities for advancement. This fact appears to have been resented by Zambians. In 1967 spokesmen for local unions at various mines opposed both the provision of training for non-Zambians and their promotion within the industry.[73] The government's attitude was more charitable, permitting the enrollment of non-Zambians in training courses and their promotion to nonsupervisory grades. However, the promotion of non-Zambians to supervisory positions has been disallowed. This kind of parochially nationalistic behavior in the economic sphere has not been more pronounced in the mine labor field than in other sectors of employment.[74] Here it signifies that a substantial though diminishing portion of the mine labor force has been relegated to second-class status on national rather than racial grounds.

The Mineworkers' Burden

The passing of the dual wage system, taken together with a satisfactory program for Zambianization of the work force and the

72. Copper Industry Service Bureau, "Origins of the Labour Force as at 31 December 1966," C.I.S.B. Filc No. 130.1.14, Sequence I; see also Patrick O. Ohadike, *Development of and Factors in the Employment of African Migrants in the Copper Mines of Zambia 1940–66*, Zambian Papers, No. 4, University of Zambia, Institute for Social Research (Manchester: Manchester University Press, 1969), pp. 2–5.

73. Copper Industry Service Bureau, C.I.S.B. File No. 90.14.9A; also Bates, p. 167.

74. Colin Legum and Anthony Hughes, eds., *Africa Contemporary Record: Annual Survey and Documents, 1970–71* (London: Rex Collings, 1971), p. B213.

advent of majority participation by the state in ownership of the industry, meant that racial issues would no longer bulk large in the process of industrial relations. Henceforth, the claims of labor would be clearly differentiated from national or racial interests. Conversely, it would no longer be possible for the government "to indulge the demands of the mineworkers as Africans"[75] in order to soften the impact of measures intended to restrain the rise of wages and enforce labor discipline.

Despite the historic achievement of racial justice in this basic industry, which had been a bulwark of white supremacy in colonial central Africa, the mineworkers' union today is no less embattled in its mission to defend the rights of labor. However, the nature of the challenge to labor has changed. There has been a decisive shift in the attitudes of most Zambian leaders away from solicitude for the rights of labor to a new emphasis upon the duties of labor in social reconstruction. The mineworkers themselves may feel relatively unprivileged by comparison with expatriates on the Copperbelt, who are generally well-to-do and, in the case of mine employees, receive substantial allowances and other benefits in addition to their basic pay.[76] Naturally, the mineworkers' union does reflect the African miners' politically potent sense of relative deprivation. Objectively speaking, however, the 48,000 mineworkers (in 1972), approximately 15 percent of all Zambian wage earners, comprise a relatively privileged sector of the working class. In 1968, the average annual earnings of mineworkers were double those of wage earners in other sectors of the economy.[77] These factors have engendered a demand for responsible trade unionism, or reasonable sacrifice on the part of mineworkers as required by the national interest.

Labor Efficiency and Wages—In colonial Zambia, the profitability of mining depended to a great extent upon the comparatively low cost of African labor. Toward the end of the colonial period, with the stabilization of the African labor force and the rise of African trade unionism, African wages in this industry rose sharply in relation to the wages of whites.[78] This trend reflected a sustained

75. Bates, p. 44.
76. Ibid., pp. 84–85.
77. International Labour Office, United Nations Development Programme, Technical Assistance Sector, *Report to the Government of Zambia on Incomes, Wages and Prices in Zambia: Policy and Machinery* (Lusaka, 1969), p. 9.
78. "Whereas equipment costs rose about 100 percent between 1947 and 1958, African and European earnings rose 248 percent and 61 percent respectively, between 1949 and 1958" (Baldwin, p. 96). "The average wages of Africans in mining

improvement in the efficiency and productivity of African labor, largely as a result of rationalization and the training of workers.[79]

In 1969 the productivity of Zambian wage earners was alleged in a controversial report, prepared under the auspices of the International Labor Office for the government of Zambia, to have declined by more than 10 percent since independence. Productivity was reported to have fallen "despite the very high rate of investment in Zambia (averaging nearly a quarter of the gross national product), which by providing the workers with more equipment ought to have raised output per head."[80] The author of this report, H. A. Turner, a professor of industrial relations at Cambridge University, adopted a challenging perspective: "The reason for this fall in labour efficiency seems to be basically that the colonial system of labour discipline has broken down and nothing has yet developed to take its place."[81]

Justifiable or not, this implicit criticism of the labor force itself underlies the policy of the Zambian government on incomes and wages; it is a burden of blame that the mineworkers, in particular, have been required to bear.[82] Indeed, this viewpoint had been expressed by governmental and management spokesmen at "productivity seminars"—public meetings conducted by President Kaunda at the main mines in January 1968. On these occasions, the high incidence of absenteeism, indiscipline, the intimidation of African supervisors, and other counterproductive practices were cited and condemned.[83]

Apart from the vexed question of trends in labor efficiency, it is clear that wage and salary levels have risen continuously and sub-

---

more than doubled between 1954 and 1962 . . . though this was partly due to upgrading, and for all sectors they rose by 90 per cent" (*Report of the UN/ECA/FAO Economic Survey Mission on the Economic Development of Zambia*, p. 31).

79. International Confederation of Free Trade Unions, Africa Research Office, "The Copper Mining Industry of Northern Rhodesia" SPEC/01/1963 (Kampala, 1963), p. 5.

80. International Labour Office, *Report to the Government of Zambia on Incomes, Wages and Prices*, p. 14.

81. Ibid., pp. 14–15.

82. Turner's thesis has been criticized on two grounds: that it is biased against labor and that its finding of a fall in productivity is rebuttable. See Michael Burawoy, "Another Look at the Mineworker," *African Social Research*, No. 14 (December 1972): pp. 253–256 and literature cited at n. 20. Burawoy argues that, in view of existing industrial conditions, management, not labor, should be held primarily accountable for the level of productivity. Ibid., p. 283.

83. Copper Industry Service Bureau, Productivity Seminar Papers (1968).

stantially since independence; the average annual increase between 1964 and 1969 was about 15 percent.[84] Among wage earners,
the well-organized mineworkers regularly establish income standards for the entire wage labor force. As Baldwin has explained,

> The copper industry is the wage leader in the unionized part
> of the economy. Union and government pressures cause a
> high copper wage scale to spread (though at a discount) to
> the railways, the government, and secondary industry in
> general. Whereas African wages are only 18 percent of
> operating costs in the copper industry, they are 40 percent of
> operating costs in the rest of the manufacturing and construc-
> tion industries. This means that a given percentage increase
> in wage costs raises total costs more in these other industries,
> and thus causes a relatively greater reduction in output and
> employment. In addition, most of the secondary industries in
> the economy face severe competition from imports. When
> they are forced to raise their prices because of an increase in
> their wage costs, they are likely to lose a substantial volume
> of sales to foreign producers. African employment, con-
> sequently, tends to be sharply reduced in these industries in
> response to wage increases.[85]

Similarly, the UN Economic Survey Mission of 1964 warned that
an unrestrained wage spiral would retard productive investment
and employment. Rising wages inhibit the ability of labor-
intensive industries to compete with imports, while the favored
wage earners have more money to spend on imported consumer
goods, contrary to national priorities for development. The mission
drew this unambiguous conclusion: "There is really a choice for
Zambia: in the next 5 years it can have big increases in wages or big
increases in employment, *not both.*"[86]

This prognosis, which presumed no significant increase in the
level of productivity, has been validated by events. Rising wages
and other inflationary costs have detracted from the planned volume of investment; meanwhile, a substantial rise in the importa-

84. International Labour Office, *Report to the Government of Zambia on Incomes,
Wages and Prices*, p. 12. It has been calculated that between 1963 and 1968, the
money wages of Zambian workers increased by 147 percent, while the cost of living
for wage earners rose by 46 percent. "The real purchasing power of the average
Zambian employee thus increased by two-thirds" (Ibid., p. 8).

85. Baldwin, p. 107.

86. *Report of the UN/ECA/FAO Economic Survey Mission on the Economic Development of Zambia*, pp. 32–33.

tion of consumer goods has increased the wasteful drain of precious foreign exchange.[87] Richard Jolly, an economic adviser to the Zambian government, has calculated that only one-seventh of the total increase in the national wage bill between 1964 and 1968 was accounted for by new jobs.[88] Furthermore, Zambia fell 17,000 short of the 100,000 new jobs that were to have been provided as a minimum goal under the First National Development Plan (1966–1970).[89] Consequently, there has been a steady and disquieting rise in urban unemployment, estimated at 8,000 to 10,000 a year during the latter 1960s.[90]

The specter of severe social tensions attributable to poverty and unemployment has cast its shadow over Zambia as a result of the dangerous disparity between urban and rural incomes. Table 2, taken from the ILO report of 1969, depicts the ominous condition with striking clarity.[91]

Professor Turner has observed that "the high pay of miners has acted as a target which has pulled up pay levels throughout the country—and continues to do so. But in the process, the mass of the population in the villages has been left far behind."[92] While farm incomes have risen moderately, the prices of urban goods

87. See Bates, pp. 68–73; and the significant essay by John B. Knight, "Wages and Zambia's Economic Development," in *Constraints on the Economic Development of Zambia*, ed. Elliott, pp. 115–117.

88. Richard Jolly, "The Seers Report in Retrospect," *African Social Research*, No. 11 (June 1971), p. 14. Jolly served as a consultant to the UN Economic Survey Mission of 1964. The leader of this mission was Dudley Seers, then director of the Economic Development Division, UN Economic Commission for Africa.

89. Republic of Zambia, Ministry of Development Planning and National Guidance, *Second National Development Plan, January 1972-December 1976* (Lusaka, 1971), p.9.

90. Charles Elliott, "Humanism and the Agricultural Revolution," in *After Mulungushi: The Economics of Zambian Humanism*, ed. Bastiaan de Gaay Fortman (Nairobi: East African Publishing House, 1969), p. 130.

91. A corroborative study is cited in Robert H. Bates, *Patterns of Uneven Development: Causes and Consequences in Zambia*, The Social Science Foundation and Graduate School of International Studies, University of Denver, Monograph Series in World Affairs, Vol. 11, No. 3 (Denver, Colo., 1974), p. 46.

92. International Labour Office, *Report to the Government of Zambia on Incomes, Wages and Prices*, p. 10. President Kaunda has summarized the situation pithily: "The average income of Zambians in paid employment in this country is already about K750 per annum. This is probably about eight times the income of the subsistence farmer. The gap between the Zambian in paid employment and his brother in the villages is proportionately greater than between the urban Zambian and the expatriate" (Republic of Zambia, *Towards Complete Independence*, Address by His Excellency the President, Dr. K. D. Kaunda, to the UNIP National Council held at Matero Hall, Lusaka, 11 August 1969 [Lusaka, n.d.], pp. 44–45).

TABLE 2

	Approximate total no. end 1968 (000's)	Approximate Annual Earnings,[a] end 1968 Kwacha	Increase in Real Terms[b] since 1964 percent
Zambian peasant farmer	800	145	3
Zambian wage earner outside mines	270	640	52
Zambian mineworker	50	1,300	35
Expatriate employee outside mines	22	4,170	25
Expatriate employee, copper mines	6	7,600	16

SOURCE: International Labour Office, United Nations Development Programme, *Report to the Government of Zambia on Incomes, Wages and Prices in Zambia: Policy and Machinery* (Lusaka, 1969), p. 9.
[a]Earnings are family earnings, including subsistence, for peasant farmers.
[b]i.e., after allowing for rise in appropriate consumers' price index.

have spiraled away from the reach of rural consumers. "The result is that the peasant farmer may now be only about half as well off in relation to the urban worker as he was in 1964. This has played an important part in the rapid flow of persons from the rural areas to the towns, causing an increase in urban population of 8 per cent per annum between 1963 and 1969."[93]

This trend is contrary to a fundamental premise of the First National Development Plan. We have noted that the planners anticipated the provision of at least 100,000 new jobs by 1970; however, they had also estimated that 185,000 to 190,000 persons would leave the educational system between 1966 and 1970. To bridge the gap between school leavers and available jobs, the planners counted on a vigorous program of rural development to absorb the energies of many young Zambians and keep them off the urban labor market.[94] This hope was not fulfilled. In 1963 the urban

93. Richard Jolly, "How Successful Was the First National Development Plan?" *African Development* (October 1970), p. Z.10; and the basic paper by C. E. Young, "Rural-Urban Terms of Trade," *African Social Research*, no. 12 (December 1971), p. 94.

94. Republic of Zambia, Office of National Development and Planning, *First National Development Plan 1966–1970* (Lusaka, 1966), p. 74.

population of Zambia comprised 22 percent of the national total. Since then, the inadequacy of rural development has resulted in "a massive exodus" of rural Zambians to the urban areas.[95] In 1971 President Kaunda solemnly declared, "We have learnt recently and to our dismay that 40 per cent of our population is urbanised."[96]

New Directions—The problems of rural development in Zambia are deeply rooted and many faceted, involving organizational, logistical, and technical dilemmas as well as economic issues.[97] For this discussion, it is most relevant that Zambian leaders have identified the existing allocation of national income in favor of relatively privileged urban dwellers as a principal cause of rural retardation.[98] In order to correct this perceived misallocation, the government has undertaken to restrain wages, control prices, and ensure that future gains by workers, whether in the form of higher wages or other benefits, shall be contingent upon demonstrated improvements in the efficiency of labor.[99] Conditions in the mining industry since nationalization have been propitious for the achievement of these aims. First, the comprehensive reevaluation of all jobs in 1970, in addition to the introduction of annual pay increments, appears to have laid a basis for industrial harmony, predisposing the mineworkers' union to accept the principle of a 5

95. Republic of Zambia, *A Path for the Future,* Address by His Excellency the President, Dr. K. D. Kaunda, as Secretary-General of the United National Independence Party on the occasion of the Opening of the Sixth General Conference of the United National Independence Party, Mulungushi, May 8, 1971 (Lusaka, 1971), p. 13.

96. Ibid., p. 21. M. E. Jackman states, "Over 40 per cent of Zambians live within 25 miles of the railway, an area including all sizeable urban centres." Between 1963 and 1969, the population of the city of Lusaka increased from 109,000 to 238,000, while that of the Copperbelt Province increased from 544,000 to 815,000. "Population Distribution and Density," in *Zambia in Maps,* ed. D. Hywel Davies (London: University of London Press, 1971), pp. 42, 44.

97. See R. A. J. Roberts and Charles Elliott, "Constraints in Agriculture," in *Constraints on the Economic Development of Zambia,* ed. Elliott, pp. 269–297; Charles Elliott, "Humanism and the Agricultural Revolution," pp. 115–143; C. Stephen Lombard, *The Growth of Cooperatives in Zambia, 1914–71,* Zambian Papers, No. 6, University of Zambia Institute for African Studies (Manchester: Manchester University Press, 1971).

98. "If you demand higher wages for the urban workers the consequent inflation will inevitably hit the majority of our own relatives in the rural areas." *Towards Complete Independence,* Address by . . . K. D. Kaunda, p. 46; see also "Rural-Urban Terms of Trade," *African Social Research,* no. 12 (December 1971), p. ix.

99. Richard Jacobs, "The Workers' Dilemma," *African Development* (October 1970), p. Z.8–9.

percent ceiling on annual wage increases. Second, the union knows that government will not tolerate strikes or other forms of disruption in the leading industry. These conditions have vastly simplified the tasks of those who are responsible for collective bargaining on behalf of the companies. With the prospect of coercive governmental machinery, including an Industrial Relations Court,[100] in the offing, neither the union nor the management companies care to incur official displeasure.

Meanwhile, other measures, intended to maximize the personal commitment of workers to national goals, have been introduced. Thus, trade unionists, including officials of the mineworkers' union, have been appointed to serve as directors of various agencies and holding companies established for state participation in the economy. Of far greater significance is the recent provision for "works councils" to be established in all enterprises in which one hundred or more persons are employed.[101] Such councils, consisting of employee and management representatives in the proportion of two to one, are intended to foster a participative form of industrial management, which Kaunda and his colleagues believe will be conducive to socially responsible trade unionism. In the mining industry, works councils might eventually participate in hiring, firing, promotions, transfers, and the enforcement of discipline. Ideally, workers might learn to accept industrial discipline as self-discipline. In theory, the union itself would continue to function as a separate and distinct organization, responsible for the conduct of negotiations concerning wages, conditions of service, and other matters that affect the interests of their members as employees rather than "industrial citizens." Kaunda has said that "the sole purpose" of this innovation will be "to raise productivity and give better service. There should be no occasion to confuse this purpose with that of the trade union."[102]

As in the case of the Industrial Relations Court, government's insistence upon works councils in the mining industry has stimulated joint protective action on the part of management and organized labor to ensure the containment of this development

---

100. This court would be empowered to interpret collective bargaining agreements and resolve disputes in accordance with the government's policy on prices and incomes. Republic of Zambia, *The Industrial Relations Act*, no. 36 of 1971, pt. 8.

101. Ibid., pt. 7.

102. Republic of Zambia, *A Path for the Future*, Address by . . . K. D. Kaunda, p. 32.

within the established framework of collective bargaining. The constitutions of works councils in this industry have been framed to provide for the nomination of employee representatives by the local branches of the union. Company officials even favor the selection of regular shop stewards as council members. From the company standpoint, the union has become an industrial ally, or buffer against the encroachment of party and government power upon the field of industrial relations. This is the logical outcome of seminationalization, wherein the union's chief purpose may be its survival as an effective force. Should the union attempt to challenge the right of the state to accumulate capital for productive investment at the expense of the better-paid workers, its survival as an autonomous organization would surely become problematical.[103] Since the state has become the majority shareholder in nearly all major industries, vigorous collective bargaining has become politically hazardous in Zambia. As Kaunda has warned, "for a union to push a claim against the State is to push a claim against the people."[104]

In 1966 the mining companies had strongly opposed large wage increases on grounds that have since become principles of Zambian public policy. At that time, the most critical of all governmental inquiries into the mining industry grudgingly conceded that "in some respects what is good for the mining companies may be good for Zambia."[105] But strictly economic values were then sacrificed to do away with a racialistic system of wages that was deeply resented by the African miners. Since then, as we have noted, racial issues have been largely eliminated from the substance of collective bargaining in the mining industry and other sectors of the

103. Bates cites Isaac Deutscher's observation to the effect that labor unions in the Soviet Union were able "to restrain the demands of their members as industrial employees by serving their interests as urban immigrants." He suggests that trade unions in Zambia might be able to render a similar service. *Unions, Parties, and Political Development*, pp. 209 and 264, n. 7.

104. Republic of Zambia, *Towards Complete Independence*, Address by . . . K. D. Kaunda, p. 44. Similarly, Turner has written, "It is to be hoped that profits *will* now rise, because by far the greater part of them will go to the Government as resources for general development. In these circumstances, to claim increased wages whenever profits are high or have increased would amount to a demand that the workers in the sector or enterprise concerned should have preferential treatment over the rest of the community, and that profits should be diverted to their own consumption instead of the general welfare" (International Labour Office, *Report to the Government of Zambia on Incomes, Wages and Prices*, p. 25).

105. *Report of the Commission of Inquiry* (1966), p. 48.

economy. Where the state predominates in ownership, foreign owners are no longer ultimately responsible for the conduct of industrial relations. This has exposed a growing fissure between the industrial working class and the government, which does not represent the interests of that class more than others. It is not surprising that management officials in the field of industrial relations comment on the unprecedented degree of "trust" on the part of both the union and the government that they have enjoyed since the takeovers.[106]

SOCIAL RELATIONS

The decade 1950–1960 was a time of fundamental change in the social order of the mining industry. It began when trade unionism replaced tribal representation for industrial purposes. Gradually, the paternalistic practice of giving weekly rations of food as well as rent-free housing to workers was abandoned in favor of an "inclusive wage." The leading directors of both groups of companies were strongly committed to the liberal principle of individual achievement unencumbered by racial barriers. Their optimism concerning the evolution of a liberal capitalist order in the Federation of Rhodesia and Nyasaland led them to adopt a broad and statesmanlike perspective on the problems of that society. The chairmen of the two groups—Anglo American's H. F. Oppenheimer and RST's R. L. Prain—were keen observers of political and social affairs; their annual statements often included commentaries that appear to have been intended rather more for the eyes of politicians and public officials than shareholders. In 1957 Prain described the change of attitude on the part of mining industry executives thus:

> In the early days the financial and technical considerations in establishing and developing a mining industry were of primary importance. Activities other than mining and prospecting were mainly concerned with serving those who were engaged in the exploitation of the country's mineral wealth. The wheel has turned full circle when mining recognises, as it does today, its own responsibility for development viewed nationally and not merely industrially.[107]

106. The class dynamics of this situation will be considered in chap. 6.
107. Sir Ronald L. Prain, "Building on a Mineral Foundation in Central Africa" (1957) *Selected Papers*, vol. 1.

In the spirit of this declaration, the two groups have contributed jointly and separately to various endeavors other than mining. During the federal era, RST specifically turned its attention to the problem of rural underdevelopment. In 1956, this group extended five-year interest-free loans to the governments of Northern Rhodesia and Nyasaland, in the amounts of £2 million and £1 million respectively, for exclusive application to African rural development. These loans were made with explicit recognition of the copper industry's historical responsibility for the increasingly dangerous economic imbalance between the industrial Copperbelt and the rural areas from which the labor force was drawn.[108] In Northern Rhodesia the government used this money to finance an intensive rural development program and related projects in the Northern and Luapula provinces, where the home villages of most of the Copperbelt workers were located.[109] A second significant attempt by RST to promote agricultural development involved the establishment of a pilot polder on the Kafue Flats. (A polder is an area of low-lying land protected by dikes to prevent seasonal flooding, while systematic irrigation is introduced.) Although long-range plans for the Kafue Flats have envisaged a large area under cultivation, RST's involvement was limited to the financing and management of a small pilot project for research purposes, which effectively demonstrated the technical feasibility of the undertaking. Despite its immense contribution to technical knowledge, the utility of capital-intensive schemes such as this one, under existing agricultural conditions in Zambia, has been questioned from an economic standpoint.[110] In 1965 the entire project was handed over to the Zambian government. The chairman of RST then disclosed that his group had spent "approximately half a million pounds on this project which was undertaken as a contribution to the development of agriculture in Zambia, and the chief asset that the Government has inherited is the data amassed in nine years of research and experiment."[111] He also remarked that findings of the

108. Roan Antelope Copper Mines Limited, *Statement by the Chairman, Sir Ronald L. Prain,* October 15, 1956.

109. This program provided a test for the "demonstration method" of agricultural development, involving intensive training courses in modern techniques for selected farmers at special training centers. It was not entirely successful. See the critique in Baldwin, pp. 201–203.

110. Ibid., pp. 204–205.

111. RST Group of Companies, *Statement by the Chairman, Sir Ronald L. Prain,* October 29, 1965.

pilot project may not be appreciated as greatly in Zambia as elsewhere: "As a result of our experiments the outside world has learned what may be done over millions of acres of similar soils in similar conditions in many different lands."[112] Although research on irrigation in this area has continued, the projected creation of a commercial polder appears to have been indefinitely postponed.

Both groups of companies have operated experimental farms for various purposes on the Copperbelt and in other parts of the country. However, the first major effort by the Anglo American Corporation Group in the field of agriculture was initiated in 1971 in the wake of a threatened shortage of food. Much to its distress, the Zambian government decided that it would have to purchase 1.5 million bags of maize from Rhodesia in addition to purchases from other countries, including South Africa.[113] Against this background, the chairman of the Anglo American Corporation announced his group's plan for agricultural development as follows:

> Zambia is suffering at present from a critical shortage of a number of basic food requirements, and considerable imports have been necessary to meet national demand. Zaminc [Zamanglo Industrial Corporation Limited] has therefore launched a large mixed farming operation, which will cost an estimated K4 million and will eventually produce a substantial proportion of Zambia's total output of maize, beef and milk. This capital expenditure is being financed by loan facilities from Zamanglo. This is the largest private investment ever to be made in agriculture in Zambia, and I am pleased that it has been possible for us to participate in this vital area of national growth. The saving to Zambia in foreign exchange as a result of the scheme is estimated at K30 million over a ten-year period.[114]

In the sphere of educational development, too, the mining groups have made significant contributions. In 1960, they financed the Northern Rhodesia Educational Trust, "on a half-grant, half-loan basis to a total which eventually reached £2 million."[115] As a

112. Sir Ronald L. Prain, "Speech by Sir Ronald Prain at Kafue Polder Lunch," July 28, 1965 (mimeo.).

113. *Africa Research Bulletin*, Economic, Financial and Technical Series 8, No. 6 (July 31, 1971): 2066–2067.

114. Zambian Anglo American Limited, *Statement by the President, Mr. H. F. Oppenheimer*, September 1971.

115. *Report of the UN/ECA/FAO Economic Survey Mission on the Economic Development of Zambia*, p. 98.

result of this supplement to governmental efforts, primary school-
ing was made available to nearly all children on the Copperbelt and
in the vicinity of Kabwe, while secondary education and teacher
training facilities in these areas were also expanded. At the time of
independence, each of the mining groups contributed £25,000 to
the University of Zambia Appeal Fund; the British South Africa
Company made a contribution of £50,000. Subsequently, the
Anglo American Corporation and RST each contributed K250,000
to endow professorships in engineering. Over and above these
specific contributions, the industry is truly described as the nation's "great training school" for industrial workers.[116] Innumera-
ble employees of the mines have moved into nonmining sectors of
the economy on the strength of skills acquired in the mining industry, often as a result of formal training or semiprofessional course
work.

Perhaps the most apparent influence of the mining companies
on Zambian society outside of the strictly industrial sphere arises
from their obligation to provide housing for the mine labor force.
This is a matter of complexity as well as great social consequence.

Mine Townships and Housing

The urban centers of the Copperbelt exist entirely by virtue of
the great industry that laid their foundations. During the colonial
period, mine townships for Africans were established on land
owned by the mining companies; they were governed by boards of
management chosen by the companies. Residence in a mine township was always contingent upon employment in the mine. Africans who were not employed by the local mine, other than wives
and children of the employees, were forbidden to remain within
the township for more than thirty-six hours without a visitor's
permit.[117]

Adjacent to each major mine a composite community—including
at the minimum a business district, a European residential sector,
and an African township—came into being. Thus it is that each of
the mine-related urban centers evolved from "twin settlements."

> . . . the dual origins of the four early centres are particularly
> marked. Of these only Mufulira has a common name for both

116. Baldwin, p. 183.
117. Northern Rhodesia, *Mine Townships,* Chapter 121 of the Laws (Lusaka:
Government Printer, 1961), pp. 164–182.

parts, and the others rejoice in separate names for their mine and municipal townships; Nchanga, Nkana and Roan Antelope are mining townships, and Chingola, Kitwe and Luanshya are their respective municipal counterparts.[118]

Whereas the European population could vote in local government elections on a property rate-payer basis, Africans were excluded from representation on the governing bodies of local authorities until the early 1960s.[119] Democratic local government was finally achieved in all local government jurisdictions other than the mine townships soon after independence.

Paternalism—In the mine townships, which are company-owned, African workers have no right to representation on the boards of management; as late as 1966, the residents of these townships were represented by extralegal councils, whose functions were mainly advisory.[120] The companies have justified this manifestation of pure paternalism in the residential sphere on the ground of their continuing financial responsibility for the maintenance of all houses in the mine townships as well as the provision of sundry services, including water, sewage disposal, electricity, and street maintenance. Until 1950, housing for African employees was rent-free. Thereafter, rents were gradually introduced and wages were increased accordingly. At no time, however, have rent revenues approximated the costs of upkeep and services borne by the companies. In 1966 direct townships costs (excluding capital expenditures), amounting to nearly £2 million, were over 70 percent higher than the revenues from rents.[121]

In Zambia it is common for employers, including the central government and local authorities, to subsidize subeconomic rents. A survey conducted on the eve of independence led to the estimate "that not more than ten to fifteen per cent of the wage earning population in urban areas is paying directly for its own rent."[122]

118. George Kay, *A Social Geography of Zambia* (London: University of London Press, 1967), p. 91.

119. Northern Rhodesia, *Report of the Committee Appointed to Inquire into the Participation of Africans in Local Government in Municipal and Township Areas* (Lusaka: Government Printer, 1960).

120. Anglo American Corporation and Roan Selection Trust, "Statement of Case on Behalf of the Anglo American Corporation Group of Companies and the Roan Selection Trust Group of Companies," app. 5, p. 25. Brown Commission of Inquiry, May 1966.

121. *Report of the Commission of Inquiry* (1966), p. 59.

122. *Report of the UN/ECA/FAO Economic Survey Mission on the Economic Development of Zambia*, app. G, p. lxxvii.

Out of a total of some 100,000 dwellings in high-density housing areas throughout Zambia in 1966, the mining companies owned approximately 40 percent, most of the others being linked to employment in the public sector.[123] Since all wages in the mining industry were above a prescribed minimum, the companies were not legally required either to provide housing for their employees or to pay a rent allowance in lieu of housing.[124] However, the companies were prepared to continue to provide housing and home services for their employees. The chief reason given by company spokesmen to the 1966 Commission of Inquiry into the mining industry was "the need to maintain a contented labor force." With candor, the companies stated that the "dominating factor" in their policies on housing and social services was "enlightened self-interest."[125]

This approach was criticized by the commission as a failure on the part of the companies to accept a "moral obligation" commensurate with their economic power. In the commission's view, it would not be enough for the companies merely to surpass the prevailing standards of the local authorities in this field, since the latter "are struggling with a legacy of neglect which they have inherited from the colonial era," while "the mining companies have only themselves to blame."[126] Specifically, the commission blamed the companies for failing to provide adequate accommodation for many of their workers, although it was also noted that between 1956 and 1964, the industry had spent over £11 million on home construction, an amount that exceeded public spending on houses during that period by £3 million. The commission also found that between 25 and 50 percent of all high-density housing in the mine townships was below an acceptable standard and recommended that most houses in these townships should be let to workers on a rent-free basis with moderate charges for services. This recommendation, based on moral rather than economic grounds, was not accepted by the companies and continued to appear as an issue in collective bargaining.

123. AAC and RST, "Statement of Case on Behalf of the Anglo American Group of Companies and the Roan Selection Trust Group of Companies," app. 5.

124. Republic of Zambia, "The Employment Act, 1965," *Supplement to the Republic of Zambia Government Gazette, dated the 1st of October, 1965*, pt. 6, p. 472.

125. AAC and RST, "Statement of Case on Behalf of the Anglo American Corporation Group of Companies and the Roan Selection Trust Group of Companies," app. 5.

126. *Report of the Commission of Inquiry* (1966), p. 56, 60.

The Limits of Paternal Responsibility—For years, the mining companies had taken pride in the human and social aspects of their paternalistic policies. Despite corporate links with South Africa, where African miners are compelled to live in bachelor quarters, and the personal ties of many European employees with that country, the Copperbelt mining companies have always encouraged their African workers to settle in mine townships with their families.[127] Since 1953, the companies have provided an extensive program of adult education in addition to many other educational and community development services.[128] Similarly, medical services provided by the mines have been rated very highly. In 1966 they employed "one quarter of the medical practitioners in Zambia . . . to serve one-sixteenth of the population."[129] By 1961 the average length of service of all African workers had risen to 5.6 years, slightly higher than that of all expatriate workers.[130] At that time, an American mining executive could fairly boast that the Copperbelt companies "have set out to be the best employers of labor in Rhodesia. They deliberately set years ago a benevolent paternalism as their goal and they have achieved this in full measure. Indeed, I have sometimes felt that the mining companies on the Copperbelt have a role in the lives of their employees and of the community that only the medieval church could equal."[131]

With the advent of independence, benevolent paternalism on the part of a foreign-owned industry became obsolete. Although living standards in the mine townships compare favorably with

127. It should be noted that the Anglo American Corporation of South Africa has tried without success to alter this aspect of South African public policy. See Gregory, pp. 572–580.

128. *Report of the Commission of Inquiry* (1966), p. 64. See also the highly appreciative appraisal of educational and other social services provided by the mining companies in Absolom L. Vilakazi, "Non-Governmental Agencies and Their Role in Development in Africa: A Case Study," *African Studies Review* 13 (September 1970): 169–202.

129. *Report of the Commission of Inquiry* (1966), p.66.

130. Copper Industry Service Bureau Limited, *Copperbelt of Zambia Mining Industry Year Book 1968* (Kitwe), p. 47. This was the first year in which the African average exceeded the European average. By 1970, the average length of African employment had risen to 9.75 years, while the European figure had fallen to 4.99. Copper Industry Service Bureau, *Mindeco Mining Year Book of Zambia 1970* (Kitwe), p. 46.

131. "Statement of F. Taylor Ostrander, Assistant to the Chairman, American Metal Climax, Inc., New York, N.Y.," *Activities of Private United States Organizations in Africa*, Hearings before the Subcommittee on Africa of the Committee on Foreign Affairs, House of Representatives, Eighty-Seventh Congress, May 8, 1961 (Washington, D.C., 1961), p.35.

conditions in other high-density housing areas, the existence of nonself-governing communities in these townships and the persistence of nonindustrial issues in labor-management relations were liabilities to the industry. Therefore the companies favored an extension of the boundaries of local government jurisdictions in mine areas to incorporate the mine townships. But they also insisted that the local authorities should take over their 40,000 high-density houses as well as responsibility for the provision of services. The companies offered to transfer the ownership of their houses to the local authorities concerned at a purely nominal valuation on condition that the number of dwellings available to mine employees would not be reduced thereafter by the new owners. They also offered to provide loan funds for new home construction and to render administrative assistance to the local authorities for a transitional period of two years.[132]

Without divestment of their houses, the companies would not favor incorporation of their townships into the local authorities, as they would then have to pay local property rates while their tenants would predominate in the local authority councils. This view was not accepted by the commission of inquiry, which declared that the right to participate in local government affairs should not depend upon property ownership. It followed, from the commission's standpoint, that divestment should not be a condition of incorporation, although legislation would be required to protect the legitimate interests of the companies as ratepayers. The commission concluded that incorporation without divestment would be desirable and that the companies should continue to provide housing and other township services for their employees.[133]

This recommendation does not appear to have reflected the mineworkers' own viewpoint. Throughout the Copperbelt, living conditions in the mine townships generally are far superior to those in the adjacent municipal townships. Gradually, substandard houses in the mine townships are being replaced by new dwellings of high quality; the waiting lists for mine township housing are much shorter than in the municipalities; extraneous—for example, political—considerations do not affect an applicant's access to housing in the mine areas; the standards of home mainte-

132. Copper Industry Service Bureau, "Amalgamation of Mine and Public Townships," C.I.S.B. File No. 70.9.3, sequence II, 1964–67.

133. Report of the Commission of Inquiry (1966), pp. 63–64.

nance, servicing, and street repair in mine townships are unmatched in other working class communities; rents in the mine townships remain subeconomic and comparatively attractive for employees at all levels of income.[134]

As might be expected, the mineworkers would not want to jeopardize their enjoyment of these advantages for the sake of extending democratic local government from the municipal to the mine townships. For their part, the companies, unwilling to contemplate incorporation without divestment, have undertaken to delegate responsibilities for certain administrative matters in some mine townships to boards of management with democratically elected majorities. Such boards exist entirely at the pleasure of the companies; their members may be removed at the discretion of the mine managements. In practice, management takes care to exclude persons who are politically objectionable to the government and ruling party from positions of local influence. For the time being, this form of political deference placates the party, which stands for abolition of the paternalistic mine township system in principle. Meanwhile, the mineworkers' union tolerates the enforcement of political conformity, whereas any attempt to do away with the separate identity of mine townships would be extremely provocative.

134. A visitor to the Copperbelt will be struck by the disparity between mine and municipality township conditions. The governmental townships are generally undercapitalized and cannot readily finance their responsibilities. In the mine townships, new housing conforms to a standard that is controversial because of its relatively high quality. Under pressure from the mineworkers' union, the companies have chosen to build attractive homes for their workers rather than a greater number of homes at a lower but acceptable standard, as the government would prefer. The union is reported to feel, contrary to government policy, that quality is more important than quantity.

FIVE

The Claims of Ideology:
RESPONSES TO THE RHODESIAN UDI
AND OTHER LIBERATION ISSUES

The preceding chapter discussed adaptations on the part of the mining industry to demands generated by various domestic interest groups—African workers, European workers, trade union leaders, party leaders, and public officials. In all such cases, the wisdom of accommodation with groups that were essential to the industry's efficient operation was apparent from the perspective of prudent self-interest. This chapter is concerned with demands upon the industry to forego relationships outside Zambia, of which Zambians disapprove for ideological reasons. As such, it tests more precisely whether international corporations domiciled in Zambia have been constrained to conduct their business in harmony with national purposes.[1]

THE CHALLENGE OF RHODESIA'S REBELLION

On November 11, 1965, the white minority regime of Southern Rhodesia issued its unlawful and unilateral declaration of independence (UDI) from the United Kingdom. That fateful step had been anticipated by Africans with foreboding since April 1964, when Ian Douglas Smith became prime minister in the territorial government of the right-wing Rhodesian Front.[2] In the face of this threat, African leaders and many supporters of the African cause had urged Britain to declare that she would neither concede nor

1. The section immediately following is based largely on my article, "Zambia's Response to U.D.I.," *Mawazo* 1 (June 1968): 11–32, as updated and expanded in "Zambia's Response to the Rhodesian Unilateral Declaration of Independence," in *Politics in Zambia*, ed. William Tordoff (Manchester: Manchester University Press, 1974; Berkeley, Los Angeles, London: University of California Press, 1974), pp. 320–362.
2. See James Barber, *Rhodesia: The Road to Rebellion* (London: Oxford University Press, 1967), pp. 192–193; and Larry W. Bowman, *Politics in Rhodesia: White Power in an African State* (Cambridge: Harvard University Press, 1973), pp. 67–69.

permit independence before the advent of majority rule.[3] Meanwhile, President Kaunda had offered to provide a military base for Britain in Zambia, from which an attack on Rhodesia could be launched in the event of an illegal seizure of power.[4] But the British government rejected the option of a military response to UDI, and did, in fact, offer to grant independence to the Rhodesian government before majority rule.[5] This offer was contingent upon Rhodesia's acceptance of various constitutional and legal preconditions, which were intended to protect and extend the existing rights of Africans and to guarantee that there would be unimpeded progress toward the goal of majority rule. At length, however, Anglo-Rhodesian negotiations collapsed over a dispute about the method that would be used to ascertain whether arrangements that might be agreed upon by the two governments would be acceptable to the African people of Rhodesia.

When the Rhodesian government finally proclaimed its independence, Britain applied a brace of economic and financial sanctions against her rebellious colony. Rhodesia was expelled from the sterling area and excluded from the London capital market. Preferential tariffs for Rhodesian exports were suspended; bans were imposed on the purchase of Rhodesia's main export crops— tobacco and sugar; Rhodesian assets in London, valued at £9 million, were frozen. In compliance with a resolution of the UN Security Council, which called upon all states to break economic relations with Rhodesia, "including an embargo on oil and petroleum products," Britain acted on December 17, 1965, to ban the sale or shipment of oil to Rhodesia by British firms. Predictably, Rhodesia retaliated by prohibiting oil shipments through her territory to Zambia. Immediate relief was provided by a dramatic and successful airlift of oil and petroleum products financed and mounted by the British, Canadian, and United States governments from De-

3. In June 1965, President Nyerere of Tanzania pointedly refused to sign the final communique of the conference of Commonwealth heads of government, on the ground that its statement on Rhodesia would permit a grant of independence before majority rule. See Donald Rothchild, "Rhodesian Rebellion and African Response," *Africa Quarterly* 6 (1966): 184–196.

4. Richard Hall, *The High Price of Principles: Kaunda and the White South* (London: Hodder and Stoughton, 1969), pp. 99–100, 112; Colin Legum, ed., *Zambia: Independence and Beyond: The Speeches of Kenneth Kaunda* (London: Nelson, 1966), p. 237.

5. Southern Rhodesia, *Documents Relating to the Negotiations between the United Kingdom and Southern Rhodesian Governments, November 1963–November 1965*, Cmnd. 2807 (London: 1965), pp. 75, 111, 124; United Kingdom, British Parliament *Hansard*, vol. 718, cols. 633–34, November 1, 1965.

cember 1965 until May 1966. Nonetheless, for thirty-two months, until the completion of a pipeline from the Tanzanian refinery at Dar es Salaam to the Zambian Copperbelt in September 1968, Zambia suffered from shortages of oil, while Rhodesia has always been able to get all she needs and more from South Africa.

Zambia's Predicament

Kaunda and his colleagues in the Zambian government never doubted that economic sanctions by themselves would not suffice to quell the rebellion. South Africa was virtually certain to defy such sanctions and assist the rebel regime in its hour of need. If sanctions failed to produce a quick kill, Zambia, which depended heavily upon Rhodesia for imports and services, would stand to incur reprisals and suffer from shortages of supply. We have seen that Zambia was almost entirely dependent upon Rhodesia Railways to carry her imports and exports. In 1965 the hydroelectric station at the south bank of the Kariba Dam provided 68 percent of all electricity used in Zambia, including some 90 percent of the electrical power requirements of the Copperbelt. The Wankie Colliery in Rhodesia supplied the massive quantity of coal that was needed to operate the copper mines. Zambian leaders were concerned that severe economic dislocations might result in unemployment, urban discontent, and political unrest. There was also the danger that prolonged economic hardships arising from a racial confrontation across the Zambezi would exacerbate racial tensions in Zambia and cause a precipitous exodus of skilled European personnel from the mines and other sectors of employment. And the Zambians knew their enemy well enough to be sure that these burdens and risks were unlikely to be rewarded by the desired overthrow of minority rule in Rhodesia.

By the end of December 1965 a number of ground rules for the bitter contest had been established on a de facto basis. Kaunda declared that he would regard Rhodesian interference with their jointly owned common services, providing electricity and transportation, as an act of war and would respond in kind. Ian Smith had said that Rhodesia would not cut off Zambia's power or interfere with Zambia's transportation rights unless Zambia allowed herself to be used as a "launching pad" against Rhodesia. Harold Wilson, the British prime minister, declared that Britain would "not stand idly by if Rhodesia cuts off power supplies to the Copper Belt."[6] At this time, Mr. Wilson's Labour government held a bare and precarious majority in the House of Commons. Kaunda appears to have been persuaded by Wilson himself that the latter would take decisive action against the Salisbury regime as soon as his parliamentary majority had been secured by a general election to be held in March 1966.[7] Kaunda's faith in Wilson was shattered in April, after the Labour party's return to power with a rousing majority of ninety-seven when the British prime minister resumed negotiations with Salisbury on a basis that did not preclude independence before majority rule.[8] Amidst reports of a softening of Britain's attitude toward the Smith regime, Kaunda threatened to propose the expulsion of Britain herself from the Commonwealth. In a radio address, he expressed his contempt for Britain's "shifty and evasive" policy; he also alleged that by holding informal talks with Rhodesian officials, Britain had extended de facto recognition to the Smith government. When Wilson managed to obtain a postponement of the forthcoming Commonwealth leaders' conference from July to September, Kaunda was moved to warn that Zambia might decide to withdraw from the Commonwealth.

At the Commonwealth conference of September 1966, Britain was urged by most of the heads of government to declare without equivocation that she would not grant independence to Rhodesia before the establishment of majority rule on a basis of universal adult suffrage. But Harold Wilson announced that he would make one more attempt to reach a settlement on less exacting terms before seeking to impose more stringent sanctions under United Nations auspices. Only after the rejection of British proposals by a confident Rhodesian cabinet in December 1966 did the Security Council, acting at Britain's behest, impose selective mandatory sanctions against Rhodesia. Unlike previous resolutions of the Security Council on this question, the vote for mandatory sanctions (under Chapter VII of the Charter) imposed an obligation of compliance on all member states. However, the emphatic condition of British participation in collective action of this kind was the understanding that sanctions would not be enforced to the extent

6. United Kingdom, British Parliament *Hansard*, Vol. 721, col. 1430, December 1, 1965; Richard Hall suggests that Wilson had decided to retaliate against Rhodesia's own supply of electricity from Kariba if Zambia's supply was sabotaged. *The High Price of Principles*, p. 128.

7. Hall, pp. 133–134.

8. Ibid., pp. 148–151.

of their escalation into "a confrontation—economic or military—involving the whole of southern Africa."[9] In view of the Security Council's resolution of April 9, 1966, authorizing a British blockade of the port of Beira in Portuguese Mozambique in order to prevent the delivery of oil intended for Rhodesia, it may be assumed that South Africa was the only real stumbling block to the unlimited enforcement of sanctions. Britain was not prepared to jeopardize her great trading and investment relationships with South Africa.[10] Since South Africa would not abandon Rhodesia, the United Nations program of economic sanctions was bound to fail, and the sacrifices made by Zambia to sustain this ineffectual policy would be, so far forth, in vain.

Enemies Within?

It would be difficult to exaggerate the magnitude of the United Nations, British, and Western failure in Rhodesia.[11] Students of the question differ as to whether the British government ever intended to strike a decisive blow for racial equality in Rhodesia. Was it Britain's purpose instead merely to induce a return to "legality" without upsetting the order of white minority rule?[12] Between December 1966, when Britain asked the Security Council to impose selective mandatory sanctions, and October 1968, Britain's official position was in harmony with the African doctrine of "no independence before majority rule." Then, at the meeting between Wilson and Smith of October 1968, British policy shifted back to the quest for a settlement that would permit independence before majority rule.

9. *United Nations Security Council, Official Records*, S/PV.1331, December 8, 1966, pp. 7, 9.
10. "Between 9 and 10 per cent of total British direct investments are in South Africa. Only Australia and Canada rank higher in importance among countries in which British companies invest directly" (Sean Gervasi, *Industrialization, Foreign Capital and Forced Labour in South Africa*, Unit on Apartheid, Department of Political and Security Council Affairs, United Nations, ST/PSCA/Ser.A/10 [New York; 1970], p. 61). South Africa also accounts for about 4 percent of Britain's export trade. In general, see Dennis Austin, *Britain and South Africa* (London: Oxford University Press, 1966).
11. See Robert C. Good, *U. D. I.: The International Politics of the Rhodesian Rebellion* (Princeton: Princeton University Press, 1973).
12. See R. B. Sutcliffe, "The Political Economy of Rhodesian Sanctions," *Journal of Commonwealth Political Studies* 7 (July 1969): 113–125; and T. R. C. Curtin, "Total Sanctions and Economic Development in Rhodesia," *Journal of Commonwealth Political Studies* 7 (July 1969): 126–131.

The consolidation of white minority rule in Rhodesia would have a profound effect upon the balance of forces in Southern Africa as a whole. Immediately, it strengthened the Portuguese position in Mozambique, while it reduced the ability of Botswana to assist the cause of liberation in South Africa or Namibia. The overthrow of white rule in Rhodesia would have deprived South Africa of a vast periphery of strategic depth. While South Africa would have retained her overwhelming military superiority in the region, an important element of South African security would have vanished, and the pressures for liberalizing change within South Africa itself might have been strengthened. Whatever doubts the South African government may have harbored concerning the legality or viability of Rhodesia's rebel regime were easily overborne when Salisbury asked Pretoria for military assistance to counter the threat of a guerrilla campaign in 1967.[13] Thus did the Zambezi River, separating Rhodesia and Zambia, become part of South Africa's effective military perimeter. And the initiative for change within the white-ruled region has fallen almost entirely into the hands of the white minority regimes.[14]

It has been suggested that South Africa views economic cooperation with Zambia as the "key" to its long-term strategy for the stabilization of a white-dominated bloc of Southern African states.[15] To be sure, the economic inducements for Zambia to accept goods and services from both South Africa and Rhodesia are not inconsiderable. Should Zambia, like Malawi, become reconciled to the logic of accommodation with the white-ruled states for economic reasons, the system of racial oligarchy in Southern Africa would be immensely strengthened and Zambia's valued self-conception as an exemplar of the liberation movement would crumble. Accordingly, Zambia has resolved to extricate herself

13. In 1966, the Zimbabwe African People's Union and the Zimbabwe African National Union began to infiltrate armed columns of trained guerrillas into Rhodesia from Zambia. Following a major incursion mounted by the African National Congress of South Africa/Zimbabwe African People's Union alliance in August 1967, units of the South African paramilitary police were deployed in Rhodesia for "field experience." J. Bowyer Bell, *The Myth of the Guerrilla* (New York: Knopf, 1971), p. 136. Since then, the Rhodesian counterinsurgency effort has involved South African personnel.

14. At this writing, opponents of white rule in Southern Africa bid fair to seize the initiative for change in Angola and Mozambique as a result of the April 1974 coup d'état in Portugal. The UN challenge to South African rule in Namibia should also be noted.

15. Gervasi, pp. 90–94.

from the coils of dependence upon white Southern Africa and redirect her trade and transportation toward the north as far and as fast as possible. To achieve this goal, many old commercial ties, corporate relationships, and personal affinities involving businessmen and other white residents of Zambia have to be ruptured or set aside.

Realistically, Zambians have been prone to mistrust the reliability of expatriates generally on the issue of disengagement from the south. Zambian officials have alleged that expatriate businessmen have been reluctant to dispense with their traditional sources of supply in Rhodesia and South Africa. White Rhodesians, South Africans, and others who have sympathized with white rule in those countries have comprised a great proportion of the professional, managerial, and technical personnel in all occupational spheres, including the civil service and the security services.[16] On the mines, 40 percent of the expatriate work force, which numbered 6,550 at the end of 1965, were South Africans.[17] Many white parents have continued to send their children to school in South Africa and Rhodesia.[18] It is commonplace for whites who live in

16. Hall, pp. 123–125.

17. Copper Industry Service Bureau, "Origins of the Labour Force as at 31 December 1966," C.I.S.B. File No. 130.1.14, sequence I.

18. Contracts for expatriate employees of the mining companies provide for the payment of allowances (including travel costs) for the education of their children in secondary schools outside Zambia. Many send their children to schools in Rhodesia and South Africa. The British-style boarding schools of Rhodesia are particularly favored by those who aspire to enroll eventually in British universities. Expatriates generally contend that adequate educational facilities are not available on the Copperbelt. I have also heard it argued in Zambia that the liberal authorities of certain multiracial boarding schools in Rhodesia have staunchly defended multiracial principles within their institutions. What was far less comprehensible to my mind was the certainty with which expatriate parents in Zambia viewed Rhodesia as a safe, secure place for their children. These questions and answers, paraphrased from a discussion with several mining executives on the Copperbelt in 1972, may be revealing:

Q. What if trouble of a military kind were to break out between Zambia and Rhodesia?

A. We have friends there who would look after the children.

Q. What about the values that your children may learn in Rhodesian schools, especially white supremacy and African subordination?

A. They would learn that here too.

Q. But at least they would also know that the President is Zambian, as are the members of his Cabinet.

A. By going there they see both sides, since they come here for vacations and see this side.

In 1973, the mining companies established their own primary schools on the Copperbelt, with governmental approval and in response to the demands of expat-

Zambia to vacation in South Africa, Rhodesia, and southern Mozambique. In 1967 Zambia ranked second to Britain as a source of white immigrants to South Africa, accounting for approximately 4,000 such persons, or 10 percent of the total number.

The mining companies, in particular, have been identified with white Southern African interests. Sir Ernest Oppenheimer was deeply committed to the unification of the two Rhodesias and Nyasaland.[19] After the federation had been established, he commented as follows:

> Circumstances have established strong ties between this group and the territories that Cecil John Rhodes brought into the Commonwealth. An inherited tradition almost demands that the corporation, which has dominant interests in Rhodes' company, De Beers Consolidated Mines, should continue his policy of fostering the development and settlement of the Rhodesias. Besides, it is good business. Our early enterprise has drawn, and continues to draw highly satisfactory rewards from Northern Rhodesia. There is, indeed, a moral obligation that we should take a leading part in assisting the progress of the Rhodesias; and more material considerations endorse this policy. For here is a young country eagerly awaiting all the development that modern civilization can offer. The scope for business in all spheres is wide; and large resources are needed for the fulfillment of even part of the ambitious programmes that the sponsors of the Federation have foreshadowed.[20]

This enthusiasm was echoed "on the broadest political grounds" by the chairman of the Roan Antelope and Mufulira copper mines, who particularly noted that the federation's declared policy of racial partnership was consistent with pending proposals favored by the companies to weaken and eventually do away with the indus-

---

riate employees. This step was necessitated by the introduction of a new public policy to delay primary school entry until the age of seven, compared with an entry age of five in British schools. However, I could not detect any interest on the part of the companies to finance the establishment of secondary schools in order to provide an alternative to the education of expatriate children in Rhodesia and South Africa. A top-ranking executive outside Zambia said simply that the government should be responsible for social projects, for which purpose the corporations pay taxes.

19. Theodore Gregory, *Ernest Oppenheimer and the Economic Development of Southern Africa* (Cape Town: Oxford University Press, 1962), pp. 461–463.

20. Quoted at ibid., p. 464.

trial color bar to African advancement on the Copperbelt.[21] During the 1950s, both groups of companies made substantial investments in the future of this interterritorial arrangement. Together they extended loans totaling £20 million to help finance construction of the Kariba hydroelectric power project; and they contributed £10 million more through surcharges on the delivery of power.[22] Both groups invested heavily in Rhodesian securities and banks; the Anglo American Corporation made large expenditures to equip the Rhodesia Railways and develop the Wankie Colliery as a vital adjunct to the copper industry.[23]

In the political sphere, both groups gave financial support to the United Federal party until 1959, when this practice became a liability in their relations with the African unions and was discontinued. At this time, the political attitude of RST diverged sharply from that of the Anglo American Corporation. By 1959 Sir Ronald L. Prain, chairman of the RST Group, appears to have reached the conclusion that the federation was failing to achieve its promise of genuine partnership between the races. His annual statement of that year noted that the legislature of Southern Rhodesia was entirely European in composition, and he ventured to say that a drastic alteration of that territory's apportionment of land between racial communities was long overdue.[24] Although Prain reiterated his support for the concept of federation, the tone of his statement suggested a disposition to reappraise that viewpoint. Two years later, before the future of Northern Rhodesia had been settled, a spokesman for American Metal Climax, Inc., told a committee of the United States Congress that "Rhodesian Selection Trust is pre-

21. Roan Antelope Copper Mines Limited, *Statement by the Chairman (Mr. R. L. Prain)*, October 1953.

22. William J. Barber, *The Economy of British Central Africa* (London: Oxford University Press, 1961), p. 124; Robert E. Baldwin, *Economic Development and Export Growth* (Berkeley and Los Angeles: University of California Press, 1966), p. 179. The present writer is informed that these contributions to the Kariba project were almost mandatory. Lord Malvern, the first prime minister of the federation, had threatened to impose an export tax on copper, which, in the opinion of top company executives, would have been extremely detrimental to the industry in the mid-1950s. While both groups favored construction of the Kariba project, a high official of RST (J. H. Lascelles) resigned from the Federal Power Board to protest the rejection of a Kafue River project in favor of Kariba. Cf. Harry Franklin, *Unholy Wedlock: The Failure of the Central African Federation* (London: Allen and Unwin, 1963), p. 114.

23. Sir Ronald L. Prain, "Building on a Mineral Foundation in Central Africa" (1957), *Selected Papers*, Vol. I.

24. Rhodesian Selection Trust Group of Companies, *Statement by the Chairman, Sir Ronald L. Prain*, October 1959, pp. 2–3.

paring, when the time comes, and the British Government and the local governments have faced up to this, to work and mine and live under an African Government in Northern Rhodesia."[25]

On the Anglo American Corporation side, Harry F. Oppenheimer, who succeeded his father as chairman in 1957, was not less devoted than Sir Ernest had been to the concepts of federation and multiracial partnership in Central Africa. In certain fundamental respects, the United Federal party of Sir Roy Welensky, prime minister of the federation between 1957 and 1963, mirrored the Progressive party of South Africa, which Harry Oppenheimer helped to inaugurate in 1959. Both parties were committed to the principle of a nonracial but qualified franchise, based on combinations of educational and economic criteria; both would have taken steps to minimize racial discrimination within an overall context of white leadership; both embodied the tradition of Cecil Rhodes's famous dictum: "Equal rights for every civilized man." Oppenheimer might well have cherished the multiracial experiment in Central Africa as an opportunity to demonstrate the validity of a political doctrine that had been rejected in his own South Africa. His annual statements as Chairman of Rhodesian Anglo American Limited in 1960 and 1961 were ardent in their defense of both the federation and the qualified or restricted franchise for multiracial countries in Africa. When the cause of federation was lost and dissolution was imminent, Oppenheimer expressed his hope for continued economic cooperation between Northern and Southern Rhodesia, "just as in pre-Federation days."[26] This outlook was shared by both groups of companies; neither would have concurred in the political logic of Kaunda's view, reported to have been privately expressed in early 1963, that an independent Zambia should be linked with Tanzania by a new railroad as an alternative to the southern route.[27] Coincidently or not, in early 1963 "one of the larger copper companies reportedly pledged financial support" to a dissident group of white Northern Rhodesians within the United Federal party, who accepted the break-up of the federation as

25. "Statement of F. Taylor Ostrander, Assistant to the Chairman, American Metal Climax, Inc., New York, N. Y.," *Activities of Private United States Organizations in Africa*, Hearings before the Subcommittee on Africa of the Committee on Foreign Affairs, House of Representatives, Eighty-Seventh Congress, May 8, 1961 (Washington, D.C., 1961), p. 38.

26. Rhodesian Anglo American Limited, *Statement by the Chairman, Mr. H. F. Oppenheimer*, October 1963.

27. Hall, p. 211.

inevitable but desired to form an anti-Kaundist alliance with Nkumbula's African National Congress.[28]

After the sweeping electoral victory of the United National Independence party in January 1964, both groups of companies adapted with apparent good will and sincerity to the new and truly African nationalist political order. Little more than one year after independence, company attitudes were tested in the conflict over Rhodesia. Like most leaders of the business community in Southern Rhodesia itself, Oppenheimer, Prain, and their associates deplored that country's unilateral declaration of independence. Yet, in the matter of disengagement from Southern Africa, Kaunda and his colleagues could reasonably fear that the mining industry might be manipulated to undermine their national policy.

Contingency Planning

To be sure, the mining companies were greatly distressed by the rupture of normal economic relations between Zambia and Rhodesia and by the prospect of their having to make costly efforts to implement Zambia's policy of disengagement. Yet they did make preparations in anticipation of the crisis, well in advance of governmental action, and they appear to have cooperated fully and loyally with the Zambian government when sanctions were imposed.

The problem of coal supply may be cited as a case in point. In 1965 Zambia consumed some 110,000 short tons of coal per month, of which about 60 percent was used by the copper industry and 30 percent by the railways. Nearly all of it was railed from the Anglo American Corporation's Wankie Colliery in Rhodesia. In addition to normal operating uses, the mining companies rely upon coal to operate their standby thermal generators in emergencies. At the time of Southern Rhodesia's UDI, the stockpile of coal on the Copperbelt was barely sufficient to keep the water pumping system in operation for thirty days. If the power supply from Kariba had been sabotaged and Wankie coal had also become unavailable, the mines would have been precariously dependent upon reserve sources of electrical power from Zaire to prevent irreparable losses from flooding.

28. David C. Mulford, *Zambia: The Politics of Independence, 1957–1964* (London: Oxford University Press, 1967), p. 305.

As a safeguard measure, the two mining groups joined with the government in August 1965 to open a low-grade coal mine in southern Zambia. The mining groups also agreed to purchase and stockpile the first 300,000 tons of this coal at a price that would cover all capital costs as well as the operating costs of this endeavor. UDI resulted in a far more extensive use of this new coal supply than had been anticipated, as increasing proportions of it were mixed with high-grade Wankie imports. But there were adverse consequences at the mines. The poor quality of this coal made for inefficient smelting; in 1968, its excessive use resulted in production cuts caused by damaged equipment. Meanwhile, the companies established a large stockpile of Wankie coal, totaling 320,000 tons, at the southern town of Livingstone. Simultaneously, the government undertook to develop a newly discovered deposit of much better quality coal, also in southern Zambia. With the 1970 installation of a washing plant to improve the thermal efficiency of this product, Zambia achieved virtual self-sufficiency in coal. However, the cost of coal to the mining companies, reflecting substantially increased transport as well as capital costs, was nearly 200 percent greater in 1972 than it had been prior to UDI.[29]

Another case of innovative adaptation to the challenge of Rhodesia involved an experiment in air transport by the RST Group with governmental participation. RST formed a wholly owned subsidiary, Zambia Air Cargoes Limited, which purchased two propjet air freighters from the Lockheed Aircraft Corporation of the United States. Operations were initiated in April 1966; subsequently, the Zambian government purchased three more air freighters for operation by Zambia Air Cargoes under contract. At peak performance, before the destruction of one plane by fire, this fleet was able to export up to 4,000 tons of copper per month from Ndola to Dar es Salaam, importing, on return flights, fuels, mining materials, and general goods. Unfortunately, the costs of this "copper airbridge" were much higher than had been estimated by Lockheed, and it was discontinued as a losing proposition in

---

29. Fuel costs are expected to be cut by the conversion of some copper smelters to furnace oil, which will be produced in large quantities as a by-product at the new Ndola petroleum refinery, scheduled to enter production in 1973. But this saving itself may be costly if it undermines the nation's new and strategically valuable coal industry.

1969.[30] While Zambia Air Cargoes made a significant contribution to the importation of essential supplies, the experimental value of its copper export venture was far greater for the mining group concerned than for the government, which defrayed a substantial part of the cost. In this instance, as in the case of the Kafue pilot polder, sponsored by RST during the latter 1950s to demonstrate the feasibility of capital-intensive agricultural methods,[31] the knowledge derived was unlikely to benefit the present generation of Zambians.

In all matters relating to transport, supply, the level of copper production, and the maintenance of employment in the event of a partial or complete shutdown of operations, the mining groups consulted regularly with members of the Contingency Planning Organization, a governmental body that functioned between December 1965 and September 1966.[32] Thereafter, many contingency planning functions were performed by a joint committee for the two groups, called the Standing Committee on Production Sharing (SCOPS). Between October 1966 and May 1967, export and supply quotas of 4:3 were fixed for the Anglo American Corporation and RST respectively. Contingency costs were also shared in accordance with this formula. Thus Anglo American defrayed four-sevenths of the cost of both Zambia Air Cargoes and the imported heavy fuel oil used as an emergency measure by the Mufulira smelter instead of coal, while RST paid three-sevenths of the cost of new road transport operations that were used for the export of Anglo American copper. When export quotas were lifted in May 1967, SCOPS continued to apportion transportation costs, supply costs, and coal stocks in proportion to each group's actual production. With the fear of comparative losses thus eliminated, the mining groups were encouraged to experiment with transport and production methods that were designed to ease the post-UDI crisis.

In both groups the top- and middle-level managers who were most intensively engaged in the search for solutions to the

30. Hall reports that Zambia Air Cargoes lost £1 million over a life span of three years. *The High Cost of Principles*, p. 210.

31. See Chapter 4.

32. The general manager of the Copperbelt Power Company Limited, then jointly owned by the two mining groups and responsible for the distribution of electricity from all sources to Copperbelt users, was a member of the Contingency Planning Organization as controller for power and fuel.

economic and logistical problems created by UDI seem to have been also sincerely dedicated to the achievement of Zambian national goals.[33] We should not be surprised to find that resident managers of the subsidiaries of multinational corporations are no less prone than resident colonial officials or expatriate scholars to identify with the interests of the country in which they live and work.[34] The sense of identification with local attitudes and values on the part of such expatriates is likely to increase as a result of their participation in a heroic effort by a beleaguered and under-privileged nation. In October 1967 a top official of one of the mining groups summarized his view of the evolving relationship between government and the companies on matters arising from the struggle over Rhodesia thus:

> At first the government did fear that we would come down on the side of Smith. We were pushed a lot and some of us felt that we should take a hard line in dealings with the government because of it. But I disagreed, and we decided to disregard kicks in the teeth and make a genuine effort to cooperate fully with government in all matters. The small day-to-day questions were basic to this relationship and the unmistakable good will of individuals on our side helped to smooth over many tight situations. Personally, I think that disengagement from Rhodesia would have been inevitable even if there had been no UDI. The government in Salisbury had treated Northern Rhodesia as if it were a colonial investment area. This was deeply resented by Zambians and they were bound to break with Southern Rhodesia.

Among company officials in the head offices of both groups, the belief in progress toward the realization of a harmony of interest between government and the industry was an article of faith. I particularly noted that Zambian nationals who held managerial positions in the mining industry, irrespective of race, almost invariably believed that the policies of their employers were essentially

33. My "subjective judgment" accords with that of Charles Harvey, who observes, "that the top management in the companies had real sympathy with Government and its aspirations" ("Tax Reform in the Mining Industry," in *Economic Independence and Zambian Copper*, ed. Mark Bostock and Charles Harvey, Praeger Special Studies in International Economics and Development [New York: Praeger, 1972], p. 141n).

34. Cf. Raymond Vernon, *Sovereignty at Bay* (New York: Basic Books, 1971), pp. 148–150.

compatible with basic national policies relating to the isolation of Rhodesia.

ASPECTS OF DISENGAGEMENT

An overall survey of Zambia's undertaking to disengage from the economic orbit of her white-ruled neighbors would include programs that have not involved the mining companies directly. One such effort was the petroleum supply program, culminating in the construction of a pipeline from Dar es Salaam to the Copperbelt by the Italian State Petroleum Company for the governments of Zambia and Tanzania. A second effort of great magnitude has involved the construction of a hydroelectric facility on the Kafue River by a Yugoslav engineering firm. As its need for electricity mounted, the Zambian government also arranged for the World Bank to finance the construction of a power station at the north bank of the Kariba Dam. When this project is completed, in 1975, Zambia should be able to dispense with the importation of electricity from the south bank station.

Since UDI, Zambia has acquired the capacity to produce certain essential materials required by the copper industry, notably, coal and explosives. Apart from electricity and emergency items, Zambian imports from Rhodesia have dwindled to insignificance. However, the redirection of commercial relations in general depends upon developments in the transport sector, and with these the mining companies have been intimately connected.

Closing an Open-Ended Risk: The Railway Crisis of 1966

In 1965 the Rhodesia Railways carried nearly all of Zambia's exports and imports over routes of approximately 1,500 miles from the Copperbelt to the ports of Beira and Lourenço Marques in Mozambique.[35] Ownership and control of the railway, excluding its Mozambique extensions, were vested jointly and equally in the governments of Rhodesia and Zambia.[36] Under the terms of an

35. The account in this section first appeared in my article, "Zambia's Response to UDI," pp. 14–17 and passim.

36. Most of this railway system was constructed during the 1890s and early 1900s. Between 1929 and 1949 it was wholly owned by the British South Africa Company. In 1949, the system was nationalized by the British and Portuguese

agreement between them, each country's trade was virtually tied
to the Rhodesia Railways. If either country diverted traffic to an
alternative route, the government of that country would have to
pay the Rhodesia Railways compensation equal to the revenue it
would otherwise have earned.[37]

In rail transport, as in other respects, Zambia's mineral wealth
benefited Rhodesia. Specifically, after 1956, high railing rates imposed upon Zambian (and Congolese) copper exports have supported the generally low rates charged for most other commodi-
ties.[38] Even with traditionally low rates for the transport of coal to
the Copperbelt, Zambian traffic earned much higher revenues per
ton-mile than Rhodesian traffic. Naturally, Rhodesia was inclined
to favor a continued high railage on copper exports, although such
rates might hinder the expansion of the copper mining industry in
Zambia. For her part, Zambia would have preferred a lower railage
as an incentive to expansion of the mining industry, since Zambia
depends mainly upon revenues from mining taxation to finance
her development. Lower railing rates would be especially desirable
to Zambia in the event of a decline in copper prices from the (often
abnormally) high levels of recent years. However, the rating pattern of the Rhodesia Railways was preserved by the Inter-
Government Agreement of December 1963, which, as noted
above, imposed a penalty on the diversion of traffic to alternative
routes.

The rupture of established railway relations occurred after UDI
as a result of Zambia's attempt to implement financial sanctions
against Rhodesia. Briefly, the Rhodesia Railways had two account-

---

colonial governments. Four years later, ownership of the Rhodesia Railways was
transferred to the Federation of Rhodesia and Nyasaland, where it remained until
the end of 1963, when the assets and liabilities were divided evenly between
Rhodesia and Zambia. For an account of the central African railway system, see
Edwin T. Haefele and Eleanor B. Steinberg, *Government Controls on Transport: An
African Case* (Washington, D.C.: The Brookings Institution, 1965).

37. Northern Rhodesia, "Agreement between the Government of Southern
Rhodesia and the Government of Northern Rhodesia relating to the Rhodesia Railways," sections 33–45, *Northern Rhodesia Gazette,* December 13, 1963.

38. Before UDI, revenues earned by Rhodesia Railways from copper shipments
alone were nearly 30 percent of total freight revenues, although copper tonnage was
only 8 percent of the total freight tonnage. See *Rhodesia Railways Reports and Accounts
30 June 1965.* R. E. Baldwin reports that "in 1957 Rhodesia Railways derived 60
percent of its Northern Rhodesian revenue from the copper industry" (*Economic
Development and Export Growth* [Berkely and Los Angeles: University of California
Press, 1966], p. 174).

ing centers, at Bulawayo in Rhodesia and Broken Hill (now Kabwe) in Zambia. Bulawayo was also the principal administrative and technical center from which most expenditures were made. But most of the revenue earned by the railway, including all freight charges on most Zambian imports, were collected at Broken Hill. The Zambian mining companies alone paid rates in excess of £1 million per month for the export of copper, and the Broken Hill account normally transferred some £1 million to the Bulawayo account every month. Interference with these payments would inevitably jeopardize the normal operations of the railway.

While Zambia agreed to support Britain's policy of sanctions against Rhodesia, she did not, as we have seen, expect that policy to succeed and was duly cautious in her approach. Although imports from Rhodesia were cut by about one-third during 1966, Zambia was unwilling to take purposeless risks that would not have the desired political effect in Rhodesia.[39] Yet money transfers to Rhodesia were scrutinized and subject to increasingly restrictive controls by the Bank of Zambia. Between UDI and March 1966, payments from the Rhodesia Railways Broken Hill account to its Bulawayo account were reduced by more than 25 percent by means of exchange control. Suddenly, in April, the Zambian government decided to block all further payments from the railway's account at Broken Hill to that at Bulawayo.

This was a precipitous and daring step for Zambia to take, since the Rhodesia Railways carried over 90 percent of Zambia's imports and exports. Unless Zambia was prepared to sacrifice her own planned development, there was no question of giving up the Rhodesia Railways for years to come. The timing of this gambit, shortly after the British Labour party's decisive victory in the general election of March 1966, may not have been coincidental, since Zambian leaders now expected the British government to act more resolutely against the rebel regime.

A disruption of rail transport would immediately affect the copper companies; ultimately, it would affect the British economy, which has relied upon Zambia for some 40 percent of its copper requirement. Perhaps Zambia hoped to induce the companies to "lobby" for a more militant policy against Rhodesia. The British government too might have been spurred to take more decisive action. Seen in this perspective, Zambia's decision to block the

39. See Hall, pp. 163–164.

transfer of railway funds to Rhodesia appears to have been a major initiative in foreign policy.

In her direct confrontation with Rhodesia, however, Zambia's position was weak. In May, following the Zambian government's refusal to reconsider its decision, the Rhodesia Railways, acting in consultation with the Mozambique Railways and the South African Railways, demanded payment in advance for all freight coming into Zambia via the Rhodesia Railways system. The railway had for some months past been requiring payments of railage in advance on shipments originating in Rhodesia. Henceforth, the Broken Hill center would be deprived of the bulk of its accustomed receipts from imports. Furthermore, it was announced that railing charges on exports from Zambia, earned outside Zambia, would have to be prepaid in Rhodesia; alternatively, the total railage could be paid on delivery at the point of destination in Rhodesia, South Africa, or Mozambique. These decisions were taken by the Rhodesia Railways Board, consisting of a chairman, three Rhodesian members and three Zambians, the latter voting against them. Theoretically, the decisions of this board were subject to confirmation by a Higher Authority for Railways, comprising two ministers from each government. A unanimous vote was required for affirmative action by the Higher Authority. But this body had been unable to function since UDI inasmuch as the government of Rhodesia had become illegal, and its acts were, therefore, null and void.

On May 24 the retaliatory payments procedure was put into effect by the Rhodesia, Mozambique, and South African railways. Copper exports were affected immediately, since the Zambian government would not permit the Zambian copper companies to make the required railing payments either directly or indirectly (through Mozambique or South Africa) to the Rhodesia Railways. On May 25, Zambia's copper companies declared force majeure on their contracts with buyers, thereby relieving themselves of liability for damages because of conditions beyond their control. On May 28 the Zambian High Court issued an injunction against implementation of the new payments procedure on the grounds that it was harmful to Zambia and could not be adopted without the consent of the (now defunct) Higher Authority for Railways. Thereupon the railways management suspended the new procedure in Zambia, although it remained in force in Rhodesia, Mozambique, and South Africa, where Zambian imports were held up pending advance payments for railage to be incurred south of the Zambezi. On May 31, the Zambian government instructed the bank of Zambia to refuse applications for foreign exchange needed to pay the railage on goods coming over the Rhodesia Railways. (Exceptions were made for medical supplies and coal, although the copper companies had actually been making dollar payments in advance for coal shipments since December 1965). At this time, Zambia was importing over 100,000 tons of general goods, exclusive of coal, per month via the Rhodesia Railways. Clearly, Zambia had overreached her striking ability and would not be able to maintain a comprehensive ban on foreign exchange for railage.

On June 3 the Zambian government relented and authorized the payment of railage to the Rhodesia Railways for goods ordered under contracts made before May 24. In addition, the Import Licensing Department of the Ministry of Commerce and Industry was authorized to permit prepayment of railing costs for an indeterminate range of "essential supplies." Thereafter, until the disruptive events of January 1973, Zambia relied upon the Rhodesia Railways for at least three-fourths of her imported general goods, exclusive of oil, for which the entire cost of railage south of the Zambezi was prepaid in Mozambique and South Africia, rather than Bulawayo.

The copper export snarl was also resolved, after much difficulty, on Rhodesian terms. Between May 29 and June 9 the copper companies railed 16,000 tons of copper, worth £10 million, into Rhodesia, where it was held up until the Zambian government would allow the companies to pay charges required by the Rhodesia Railways. Further shipments were prohibited, and by mid-July there were 90,000 tons of copper awaiting export from the Copperbelt. Amid rumors that the copper companies might restrict production and retrench the size of the work force, Zambia's Parliament enacted a law that empowered the president to prohibit the dismissal of employees during periods of public emergency.[40]

On July 22 the Zambian government ended the impasse by announcing that copper shipments via the Rhodesia Railways could be resumed. It was agreed that the copper companies would pay the railage incurred within Zambia to the Zambian section of the

---

40. Republic of Zambia, *Debates of the Third Session (Resumed) of the First National Assembly*, July 21, 1966, cols. 17–82. Regulations under this act were in effect from August 3–25, 1966.

Rhodesia Railways. Arrangements were made whereby an agency company, or intermediary, associated with each of the two copper mining groups would take title to the copper at the Rhodesian border and pay the railage due from there to the seaports, at which points, title to the copper would be transferred to sales companies associated with each group. While these sales companies are registered in Great Britain, the two intermediary companies are registered in Switzerland.[41] By this device, the rail payments issue was resolved and the crisis ended without a technical breach of sanctions by the Zambian producers, their British customers, or either the British or Zambian governments.

Once before, at the time of UDI, Zambia may have come close to the brink of all-out economic warfare against Rhodesia. It has been suggested to me that the possibility of a total break with Rhodesia was seriously considered by the Zambian cabinet in December 1965.[42] Had Zambia sealed her border with Rhodesia, thereby preventing both the importation of coal and the export of copper, the crisis might have been brought to a head. An imaginative commentator has suggested that the copper companies might then have become the "most insistent and powerful lobbyists at Westminster for Britain to restore normal relations at all costs; they would have advocated the use of troops in Rhodesia to end the crisis."[43] This scenario is intriguing, as it would have compelled the companies to choose between their basic economic interests and what might be described as a cozy but cautiously critical relationship with the white regimes of Southern Africa. Doubtless, the risks incurred by Zambia would have been enormous. Among them were the following: an indeterminately great loss of revenue from copper exports that would set back the country's economic development; prolonged idleness at the mines and urban discontent as a result of

41. This matter was so sensitive at the time that officials of the two groups were unusually reluctant to divulge the names of the Swiss intermediary companies long after the arrangements had become routine. I am informed that they are, for the Anglo American Corporation, Union Investment Company, which is listed in annual reports of the Anglo American Corporation of South Africa prior to 1971 as a mining finance and investment company, administered outside the group; and, for RST, Ametalco S.A. (Geneva), a wholly owned subsidiary of the RST sales organization.

42. President Kaunda has disclosed that Zambia did offer "to make a total break with Rhodesia" at the time of UDI on condition of adequate British assistance. Republic of Zambia, "President Kaunda's Press Conference," May 12, 1966, "Background," No. 12/66.

43. Guy Arnold in *The Times of Zambia*, December 9, 1967.

consumer goods shortages and unemployment; the possibility of disastrous floods in underground mines if the electrical power supply failed when coal stocks were exhausted. On the other hand, the disruption of rural life would have been minimal, and a popular government in a state of emergency might have weathered the storm for an indefinite period of time. In any event, the British government was anxious to avert the assumption by Zambia of any such open-ended risk taking, and appears to have exerted a restraining influence on the Zambian leaders in December 1965.[44]

Once again, in April 1966, Zambia seemed ready to risk everything in an attempt to provoke action by the British. By prohibiting the payment of funds, including copper railing charges to the Rhodesia Railways, Zambia put British interests and those of the copper companies directly in the line of fire. With what result? "The British Government," said Foreign Minister Kapwepwe, addressing the UN Security Council, "flew immediately to say 'Don't close it' [the border]—and yet they were responsible for the sanctions. They said they were prepared to pay money for transporting their copper; they were prepared to pay Smith the foreign currency."[45]

Eventually, as we have seen, a face-saving procedure was devised to permit payment of the railage. Zambia's moral position was unimpaired, although her attempt to bring the sanctions war to a climax had misfired. Clearly Britain, which imports 40 percent of her copper from Zambia, did not want Zambia to endanger the flow of copper exports. Zambia had been prepared to pay a great price for the sake of a decisive stroke against Rhodesia. Only Britain could

44. A report to this effect was filed from Lusaka by Anthony Lewis in *The New York Times International Edition*, August 17, 1966: "Zambian leaders . . . say resentfully that they were taken in by Mr. Wilson last winter on the issue of the British sanctions program.

"The story told is that Zambia wanted to begin last December to cut off her Rhodesian trade, but Britain resisted the idea and said she would not help Zambia in the difficult economic transition.

"The reason assertedly given was that the Rhodesian rebels would fall under the weight of sanctions in a few weeks anyway, and that Britain did not want to upset the trade patterns for a Rhodesia about to be restored to grace.

" 'If Britain had not bluffed us,' a member of the Zambian Government said, 'we'd be much farther along now to where we must go.' "

45. *United Nations Security Council, Official Records*, S/PV. 1336, December 13, 1966, p. 9.

deliver that stroke. Unwilling to do so, Britain was anxious to avert the costs of extreme measures to herself, Zambia, and the copper companies. Britain's tactical position in mid-1966 was described succinctly by *The Times* of London: "The British case has been that Zambia should cut its trade with Rhodesia first, and only discontinue the use of the Rhodesia Railways when assured of alternative routes and alternative supplies of coking coal."[46] When a British minister of state urged this strategy on Zambia in July 1966, it was rejected with obvious justification in Lusaka on the ground that Zambia would be exposed to immense economic dangers without adequate reason to expect that the cause of African liberation in Rhodesia would be thereby advanced.[47]

Zambia's continued willingness to run open-ended risks was asserted by her foreign minister in December 1966, during the course of his prescient argument to the UN Security Council that Britain's proposal for selective mandatory sanctions would prove to be ineffectual. At this time, a specific proposal submitted on behalf of the African group of states to tighten sanctions by including coal on the list of prohibited Rhodesian goods was supported by Zambia but not, however, accepted by the Security Council. Had coal imports from Wankie been prohibited at that juncture, copper production in Zambia would have been interrupted. Subsequently, in May 1968 and March 1970, the Security Council imposed comprehensive nonmilitary sanctions against Rhodesia that were binding on all member states. The latter resolution enjoined member states to "immediately interrupt any existing means of transportation to and from Southern Rhodesia."[48] Neither Zambia nor the other landlocked states bordering Rhodesia (Botswana and Malawi) would be required to implement this injunction.[49] After 1966, Zambia pursued the goal of disengagement from Southern Africa without the pressure of a moral obligation to incur risks that might have been taken earlier for the sake of effective concerted action against Rhodesia.

46. *The Times* (London), August 23, 1966.
47. Hall, pp. 163–164.
48. S/RES/277 of March 18, 1970.
49. Article 50 of the Charter of the United Nations provides that any state which "finds itself confronted with special economic problems" as a result of enforcement measures taken by the Security Council "shall have the right to consult the Security Council with regard to a solution to those problems."

156THE CLAIMS OF IDEOLOGY

Old Ties and New Routes

The railway crisis of 1966 virtually nullified those international and commercial agreements that had obligated both governmental and business organizations in Zambia to support the Rhodesia Railways at the expense of other routes.[50] Henceforth, decisions concerning Zambia's use of this system would turn on calculations relating to necessity, convenience, and her vulnerability to reprisals in the form of punitive rates that would be charged by the Rhodesia Railways to compensate for an insufficient volume of traffic. Before UDI, the net tonnage of imports per month via the Rhodesia Railways averaged approximately 215,000 short tons, including 100,000 tons of coal and coke, 15,000 tons of petroleum products, and 100,000 tons of general goods. By September 1966, the total net tonnage had fallen to 170,000 tons; coal was down to 67,000 tons, but general goods had actually increased to 103,000 tons. At this time, a mere 15,000 tons of general goods entered Zambia via all other routes, including rail, road, and air transport. By 1968 the import capacity of the alternative routes had been increased to 40,000 tons per month, approximately 25 to 30 percent of all dry cargo imports. For several reasons, both logistical and financial, this degree of dependence upon the Rhodesia Railways seemed unlikely to be altered significantly until the projected rail link to Tanzania had been completed.[51] Meanwhile, Zambia would attempt to maximize her use of alternative rail and road routes as follows.

The Angolan Rail Route.—Zambia Railways, created in June 1967 when Rhodesia Railways was formally divided between the two countries by action of the Rhodesia Railways Board, connects with the Zaire railway system (KDL or Katanga-Dilolo line; formerly,

50. This section updates an earlier version in my article, "Zambia's Response to UDI," pp. 20–25.

51. In 1968, the Zambian government informed the secretary-general of the United Nations that 25 percent of Zambia's transported foreign trade had been routed away from the Rhodesia Railways. Financial pressures appear to have reinforced Rhodesia's logistical hold over Zambian trade thus: "The remaining traffic still moved by the Rhodesia railways is the outcome of calculations by the Southern Rhodesians of the largest amount of money they consider they can safely extort from Zambia and the largest amount of traffic Zambia can route through Southern Rhodesia without paying more. Any further attempt to direct traffic from the Southern Rhodesian route would result in additional payments to Southern Rhodesia for less traffic, which Zambia could not afford" (UN Doc. S/8786/Add.2, 10 October 1968, p. 5).

MAP 5.

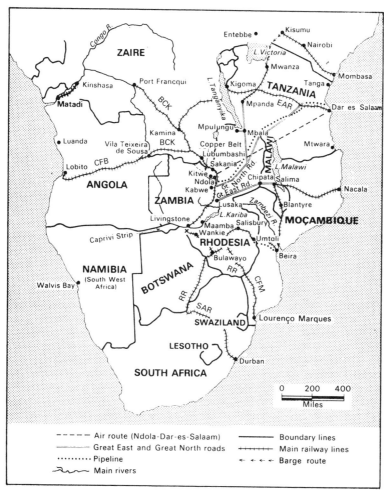

Zambia's rail, road, and other main supply routes.

BCK or Chemin de Fer du Bas Congo au Katanga), as shown in map 5. One branch of the KDL connects with the Benguela Railway (CFB or Caminho de Ferro de Benguela) of Angola, terminating at the Atlantic port of Lobito. This route from the Zambia copperbelt is much the same length as the southern routes to Beira and Lourenço Marques. Moreover, the port of Lobito is some 2,000 miles nearer to destinations in Europe than are the seaports of Mozambique.

The Benguela Railway, opened in 1931, was constructed by a

British firm, Tanganyika Concessions Limited (TANKS), which also acquired about 15 percent of the Belgian (Congolese) mining company, Union Minière du Haute-Katanga. TANKS owns 90 percent of the Benguela Railway while 10 percent belongs to the Portuguese government of Angola. For many years, the BCK/Benguela line was denied access to the lucrative trade of the Copperbelt. Thus in 1936, the Northern Rhodesian copper companies agreed to ship all of their production via the Rhodesia Railways for the next twenty years. In exchange, the mining companies were given very low rates on both their copper exports and their imports of coal from the Wankie Colliery in Southern Rhodesia. To assure the continuation of two-way (copper/coal) traffic, the mining companies also agreed not to develop hydroelectric power as a substitute for coal.

When this agreement expired in 1956, rates on copper from Northern Rhodesia were raised from about £3 per ton to £14.85. By then the copper companies wanted a second route to relieve congestion on the Rhodesia Railways. In 1956, an inter-railway agreement between the Rhodesia, BCK, and Benguela railways stipulated that a maximum of 20 percent of total copper exports from Northern Rhodesia could be shipped via the Lobito route. It was also agreed that both routes would charge identical rates for Northern Rhodesian copper. After this agreement was renewed in 1960, the Rhodesia Railways acted unilaterally to offer the copper companies a substantial rebate on exports diverted to it from the BCK/Benguela system. As a result, the Lobito route was virtually abandoned by the Northern Rhodesian (later Zambian) producers for several years.[52] Interest in the Lobito route was renewed prior to UDI when the copper companies found it necessary to supplement the coal-carrying capacity of the Rhodesia Railways. By the end of 1965 small quantities of South African coal and Zambian copper were being transported via the BCK/Benguela system. But it remained for the railway payments crisis of 1966 to stimulate a massive redirection to the Lobito route.

It will be recalled that in June and July 1966, an immense stockpile of exportable copper, about 90,000 tons, accumulated at the Copperbelt mines. From July 12 to 15, ministerial talks concerning rail transport were held at Kinshasa, capital of the Democratic Republic of the Congo (later Zaire), including representatives of

52. See Haefele and Steinberg, *Government Controls on Transport: An African Case;* and Baldwin, pp. 171–174.

the Congo, Zambia, and Tanzania, in addition to observers from the several railway systems involved.[53] An agreement was reached to facilitate the export of 40,000 metric tons of copper per month, equal to about two-thirds of Zambia's current copper exports, via Congolese and related routes.[54] However, various technical and logistical impediments foiled the implementation of most of this agreement. Moreover, the crucial Benguela Railway insisted upon a five-year guarantee, backed by the Congolese and Zambian governments, for 20,000 metric tons per month at a fixed railage that would be 25 percent higher than the rate then in effect. Since this guarantee could not be obtained, the agreement as a whole never came into force and traffic via the Lobito route did not attain the desired level until the transportation crisis of 1973, which is discussed below.

Nonetheless, the Kinshasa agreement represented a real achievement for Zambian diplomacy. Copper shipments via the Lobito route were sustained at more than 10,000 metric tons per month for nearly a year, until acts of sabotage in both Angola and the Congo, attributed variously to Angolan freedom fighters, Tshombist saboteurs, and mercenaries, disrupted transportation in 1967. Periodic incidents of this kind have served to underscore the hazards of reliance upon exit routes through countries that are liable to experience racially based military conflicts for years to come. It was also seen that the Portuguese would take reprisals against Zambian and Congolese traffic for guerrilla activities thought to be supported by either country.[55] Despite these risks, an agreement between Zambia and Zaire in December 1967, reaffirming the principle of complete cooperation between these two countries in the field of rail transport, called for the negotiation of a new railway agreement by the BCK, Zambia, and Benguela railways to supplement the Kinshasa decisions and replace the inter-railway accords of 1956 and 1960. The Benguela Railway has since undertaken to make major improvements that are expected

53. The railways represented were the Congo railway companies, namely, the BCK, Otraco (from Kinshasa to Matadi), and Chemin de Fer aux Grands Lacs Africains (CFL, between BCK and Albertville), the Benguela Railway, and East African Railways and Harbours. The Zambian delegation, led by the minister of transport and works, also included the administrator of the Zambian section of the Rhodesia Railways and an official of the mining companies.

54. Republic of Zambia, "Statement on Kinshasa Railway Talks," July 15, 1966, "Background," No. 16/66.

55. See Douglas G. Anglin, "Confrontation in Southern Africa: Zambia and Portugal," *International Journal* 25 (Summer 1970): 510–511.

to double the capacity of this route by 1974. Recently, it has been used to carry not less than 20 percent of Zambian copper exports, and frequently more, per month.[56]

The Limits of Disengagement.—Among the alternative routes that were pressed into service on an emergency basis both to supply Zambia with vast quantities of petrol and to facilitate a maximum disengagement from the Rhodesia Railways, pride of place belongs to the Great North Road, which runs 1,200 miles from central Zambia to Tanzania's seaport capital of Dar es Salaam. This road has been extremely difficult to maintain during the heavy rains between November and April. In the aftermath of UDI, it was excessively overburdened with heavy traffic; its deplorable condition and high accident rate earned it the apt nickname of "hell run." Commercial traffic on the Great North Road has been organized primarily by Zambia-Tanzania Road Services Limited, a joint venture involving the Zambian and Tanzanian governments and the Fiat organization of Italy. This enterprise has activated a large fleet of trucks, including dual purpose tankers while they were needed, to carry imports and copper exports on the Great North Road. Despite these efforts, export tonnages via road to Dar es Salaam have not normally exceeded 15,000 tons per month, which is comparable to the performance of the Benguela Railway before 1973. While the companies have cooperated fully with Zam-Tan Road Services, they have also dreaded the potential appearance of a truck-bound stockpile of valuable copper stuck in the mud of the Great North Road. Preparations to improve this road and relocate portions of it were made by the Tanzanian and Zambian governments in 1966–1967; but completion of the work was delayed until 1972, by which time a bituminized highway had been constructed with financial assistance from Britain, Sweden, and the United States, as well as the World Bank.

Another significant route is the Great East Road, extending more than 500 miles from Lusaka to Salima in Malawi, which is connected by rail with the port of Beira in Mozambique. The cost of

56. In 1971, the Zambian government entered into an agreement with Tanganyika Concessions, predominant owner of the Benguela Railway Company, providing for the transport of at least 20 percent of Zambia's copper production for a period of three years, subject to penalty payments for shortfalls. In return, the Benguela Railway agreed that it would not increase tariffs and would pay rebates to the Zambia Railways for shipments in excess of 22.5 percent of production. "Copper Railway Agreement" (typescript).

shipping copper via this route is over 20 percent higher than that of either the Lobito route or the route to Dar es Salaam; the average transit time of forty-six days is far inferior to that for Lobito—fourteen days—or Dar es Salaam—11 days. From time to time, transport directors have experimented with other, less developed, routes: a road branching from the Great North Road to the southern Tanzanian port of Mtwara, where improvements of the airport and harbor facilities have been financed by the Zambian government; a branch from the Great North Road via Mbala to the railhead at Mpanda, Tanzania, which is linked by rail both to Dar es Salaam and to the Kenya railways via ferry from the lake port of Mwanza; a branch from Mbala to Mpulungu on Lake Tanganyika, where barges connect with the Tanzania railways at Kigoma. While these experimental routes have been used sparingly, the costs of developing them have been defrayed by the Zambian government, and they have continued to attract interest in view of the present limitations of the congested port of Dar es Salaam.

Despite these strenuous and costly efforts to develop reliable new routes,[57] the Zambian copper industry has been compelled to use the Rhodesia Railways to carry a large percentage of its exports. Before 1973, the Lobito route never carried anything near the Kinshasa agreement target of 31,000 metric tons per month; it often failed to reach the 15,000 tons that it was thought able to carry in mid-1966. Given the availability of more than 60,000 short tons of exportable copper per month, it was possible, in an average month during 1967–1968, to ship it via various routes about as follows:

via rail to Lobito	15–16,000 tons
via road to Dar es Salaam	15–16,000 tons
via air to Dar es Salaam	3– 4,000 tons
via road to Malawi and rail to Beira	4– 5,000 tons
via miscellaneous routes	2– 3,000 tons
via Rhodesia Railways to Beira and Lourenço Marques	20–22,000 tons
	59–66,000 tons

57. In October 1968, the Zambian government estimated its net contingency costs resulting from the Rhodesian crisis at the figure of K142.4 million. UN Doc. S/8786/Add.2, 10 October 1968, pp. 6–7.

The actual decision on each month's export allocation to the various routes, including the Rhodesia Railways, has been made by officials of the ministry responsible for foreign trade after consultation with officials of other ministries and the mining companies. In practice, more often than not, one or another alternative route has fallen short of its expected capacity. To Zambia's acute distress, attacks by nationalist guerrillas in Angola put the Lobito route out of commission for several weeks in both 1968 and 1969. The Great East Road was also disrupted by the sabotage of a bridge over the Luangwa River in 1968, presumably by Portuguese agents in retaliation for the intensification of guerrilla activities in nearby Mozambique. From time to time, stretches of the Great North Road have been rendered inoperative by torrential rains. Consequently, until 1973 Zambian copper exports via the Rhodesian rail route rarely dipped beneath 20,000 tons or one-third of the total; they were often considerably higher. Indeed, the Rhodesian authorities eventually required Zambia to ship a minimum of 22,700 metric tons of copper per month via the Rhodesia Railways. Failure to comply with this requirement is penalized by the imposition of a surcharge of 50 percent on all Zambian imports using that railway.

Zambia's release from dependence upon the transportation systems of white-ruled Southern Africa is promised by the construction of a 1,000-mile Tan-Zam railway between the Zambian center and Dar es Salaam. This project has been a cherished goal of Zambian and Tanzanian leaders since 1963. But a World Bank study, requested by Kaunda in 1964, had resulted in a negative report that favored the much less costly alternative of an improved Tan-Zam highway. When Zambia became independent, the People's Republic of China expressed an interest in undertaking the project. President Nyerere was immediately receptive; Kaunda's enthusiasm for closer relations with China was kindled during his visit there in 1967.[58] China then offered to build the Tan-Zam railway on the basis of a £100 million interest-free loan. An agreement between China, Tanzania, and Zambia was concluded and a survey undertaken by Chinese engineers. Subsequently, it was reported that the interest-free loan would amount to K286.6 million (£168 million), repayable over a period of about thirty years beginning in 1985. This loan is expected to cover costs of construction, rolling stock, and the improvement of port facilities at the congested harbor of

58. Hall, p. 218.

Dar es Salaam. For their part, Zambia and Tanzania have agreed to purchase consumer goods from China equal in value to the local construction costs that will be incurred by the Chinese. Actual construction was begun in 1970 and has proceeded ahead of schedule. Completion is now anticipated in 1974. Although the eventual carrying capacity of this railroad, 7 million tons per year (both directions), would more than suffice for Zambia's current needs, Zambian reliance upon it may be restricted by the administration and capacity of port facilities at Dar es Salaam.

A sudden, unanticipated test of Zambia's ability to dispense entirely with routes through white-ruled countries materialized in January 1973. In reprisal for the actions in Rhodesia of nationalist guerrillas alleged to operate from Zambia, the Salisbury government closed its border with Zambia, demanding an assurance from Lusaka that henceforth the guerrillas would be curbed. Although copper exports via the Rhodesia Railways were specifically exempted from this embargo, Zambia decided to discontinue them on the ground that Rhodesia would not return the empty railway wagons, which normally carry imported goods. Doubtless, the Rhodesians would be faced with a drastic loss of railage revenue, estimated at R$1 (U.S. $1.4) million per month. But Zambia in turn would have to expand the import capacity of her alternative routes by up to 75,000 tons per month in order to bring in vital machinery and spare parts required by the mining industry, coke (heretofore supplied by the Wankie Colliery in Rhodesia) for the Broken Hill lead and zinc mine, and general goods of every description.[59]

With spirited determination, the Zambian government rejected Rhodesian overtures to resume transport relations and resolved to press the new routes into emergency service. At this time, the Tan-Zam railway reached to within 150 miles of the Zambian frontier, and a large fleet of trucks could be mobilized to ply the recently reconstructed Great North Road. Zambian officials confidently asserted that, if need be, the entire export trade in copper could be shipped via the port of Dar es Salaam. In fact, some 53 percent of Zambia's copper was shipped via the Angolan rail route during the first six months of 1973, while 41 percent went via Dar es Salaam and 5 percent via Mombasa, Kenya.[60] (It was noted that

59. *Report of the Security Council Special Mission Established Under Resolution 326 (1973)*, UN Docs. S/10896, 5 March 1973 and S/10896/Add.1, 6 March 1973.
60. *Barclays International Review* (October 1973), p. 26.

Portugal, regretting the loss of rail and sea revenues at Beira, deplored Rhodesia's precipitous action. South African businessmen
were also upset by the loss of their easy access routes to Zambian
markets.) The crunch for Zambia would come on the import side,
depending upon the capacity of Dar es Salaam and other East
African ports—Mtwara and Tanga in Tanzania, Mombasa in
Kenya, and Malawi's new outlet to the sea at the port of Nacala in
Mozambique—to accommodate Zambia's need.[61] It was also
suggested that Kaunda's government would not regret an unlooked-
for opportunity to cut back nonessential imports and thereby
improve a deteriorating balance of payments position, while the
nation might be rallied to greater collective efforts on the basis of
moral and patriotic incentives.

LIBERATION AND STABILITY
IN SOUTHERN AFRICA

Historically, no interest contributed more than the mining
groups to the economic integration of colonial Zambia into Southern Africa. Yet, as denizens of independent Zambia, the mining
companies adapted quickly and realistically to the situation created
by resurgent white racialism in Rhodesia. Thus far, we have
examined their compliance with major aspects of Zambia's policy
of economic disengagement from Southern Africa. But Zambia's
policy on Southern Africa looks beyond economic disengagement
toward the positive goal of African liberation. Does this extrater-
ritorial aspect of Zambia's policy give rise to conflicts of interest
with her business partners in the mining field?

Reconciling to Racial Rule in Rhodesia

Zambia's militant response to the Rhodesian declaration of independence nullified certain basic assumptions of long-term

61. Tanzania's government rose to this occasion by diverting its own imports to
the northern port of Tanga, thereby freeing facilities at the port of Dar es Salaam to
handle Zambian goods. The port of Mtwara was also reserved for Zambian trade.
Africa Research Bulletin, Economic, Financial and Technical Series 10, no. 1 (February
28, 1973): 2613–2614. However, the port of Dar es Salaam is administered by the
East African Economic Community and serves Burundi, Rwanda, and Uganda in
addition to Tanzania and Zambia. Steep increases in port handling charges and
congestion have been matters of concern for Zambia. Thomas A. Johnson in *The
New York Times*, June 2, 1974.

economic policies that had been adopted by both mining groups for their operations in central Africa. From their standpoint, the existing arrangements for fuel, power, and transportation were excellent and therefore painful to abandon. Given its special interests in the Wankie Colliery and the Rhodesia Railways, which rented rolling stock from an Anglo American subsidiary, and its natural tendency to promote integrative relationships among the national economies of this region, the Anglo American Corporation was far more deeply committed than RST to the established patterns of interdependence.[62] From the Anglo American standpoint, the aftermath of UDI was nothing less than a logistical disaster. Yet the challenges of this crisis period were not without positive value to the corporation. Specifically, they provided a useful test for the political theory of Anglo American's distinctive "group system" of corporate organization. In theory, this system provides for effective central control through the assignment of trusted managers to subsidiaries along with the continuous supply of both administrative and technical services. At the same time, the managers of major subsidiaries are notably autonomous in the exercise of authority within their spheres of operation.[63] Despite its multifaceted involvement within the network of Anglo American Corporation relationships in central and southern Africa, ZAMANGLO was able to conduct its affairs as a Zambian company with a Zambian national point of view. Similarly, Anglo American Corporation Rhodesia Limited (AMRHO) was also able to exercise autonomy as a Rhodesian national company. In brief, experience would show that within a region torn by conflict the individual subsidiaries of a single industrial group could operate in

62. In 1970 the assets of RST in Rhodesia were reported to include a real estate company, a modest portfolio of investments, and a much larger holding in loans. Roan Selection Trust Limited, *Explanatory Statement for Meetings of Shareholders To Be Held on 6th August, 1970*, June 30, 1970, app. J–2–3. These assets have been blocked in Rhodesia by exchange control regulations in force since the unilateral declaration of independence. RST continued to explore for minerals in Rhodesia until 1968, when these operations were discontinued; many of the employees were then transferred to an RST-managed mining enterprise in Botswana.

63. This feature of Anglo American Corporation's management in Zambia has been remarked by M. L. O. Faber: "Within AAC, the major policy decisions seemed to be made by a small group of younger men sent to Lusaka especially for the purpose and enjoying a very large measure of autonomy" (*Towards Economic Independence: Papers on the Nationalisation of the Copper Industry in Zambia*, ed. M. L. O. Faber and J. C. Potter [Cambridge: Cambridge University Press, 1971], p. 7).

accordance with the dictates of the discordant foreign policies of
their respective host states in order to safeguard their local positions and thereby serve the interests of the group as a whole.[64]

While the managers of individual subsidiaries are constrained by
the requirements of effective performance to function in accordance with local values, the directors of the various companies
identify with the group as a whole. Many directors and alternate
directors are members of the boards of several companies in the
group. Some directors are also managers; in their managerial
capacities they would be expected to acquire a feel for the values of
the societies within which they operate, without, however, losing
sight of the overall interests of the group. H. F. Oppenheimer
appears to be the chairman of all major autonomous companies in
the group. The annual chairman's statement for each company
reflects the point of view of its directorate, tempered by an appreciation for local values. Naturally, the most authoritative and
comprehensive exposition of the position of the group as a whole
appears in the chairman's statement for the parent company,
Anglo American Corporation of South Africa Limited. Since the
parent company is domiciled in the dominant state of the region,
where most of the directors live, one might expect it to reflect the
values and preoccupations of South African businessmen. This it
does. Yet Harry Oppenheimer and many of his business associates
are long-time critics of South African racial policies;[65] his ideological home was Southern Rhodesia during the era of Welensky and
Whitehead, a home that was wrecked by the electoral debacle of
1962.[66] Consequently, the chairman's statement for the parent

64. It is certainly not uncommon for business groups in hostile nations to collaborate systematically in order to serve their long-term mutual interests. A significant study of one such case, involving the national industrial federations of
Great Britain and Germany on the eve of World War II, is Louis H. Orzak, "The
Dusseldorf Agreement: A Study of the Organization of Power and Planning," *Political Science Quarterly* 65 (September 1950): 393–414. The present case is distinctively
more typical of the latter twentieth century, since it illustrates collaboration between
members of a single corporate group—the Anglo American Corporation—rather
than members of a traditional cartel or group of national federations.

65. See Colin Legum and Margaret Legum, *South Africa: Crisis for the West* (Lon-
don: Pall Mall Press, 1964), pp. 117–123; for a recent statement of this criticism see
Anglo American Corporation of South Africa Limited, *Statement by the Chairman Mr.
H. F. Oppenheimer,* May 1971, pp. 2–3.

66. Sir Edgar Whitehead was prime minister of Southern Rhodesia between
1958 and 1962. His government (United Federal party) was hostile to African
nationalism but prepared to collaborate with Africans to institute reforms, including

company reflects a value position that is not exemplified by any one of the existing organizations of state power in southern and central Africa. Typically, it synthesizes the values of the group as a whole in forthright, lucid, and overtly political prose.

In 1967 Oppenheimer announced that his group's Rhodesian subsidiary had embarked upon a new venture in nickel mining. His view of the sanctions campaign, then in its second year, was as follows:

> Whatever the rights or wrongs of the U.D.I. dispute, I cannot believe that either British interests or the interests of any of the Rhodesian peoples will be advanced by destroying the Rhodesian economy. The sanctions policy might perhaps have been justified had it produced, as the British Government apparently supposed it would, rapid political results. It might not have done much harm if, as the Rhodesian Government apparently supposed, it had rapidly proved a failure and been abandoned. As it is, we have in Rhodesia the worst of both worlds: the Rhodesian economy is being slowly throttled, and no political result favourable to British interests is being obtained.[67]

It seems fair to characterize this declaration as a plea for the primacy of business as usual, somewhat closer to African values than to those of the dominant white Rhodesians, since it does contemplate the overthrow of their regime with equanimity. It also contrasts sharply with the African viewpoint inasmuch as it accepts the survival of the white supremacist regime with equal equanimity. Several months later, it was disclosed that the new nickel mine would involve an expenditure of approximately £10 million on development and prospecting, "the largest capital investment in a Rhodesian company since the Unilateral Declaration of Independence nearly two years ago."[68] The Zambian government's predictably angry reaction was not assuaged by Anglo American protestations that the corporation planned to invest £40 million in Zambia during the next four years and that the entire

---

the abolition of racial restrictions on land ownership, the gradual elimination of segregationist practices, and some liberalization of the nonracial but qualified franchise. It was turned out of office by the frankly white supremacist Rhodesian Front in the election of December 1962.

67. Anglo American Corporation of South Africa Limited, *Statement by the Chairman, Mr. H. F. Oppenheimer,* May 1967, p. 4.

68. *The Times* (London), October 6, 1967.

cost of the Rhodesian venture would be financed from funds within Rhodesia.[69] From the group's viewpoint, AMRHO was just getting on with its business, which the Zambian government should try to understand. A high official of the corporation in Zambia was reported to have explained that the corporation had "an obligation to its investors to promote their interests despite UDI. The decision was not to be understood as 'approval for the rebel regime but rather as confidence for the long-term stability of that country.' "[70] The situation was obviously an awkward one for officials of the Zambian subsidiary. It would have been more awkward yet had it come to light that ZAMANGLO itself held 47 percent of the shares in AMRHO. While this knowledge would have added insult to injury in Zambia, it would not have affected Zambian perceptions of reality, since it was clear in any case that the directorates of both subsidiaries overlapped substantially with the directorate of the parent company.

In 1968 Oppenheimer once more deplored the politically futile sanctions campaign, which, in his view, had resulted in "the slowing down of development, the hardening of white attitudes to African aspirations and the embitterment of relations with Great Britain. Nothing of this," he argued, "will serve to promote a return to legality or a peaceful and liberal evolution of race relations within the country." He also referred to the report of a constitutional commission in Rhodesia, which had abandoned the theoretical possibility of eventual majority rule in favor of a purely theoretical and distant possibility of political parity between Africans and Europeans. "It may be," he speculated, "that changing attitudes sinde U.D.I. have made this policy of racial parity the only practical way of ensuring a significant African participation in Government in the near future." The idea, he felt, should "be studied on its merits and not rejected out of hand because it conflicts with the previously accepted formula."[71] These statements appeared to

69. *The Times of Zambia*, November 17, 1967; Anglo American Corporation of South Africa Limited, *Statement by the Chairman, Mr. H. F. Oppenheimer*, May 1968, p. 5. In 1969, the total value of AAC investments in Rhodesia appears to have been less than one-fifth of the value of its investments in Zambia. *Anglo American Corporation of South Africa Limited 1969 Annual Report*, p. 51; and see chap. 2. Yet in 1973, Mr. Oppenheimer observed that "Anglo American Corporation Rhodesia Limited has interests in nearly every sector of the Rhodesian economy." *Zambian Anglo American 1973 Annual Report*, p. 5.

70. *The Zambia Mail*, November 17, 1967.

71. *Statement by the Chairman, Mr. H. F. Oppenheimer*, Anglo American Corporation of South Africa Limited, May 1968, p. 6.

warrant the view that for the time being, within Rhodesia, the corporation would march in step with the partisans of strictly racial rule.

Investing in White Supremacy: Angola, Mozambique, and Namibia

Since 1922 the Anglo American Corporation has participated directly or indirectly in the ownership of the Companhia de Diamantes de Angola (Diamang), which holds mining rights in most parts of Angola. Binding argeements provide for the sale of this company's entire output to the Diamond Corporation, a marketing subsidiary of De Beers Consolidated Mines, which also holds the Anglo American Corporation's interest in Diamang.[72] This company is "exempt from taxation both as to import duties on plant and materials and export duties on diamonds."[73] In return, the Portuguese government of Angola receives 50 percent of net profits after the payment of management fees. In 1970, payments from Diamang to the Angolan government totaled some 968 million escudos ($32 million).[74] Subsequently, this company in association with De Beers Consolidated Mines launched yet another large diamond enterprise with the Angolan government as a minority shareholder.[75] In Mozambique, subsidiaries of the Anglo American Corporation have undertaken various ventures involving minerals, sugar, and fisheries. Recently, subsidiaries of the corporation have joined in the search for oil in both territories and Namibia. In view of South Africa's dependence upon external supplies, primarily from the Middle East, oil exploration in southern Africa is a matter of high priority for the South African government.

Cabora Bassa.—In Mozambique, the Anglo American Corporation has assumed the leadership of an international consortium organized to finance the construction of a high dam and hydroelectric facility at Cabora Bassa on the Zambezi River, some 80 miles from the Zambian frontier. This project has been condemned by the African liberation movement and the government of Zambia as a racialist political stratagem designed to consolidate white supremacy and Portuguese rule in Mozambique. When it is completed,

72. Gregory, pp. 130, 375, and passim.
73. Walter E. Skinner, comp., *Mining Year Book 1964* (London, 1964), p. 75.
74. UN Doc. A/8723 (Part III), pp. 17–18.
75. I am indebted to Gerald J. Bender's work in progress for this information.

Cabora Bassa will rank as the largest hydroelectric facility in Africa, by far surpassing the Aswan power facility in Egypt. It will provide low-cost electricity to users in at least four countries, including Malawi, Rhodesia, and South Africa. In fact, the project became feasible when, in 1969, the South African Electricity Supply Commission agreed to purchase most of the electrical power that would be generated.[76] The plentiful supply of inexpensive power is expected to stimulate development of an iron and steel industry based on the rich deposits of iron ore in this area of Mozambique. Vast improvements in transportation by road, rail, and river have also been envisaged, including the construction of a rail line linking Cabora Bassa to the Malawi railways and thence to the newly developed port of Nacala in northeastern Mozambique. Finally, the project is intended to spur agricultural development in the Zambezi basin by means of extensive irrigation and, in African eyes, the dreaded settlement of an indeterminate number of Portuguese immigrants.

In 1969 the Portuguese government awarded a contract for the project to a consortium made up of numerous companies from six countries—South Africa, West Germany, France, Italy, Sweden, and Portugal. However, the Swedish firm withdrew in the face of domestic protests, organized by opponents of white supremacy in Southern Africa, by claiming that its participation would have involved a violation of United Nations sanctions against Rhodesia, which is prohibited by Swedish law. Italian participation subsequently came to an end when the Italian government, responding to appeals from Zambia and Tanzania, decided not to extend export credits to the Italian firm concerned.[77] Among the remaining firms, French and German participation, estimated at about $95 million each, now accounts for some 60 percent of the total investment, followed by financial commitments from South Africa and Portugal. The contract's total value is reported to exceed $300 million.

---

76. The South African state agency is reported to have agreed to buy 680 megawatts starting in 1975, and larger quantities up to 1,470 megawatts each year beginning 1981. At present, South Africa accounts for 57 percent of all electricity consumed in Africa. World Council of Churches, Programme to Combat Racism, *Cabora Bassa and the Struggle for Southern Africa* (London, 1971), pp. 8–9. Electricity imported from Cabora Bassa would not come to 10 percent of South Africa's total requirement.

77. Ibid., pp. 15–19.

Kaunda's personal opposition to this project has been vehement. He has expressed his views forcefully during visits to several European capitals; his personal influence is thought to have been a major factor in the Swedish and Italian withdrawals. On one occasion he acted to expropriate (with compensation) a foreign-owned shareholding in a Zambian transportation company because the shareholders concerned had accepted a contract from the Cabora Bassa consortium. At the same time, he announced that other companies in Zambia were being investigated on similar charges. His warning to the foreign investors under suspicion was categorical: "I want to warn these companies that they must make a choice—they have to choose either us or our enemies. If and as soon as I have proof that any firm is involved in Cabora Bassa, we will have to ask them to either pack up and go or we will take them over, depending on how important they are in the national interest."[78]

Yet there is no indication that this rule has been applied to the Anglo American Corporation, which has undertaken to direct the operations of the entire consortium. As in the case of its operations in Rhodesia, the activities of the Anglo American Corporation in Mozambique do not appear to endanger its position in Zambia, despite the fact that these activities have been condemned by the Zambian government. Conversely, the corporation has demonstrated once again that its obedience to the dictates of any national political doctrine goes no further than the jurisdiction within which that doctrine enjoys official sanction. The principles of the Zambian government would not be permitted to influence corporation policies in Mozambique any more than the doctrines of the South African government would be allowed to warp corporation policies in Zambia.

Anglo American and AMAX in Namibia.—In 1965 mining accounted for 46.6 percent of gross domestic product in arid and sparsely settled Namibia, compared with 16.8 percent attributable to agriculture.[79] Among the minerals of this country, diamonds hold pride of place. The principal producer is Consolidated

78. Republic of Zambia, *"Take Up the Challenge . . . ,"* Speeches made by His Excellency the President, Dr. K. D. Kaunda, to the United National Independence Party National Council, Mulungushi Hall, Lusaka, November 7–10, 1970 (Lusaka: Zambia Information Services, 1970), p. 62.

79. Muriel Horrell, *South-West Africa,* South African Institute of Race Relations (Johannesburg, 1967), p. 46.

Diamond Mines of South-West Africa Limited, a coastal and offshore enterprise in and adjacent to the southern Namib Desert, which has been described as "the richest source of gem diamonds in the world."[80] This company is controlled by the Anglo American Corporation through its associated company, De Beers Consolidated Mines Limited. Recently, a spectacular mineral boom has attracted numerous mining and prospecting firms to Namibia. In one case, the Atomic Energy Authority of Great Britain has contracted to purchase large quantities of uranium from a new mine at Rossing, which is owned by the (British) Rio Tinto-Zinc Corporation in association with the Industrial Development Corporation of the Republic of South Africa and the (South African) General Mining and Finance Corporation.[81] Subsidiaries of the Anglo American Corporation are among the companies to which concessions have been awarded by the South African government to prospect for uranium in this area.[82]

At present, nearly all mining revenues in Namibia are derived from the operations of Consolidated Diamond Mines and one other company, Tsumeb Corporation Limited, a copper, lead, and zinc mining enterprise in the northern part of the territory. Tsumeb Corporation is mainly owned by two American companies—Newmont Mining Corporation and American Metal Climax—each of which holds 29.6 percent of the equity. Selection Trust Limited of London, the largest single shareholder in AMAX, owns 14.2 percent; the balance is owned mainly by institutional investors in South Africa. While Tsumeb Corporation is managed by the Newmont Mining Corporation, the chairman of AMAX, I. K. MacGregor, is, at the time of writing, chairman of Tsumeb as well. "Over the past ten years, AMAX has received an average of $4,100,000 per year in dividends from Tsumeb after US taxes, representing approximately 7% of AMAX average net earnings."[83]

Tsumeb Corporation attracted worldwide attention in December

80. *De Beers Consolidated Mines 1966 Annual Report*, p. 32.

81. See Richard West, *River of Tears: The Rise of the Rio Tinto-Zinc Mining Corporation* (London: Earth Island, 1972), pp. 56–75.

82. *Anglo American Corporation of South Africa Limited 1971 Annual Report*, p. 371.

83. American Metal Climax, Inc., *Report on Tsumeb Corporation Limited*, February 25, 1974; also Namibia Support Group, "United States Complicity in Underdevelopment in Namibia: The Tsumeb Corporation" (New York, 1972), p. 6; and Winifred Courtney and Jennifer Davis, *Namibia: United States Corporate Involvement* (New York: The Africa Fund, 1972).

1971 as a result of a general strike by African workers in Namibia. The vast majority of African workers in all enterprises, including the mines, are recruited from among the Ovambo people of northern Namibia, who constitute more than half of the 600,000 Africans in the entire country. (The total white population in this immense territory of 318,000 square miles numbers only some 100,000.) Workers from the African reserves are employed on a fixed-term contract basis; they are housed in compounds that are segregated on a tribal basis and, to a large extent, in barrack-type accommodations, since the vast majority of contract workers are not permitted to bring their families out of the reserves.[84] Tsumeb Corporation is the largest single employer of contract labor in the country. In 1971, Tsumeb employed some 5,300 Africans, nearly half of all Africans employed in the country's mining sector.[85] The great majority of them were recruited by the South West Africa Native Labor Association, a state agency in which the major employers are represented. Contracts were normally for periods of one year, with the possibility of a six-month extension. In 1971, the average wage for African workers at Tsumeb was the equivalent of $28 per month; the minimum wage was $21 per month. By contrast, the lowest-paid white employee earned $444 per month plus bonuses.[86] As in South Africa, African workers were denied freedom of movement outside the area of their employment. They were also denied the most elementary rights of collective bargaining and the right to strike.

Given these draconian conditions, the workers' uprising of December 1971 had an electrifying effect. Amazingly, in view of the distances involved, it spread rapidly from the capital at Windhoek, where over 5,000 workers in all sectors of employment went on strike, to the country at large, including the mines. All told, more than 12,000 workers throughout Namibia participated in the strike, including more than 4,000 employees of the Tsumeb Corporation.

The demands of the strikers included abolition of the contract labor system as well as all restrictions on freedom of movement and racial discrimination in employment.[87] They also asked for representation in any negotiation for a settlement. Pursuant to

84. Horrell, pp. 71–73.
85. Ibid., p. 56, and "United States Complicity," p. 7.
86. Ibid., p. 9.
87. For the principal demands of the strikers, see George M. Houser, "Statement to the UN Council for Namibia," January 19, 1972 (mimeo.).

their wishes, and "presumably to avert possible disturbances," the strikers were returned to the northern reserves by the South African authorities.[88] Then an agreement was negotiated between South African officials (representing the Ministry of Bantu Administration and Development) and appointed tribal authorities from the Ovambo and Okavango areas. As a result, the hated recruitment agency was abolished and the labor recruitment system was revised to clarify and liberalize cautiously the conditions of work for individual employees. At Tsumeb, new pay rates for Africans were introduced, including a 25 percent increase of the minimum wage.[89] However, the workers did not gain collective bargaining rights, nor the right to strike; nor did they participate in framing the new agreement. The pass laws remain in effect, and it is still illegal for the familes of contract workers to leave the reserves. Furthermore, twelve alleged leaders of the strike have been prosecuted in Windhoek, and official violence has been reported in the Ovamboland district, where a state of emergency was proclaimed in February 1972.[90]

As a result of these events, an American committee known as "Episcopal Churchmen for South Africa" filed stockholder motions with Newmont Mining Corporation and AMAX calling upon these companies to "recognize the United Nations as the lawful authority" in Namibia and to allocate profits from Tsumeb to "an independently administered trust fund" pending United Nations control of the territory. They further requested each corporation to make a full disclosure of its involvements "directly or indirectly" in Namibia and South Africa.[91] These motions were predicated on an advisory opinion by the International Court of Justice in June 1971, to the effect that all states

> are under obligation to recognize the illegality of South Africa's presence in Namibia and the invalidity of its acts on behalf of or concerning Namibia, and to refrain from any acts and in particular any dealings with the Government of South Africa implying recognition of the legality of, or lending support or assistance to, such presence and administration.

88. UN Doc. E/CN.4/1076, 15 February 1972, p. 16.

89. "United States Complicity," p. 9.

90. Judge William H. Booth, "Report: International Commission of Jurists," March 1972 (mimeo.).

91. Summarized in American Committee on Africa, "Strike in Namibia" (New York, January 7, 1972), app. 6 (mimeo.).

This opinion, capping twenty-five years of efforts to assert United Nations authority over this former mandated territory,[92] has been accepted by the United States government. In fact, the United States had previously announced that it would not protect any rights of American investors in Namibia acquired through the South African government after the adoption of a resolution by the General Assembly purporting to terminate the mandate in 1966.[93] The churchmen, representing the views of Americans who believe that more positive actions should be taken by the United States government and the two American corporations concerned, hoped to challenge the continued payment of taxes by Tsumeb to the South African government, reported at $14 million in 1970.[94] However, their motions to this effect were stricken from the proxy statements for the 1972 annual meetings of both Newmont Mining and AMAX by the Securities and Exchange Commission at the request of these companies. In their briefs to the commission, the companies argued that normal business operations should not be prohibited on account of unresolved "political claims," including controversial opinions of the International Court of Justice.[95] But one motion proposed by the churchmen, calling for full disclosure of involvements in Namibia and South Africa, did appear in the proxy statements. In the case of AMAX, management opposed this motion on the ground that neither American nor international law would be held to penalize a company for acting in compliance with "the laws of the authorities in *de facto* control" of a given country; nor does such compliance signify that the company concerned has taken a position "as to the *de jure* standing of any such authorities."[96] Evidently, AMAX and its partners were intending to do business as usual at Tsumeb. The AMAX annual report merely commented that in response to a strike against the contract labor system, "an entirely new system of direct employer-employee agree-

92. The mandate had been entrusted to South Africa by the League of Nations in 1920.

93. The legal position and American policies are reviewed in United Nations Association of the U.S.A., *Southern Africa: Proposals for Americans* (New York, 1971), pp. 57–63. In his 1972 message to Congress on "the state of the world," President Nixon declared that "South Africa is obliged to quit Namibia."

94. "United States Complicity," p. 9. AMAX reports that income taxes alone paid by Tsumeb Corporation between 1963 and 1972 averaged $8,435,000 per year. *Report on Tsumeb Corporation*, p. 5.

95. Barry Newman, "Namibia: A Major Test for the UN," *The Wall Street Journal*, March 24, 1972.

96. American Metal Climax, Inc., *Proxy Statement*, April 6, 1972, p. 20.

ment was put into effect."[97] This hardly reflects the reality of industrial and political peonage indicated by the present account.[98]

The involvement of AMAX with Tsumeb Corporation is less provocative to Zambians than Anglo American Corporation's participation in the scheme at Cabora Bassa. Thus far, Zambia has not specified capital investment in Namibia as a hostile act. Yet, occupied Namibia, like colonial Mozambique, poses a threat to Zambian security. There have been alleged violations of Zambian territory and air space by South African soldiers and aircraft based in the Caprivi Strip, which has become a strategic military outpost for South Africa. It would be plausible for Zambians to conclude that AMAX's policy of compliance with the political status quo in Namibia is detrimental to African and Zambian interests. Yet this matter does not appear to have been raised by the Zambian government in its dealings with AMAX or RST. AMAX officials have indicated to me that they do not anticipate pressures from Zambia on the question of AMAX investments or policies in Namibia or South Africa. It appears to be their realistic view that the only serious threat to these policies is posed by radical critics within the United States.

Conclusion

During the era of Zambian independence, the mining companies have found it both necessary and prudent to make numerous concessions to official Zambian conceptions of morality in the conduct of foreign economic relations. From the company standpoint, these constraints, or claims of ideology, have been both costly and distasteful. Nonetheless, the mining industry's record with respect to the activities that have been surveyed in this chapter is one of complaince and genuine cooperation. This much said, it must be added immediately that the claims of Zambian ideology have had no effect on the conduct of the companies in other national jurisdictions.

97. *AMAX 1971 Annual Report*, pp. 14–15.

98. A more forthright statement by AMAX in 1974 reports Tsumeb's opposition to the enforced separation of black miners from their families and other racially oppressive conditions. However, this statement makes no concession to the antiapartheid lobby: "As an international company with investment interests in many countries, AMAX does not intervene in the political policies of host countries. . . . AMAX anticipates that Tsumeb will continue to work constructively with any government responsible for the administration of the country, now or in the future." *Report on Tsumeb Corporation*, pp. 17–18.

Within Zambia, the companies have been prepared to assist national leaders in their drive for economic disengagement from white-ruled Southern Africa. We have seen that the Zambian government itself has been disposed to pursue this goal with "deliberate speed" or caution, so as to minimize the danger of serious economic disruption.[99] Such realism on the government's part may have helped to reconcile the companies to Zambia's long-range goal of disengagement. But the goals of Zambian ideology transcend the near horizon of economic disengagement from Southern Africa to envisage the liberation of all subjugated Africans in that region. This study has adduced no evidence of any concession to liberationist ideology by the mining magnates in respect of their activities in white-ruled Southern Africa.[100] Nor does it appear that the substantial contributions of the parent mining houses to the economic viability of white supremacist rule in Angola, Mozambique, Rhodesia, or Namibia have been detrimental to their relationships with Zambia.

The mining magnates justify their professed rule of conformity to local law and custom on strictly economic grounds. Apart from an occasional private comment, I have neither seen nor heard the corporate policy of adaptation to widely diverse political conditions within the Southern African region defended in explicitly political terms. Yet the potential political significance of corporate expansion within the region on an interstate basis should not be minimized. The Anglo American Corporation, AMAX, and various other corporations have mutual interests in the maintenance of political stability in this region and in the preservation of a political climate that is favorable to both corporate enterprise and the establishment of mutually beneficial interstate economic relationships. These interests are served by investing in all parts of the region, as for example in Botswana, a staunchly nonracial African state, where AMAX and the Anglo American Corporation jointly control a new mining enterprise. In Zambia, the strongest and most influential nonracial state within the traditional economic orbit of white-dominated Southern Africa, the political priorities of the

99. The theme of creative tension between the competing norms of *realpolitik*—the realistic pursuit of a narrowly defined national interest—and self-denying revolutionary idealism is developed in Sklar, "Zambia's Response to the Rhodesian Unilateral Declaration of Independence."

100. Given the imposition of mandatory economic sanctions against Rhodesia by the United Nations, RST's discontinuance of its activities there in 1968 does not appear to be inconsistent with this statement.

mining magnates for Southern African development have been challenged in the name of liberation. The mining companies have much at stake in Zambia; and they can surely learn to live with the inconvenient but, from a moral and psychological standpoint, entirely reasonable state policy of economic disengagement. Beyond this possibly inescapable necessity, it would be in the interests of the corporations to foster peaceful coexistence and some kind of stable accommodation between Zambia and her neighbors. Their ability to promote accommodation at the expense of liberationist values depends largely upon their ideological impact within Zambia. This must now be considered.

SIX

Power and Development

In Zambia, as in many other postcolonial and nonindustrial countries, the state is conceived and appraised mainly in terms of its contribution to development.[1] Development, itself, is a value-laden idea, connoting progress toward the achievement of desired goals.[2] Zambian opinion does appear to reflect a fairly wide agreement on the values of development, to wit, improvement in the quality of life, maximized equality of opportunity, progress toward substantive social equality, and a high degree of democratic or popular participation in the conduct of public affairs.

The political aspect of development, as distinct from those value premises that involve political goals, may be understood to signify the improvement of a society's ability to control the rate and direction of change. The concept of control is crucial to this definition, as it implies the ability to formulate and implement strategies for solving problems and achieving goals. In newly developing countries, drastic changes in the organization of authority are frequently required to facilitate the effective exercise of social control. In Zambia, organizational reform has featured a pervasive program of state participation in the ownership and management of industries. The giant copper industry is Zambia's sole significant source of wealth. An immense asset to the nation, this industry is also the source of grim challenges and major national problems, among them the country's costly and resented dependence upon expatriate manpower and the disastrous imbalance of economic development, in particular, the chronic retardation of rural development. By means of state participation in this industry and other enterprises, the government has endeavored to create a capacity to exercise social control that will be adequate for the realistic pursuit of its purposes.

1. This conception of the state is discerningly distinguished from liberal and communist conceptions in C. B. Macpherson, *The Real World of Democracy* (London: Oxford University Press, 1966).
2. See Gunnar Myrdal, *Asian Drama: An Inquiry into the Poverty of Nations* (New York: Random House, 1968), pp. 49–69.

This study conceives state participation in the mining industry as a new phase in the long and controversial relationship between the people of central Africa and the mining companies. No longer do the African people concerned act only in response to conditions that have been shaped by imperial or company decisions. As citizens of the Republic of Zambia, they are now collectively able to choose between alternative paths of development. For the time being, they have chosen to try state participation in partnership with the established mining groups. The political features of the joint ventures that have been inaugurated may be discerned tentatively through the dawning haze of a new era.

THE QUESTION OF CONTROL

The nature and extent of corporate power in the independent states of Central Africa has been a matter of vehement debate for several years. Shortly before Zambian independence, an American anthropologist, Alvin W. Wolfe, advanced a provocative hypothesis. Based upon his study of the common interests and interlocking directorates of nine major mining and investment companies in central and southern Africa, from "the Cape to Katanga," Wolfe perceived a tendency for the countries of this vast region to become increasingly interdependent in the economic sphere despite their political differences. His major hypothesis was stated as follows: "as political empires dissolve, states [in this region] become weaker relative to the supranational mining system."[3]

Subsequently, political developments in the aftermath of Rhodesia's unilateral declaration of independence reversed the tendency toward economic integration within the central and southern African subcontinent. Zambia has systematically reduced her economic dependence upon white-dominated Southern Africa; consequently, Zaire has also become less accessible to economic penetration from that quarter. In contrast, economic relations between South Africa and three other trans-Zambezian countries—Angola, Malawi, and Mozambique—have been strengthened. If, as Wolfe has hypothesized, the power of the great corporations waxes vis-à-vis the new and emergent states, the South African

3. Alvin W. Wolfe, "The African Mineral Industry: Evolution of a Supranational Level of Integration," *Social Problems* 2 (Fall 1963): 163.

capitalist dream of subcontinental economic interdependence may yet become a reality.

Wolfe's critics have directed valid criticisms against certain aspects of his argument. For one, his suggestion to the effect that interlocking directorates imply a harmony of interest and uniformity of purpose among distinct corporate groups is untenable. As Michael Faber has observed, "ultimate control" is a far more important criterion than interlocking directorships when it comes to judging the nature of relationships between potentially competitive business corporations.[4] Another critic, F. Taylor Ostrander, has argued that in the field of mining, "mixed participations in ownership" are inevitable for various reasons—multiple claims to prospecting areas, risk sharing, expedient combinations of various types of resources, capital formation, and the relative fewness of highly efficient companies. However, he contends, diversified ownership involving minority interest representation on boards of directors does not signify collusive control in the manner of a financial octopus.[5] In Zambia, prior to state participation, the two groups of companies were separately and independently controlled despite their many joint activities and formal connections. We must conclude that the actual significance of an interlocking directorship arrangement cannot be inferred from the fact of its mere existence. Corporate power groups, like national power groups, normally have their listening posts and accredited representatives in the camps of their competitors and potential enemies. The degree of solidarity or conflict involved in any such relationship is always a matter for strictly empirical determination.

Faber has also rebutted Wolfe's statement to the effect that "the continuing process of political decolonization enhances the freedom of action of this essentially private [corporate] system."[6] In Faber's opinion, decolonization results in a shift of power from the business corporations to the newly independent states. His rival thesis is summarized as follows:

4. M. L. O. Faber, "Corporate Policy on the Copperbelt," in *Towards Economic Independence: Papers on the Nationalisation of the Copper Industry in Zambia*, ed. M. L. O. Faber and J. G. Potter; University of Cambridge, Department of Applied Economics, Occasional Paper 23 (Cambridge: Cambridge University Press, 1971), p. 17.

5. F. Taylor Ostrander, "The Role of Foreign Private Capital in Africa," in *Southern Africa in Transition*, ed. John A. Davis and James K. Baker (New York: Praeger, 1966), p. 360.

6. Wolfe, p. 160; Faber, p. 15.

So there we have it—an alternative theory demonstrating the diminution of the local power of the Big Mining Groups, their further subordination to local nationalist interest, their diminished power to control local conditions through prominent shareholders in the Imperial countries, their replacement of old-type 'Boss Businessmen' by young executives whose attitude is sympathetic towards local African aspirations, and the progressively smaller scope offered for any sort of amalgamation, action, or 'conspiracy' on a supra-national plane.[7]

Even before the advent of state participation in Zambia, the freedom of action of the mining companies had been substantially curtailed. But the strength of the corporate enterprise system in central Africa may not depend upon or be affected by "freedom of action" on the part of businessmen. Decolonization does entail an enormous increase in political complexity, resulting in the establishment of new conditions of effective action by private interest groups. Such conditions are far more exacting in their requirements than those to which businessmen had been accustomed during the era of colonial rule. By adapting to the new order, resourceful international companies may yet preserve and enhance their positions of power vis-à-vis the state.[8] In my view, therefore, Wolfe's critics have not invalidated his major hypothesis, to wit, "as political empires dissolve, states [in this region] become weaker relative to the supranational mining system."[9] As his critics show, Wolfe does not adequately support his position, but the rival thesis offered by Faber is vulnerable to equally strong objections. I will attempt to answer the question—"Who controls?"—on independent grounds.

The Doctrine of Domicile

In the face of constraints upon their freedom of action arising primarily from Zambia's principled participation in the program of

7. Faber, p. 39.

8. For example, in Zaire, the Belgian-owned mines were nationalized outright in 1967. Yet the former owners have secured a powerful position within the new industrial structure. See chap. 3.

9. Wolfe, p. 163. In addition to the source cited, Wolfe has written several papers of a political nature in which he has alleged that the collective influence and power of the mining corporations has been exerted in opposition to African nationalist goals in Zambia, Zaire, and Southern Africa. These papers have provoked commentaries from diverse standpoints. However, the hypothesis quoted here does not appear to have been rebutted in any of the latter commentaries.

United Nations sanctions against Rhodesia, the Zambian-based, foreign-owned mining companies professed their unconditional loyalty to Zambian national authorities in cases of conflict between national policies and the wider interests of their shareholders. With respect to transport policies, the development of domestic coal resources, and the various phases of contingency planning, the companies performed, as we have seen in chapter 5, to the general satisfaction of Zambian officials. Similarly, the companies have been commended for their efforts to accelerate Zambianization within the mining industry at the expense of their expatriate employees.[10] Their reluctant but nonetheless substantial contribution to the establishment of a metal fabricating plant in Zambia, noted in chapter 3, represents a further concession to Zambian economic policy at the expense of their affiliates and customers abroad.

Spokesmen for the mining companies often contend that business corporations are bound by necessity to comply with the precepts of local law and authority. This viewpoint has been expounded succinctly by F. Taylor Ostrander, an official of AMAX and specialist in African affairs:

> Corporations have to live with whatever political system is in control. Sometimes their managements approve of these political systems, sometimes they do not. There is little they can do about it. The policy of most corporations is to stick to their business in the hope that those who determine political policy in a country will allow them to produce, to give employment, to make profits, and to pay their taxes.[11]

This attitude is regularly assailed from a liberationist standpoint wherever business corporations form part of a national power structure that perpetuates colonial or racial oppression, as in colonial Zambia or white-ruled Southern Africa. However, in the event of a transfer of power to majoritarian nationalists, as in postcolonial Zambia, the same company viewpoint becomes an unexceptionable, if less than entirely credible, virtue. Indeed it would be nothing short of miraculous for the new nationalist leaders to accept the benign declarations of alien businessmen at face value. After a decade of operations in sovereign Zambia, during which time they have acceded to governmental demands for state partici-

10. See chap. 4.
11. Ostrander, p. 361.

pation and have complied with policies for economic disengagement from Southern Africa, the mining magnates may at last hope
that a measure of real trust has been earned.

The basis of corporate planning for a prolonged relationship between the international mining companies and Zambia may be
identified and without undue formality termed "the doctrine of
domicile." Briefly stated, this idea implies that there is no necessary inconsistency between the properly defined claims of foreign
ownership in a Zambian national enterprise and uncompromising
loyalty to the Zambian government on the part of those who are
collectively responsible for the company's performance. In general,
the doctrine maintains that affiliates of international business corporations are truly able to conform to the policies and national
interests of their host governments irrespective of the policies and
interests of other governments, including the governments of
those relatively powerful countries where parent companies are
likely to reside.

Raymond Vernon, a foremost student of multinational enterprise, has argued that the American government and American
multinational firms should respect the local identities of
American-owned subsidiary companies abroad as the indispensable basis for the entitlement of such subsidiaries to national treatment. The American government, he believes, should scrupulously refrain from attempts to control the behavior of subsidiaries
abroad through the application of pressure to their American parent companies. Conversely, subsidiaries abroad "must relinquish
the right to appeal to the United States for help."[12] Vernon's assessment of the prevailing hostility to multinational business in
many less-developed countries is realistic. The crux of the problem, he states,

is to be found in the inherent nature of the multinational
enterprise, as the leaders in the host countries see it. These
enterprises draw their special strengths from the ability and
opportunity to think in terms that extend beyond any single
country and to use resources that are located in more than
one jurisdiction. These characteristics are seen as posing a
threat for government leaders bent on control, for local

12. U.S., Department of State, Office of External Research, "Conference on the
Multinational Corporation," Proceedings, February 14, 1969, p.38 (mimeo.).

businessmen who aspire to compete, and for intellectuals who are hoping to challenge the status quo.[13]

Yet he believes that joint ventures and other measures to provide for local control will facilitate the increasing acceptance of multinational enterprise.[14] Furthermore, he points out, the managers of multinational enterprises are fortified by the sincere belief that a sound investment is beneficial to all concerned.

> Whereas the political philosophers of host countries often proceed from the assumption that when the enterprise gains the country loses, the ruling assumption in the multinational enterprise is that all parties gain from its operations. On this assumption, the fundamental contradiction between a global and a national view can be reduced to tolerable proportions.[15]

The crisis in central Africa caused by Rhodesia's unlawful declaration of independence under white minority rule posed an exacting and possibly historic test of the contention that multinational enterprises can reduce to "tolerable proportions" severe conflicts of value between their local commitments and their general interests. It would be difficult to imagine a more painfully revealing case. The companies concerned—subsidiaries of South African and American corporations before their transformation into joint ventures between the Zambian government and the former majority shareholders, with management entrusted to the latter— demonstrated their autonomy and reliability as good corporate citizens of Zambia by their compliance with national policies, as narrated in chapter 5. The fact that overt resistance to national policies on their part would have entailed coercive action by the Zambian government does not negate the significance of compliance in good faith in support of sanctions against Rhodesia and disengagement from Southern Africa, at the expense of economic values espoused by their parent companies abroad. The case of the Anglo American Corporation is particularly clear-cut, since the directors of that group of companies are on record as being opposed to economic sanctions against Rhodesia and in favor of a liberalized form of "white leadership" for an indefinite period in South Africa, which cannot be reconciled with Zambia's commitment to the val-

13. Raymond Vernon, *Sovereignty at Bay: The Multinational Spread of U.S. Enterprises* (New York: Basic Books, 1971), p. 265.
14. Ibid., pp. 265–266.
15. Ibid., p. 147.

ues of African nationalism. While American Metal Climax has not officially challenged the logic of disengagement from Rhodesia, spokesmen for that company have justified its investments in South Africa and Namibia on the dubious ground that economic development there will enhance the prospects for peaceful social change, favorable to the African people.[16] Both companies are strongly opposed to the militant liberation movements favored by the Zambian government. Both draw the line on subservience to Zambian national policy at the Zambian frontier and adopt similar postures of good corporate citizenship in the white supremacist states of Southern Africa.

The doctrine of domicile is an ideological notion, relevant to the value premises of multinational corporations. It affirms that the individual subsidiaries of an international business group do operate in accordance with the requirements of divergent and conflicting state policies. Ultimately, the aim of local adaptation is to promote the interests of the enterprise as a whole. It may be objected that at bottom the interests of multinational corporations are incompatible with the interests of host states, particularly in the circumstances under consideration in this study. The doctrine of domicile may serve to mask underlying conflicts of interest that cannot be reconciled. The question of African liberation may illustrate one such conflict. So long as Zambia's commitment to liberation in Southern Africa does not color Zambian expectations of corporate conduct, inconsistencies between the local and regional viewpoints of mining industry leaders may indeed be minimized. Yet the mere fact of inattention to liberationist values in the conduct of this relationship may not be without significance. If revolutionary idealism is allowed to subside within the Zambian regime, habitual reliance upon economic relationships with multinational corporations may eventually breed an accommodationist attitude toward neighboring states that will detract from Zambia's determination to harbor and support militant liberation movements. It is at least arguable that Zambia would then have compromised a real racial interest at no small cost to herself in self-esteem and morale.

16. A letter to this effect from the chairman of AMAX to the United Church of Christ is quoted in Winifred Courtney and Jennifer Davis, *Namibia: United States Corporate Involvement* (New York: The Africa Fund, 1972), p. 21; see also Ostrander, pp. 357–338; a valuable survey of arguments on both sides of this issue is presented in William A. Hance, ed., *Southern Africa and the United States* (New York: Columbia University Press, 1968).

The thesis of compatibility between the local and general interests of an international business group, implied in the doctrine of domicile, may also be questioned in relation to matters of economic policy. Since the takeover of majority ownership in the copper industry by the state, various attempts have been made by the responsible state agency—MINDECO until September 1973; thereafter the Ministry of Mines and Mining Development—to integrate parallel operations of the two new joint ventures, Nchanga Consolidated Copper Mines (NCCM) and Roan Consolidated Mines (RCM). This policy, termed rationalization, has been pursued with varying degrees of success in several areas, including technology, production, purchasing, stores control, marketing, public relations, mine safety procedures, and industry-wide training.[17] The unexceptionable aims of rationalization have been to improve efficiency and reduce costs. However, it is alleged that the "forty-nine percenters"—former majority shareholders—have been reluctant to implement recommendations that conflict with their vested interests. For example, MINDECO's goal of a common purchasing system would undermine established supplier relationships. Naturally, the mining companies prefer to purchase materials from industrial affiliates within their respective groups or from suppliers in which their parent companies have interests. To an extent, the mining companies may have been cool toward the creation of certain domestic, state-supported manufacturing ventures, such as cable fabrication, the manufacture of explosives, and the production of welding electrodes, because of their links with foreign suppliers. Almost certainly, there would be resistance to any government policy that tended to discourage purchases "within the family." Similarly, the establishment of a national metal marketing company, as directed by President Kaunda in 1973,[18] will be perceived as a setback for the mining groups.

Economists point out that integrated international firms normally attempt to maximize their profits in jurisdictions where the rate of taxation is most favorable. As Raymond F. Mikesell has observed, "integrated firms are interested in maximizing after-tax profits of the parent firm and not the before-tax net revenues of individual producing affiliates. Instead they may deliberately sac-

17. Republic of Zambia, *Mindeco Limited, Executive Chairman's Statement, 1971.*
18. Republic of Zambia, *Address by His Excellency the President, Dr. K. D. Kaunda, at the Press Conference on the Redemption of ZIMCO Bonds,* State House, Lusaka, August 31, 1973.

rifice net earnings in one affiliate in favor of larger earnings for another."[19] This observation, like the experience surveyed above, appears to cast doubt on the potential compatibility between the local and general interests of an international business group. Yet Mikesell himself is inclined to stress the opportunities for solutions to conflicts that serve the long-term interests of international companies and host countries alike.[20] While the mining companies in Zambia may be reluctant to comply with specific proposals for rationalization, they are unlikely to withhold such compliance when it is clearly required to protect the principal interests that they have at stake.

In sum, it may be presumed that the doctrine of domicile as an interpretation of corporate ideology will also appeal to the leaders of newly developing host countries who would like to establish stable relationships with international business organizations. The doctrine implies that both the corporation and the foreign state in which its parent company resides will yield to the state in which the subsidiary is domiciled in matters of local policy, both domestic and foreign. Positing a mutuality of interest, this interpretive formulation justifies corporate expansion while it also legitimates large-scale foreign investments in the eyes of the host country. As set forth here, it is a proposition about interest and value, which says nothing about the actual division of power.

Formal Control

The nationalization agreements negotiated by the Zambian government with each of the two groups of companies prescribed similar conditions of management for the two jointly owned operating companies—NCCM and RCM.[21] In each case, the gov-

19. Raymond F. Mikesell, "Conflict in Foreign Investor-Host Country Relations: A Preliminary Analysis," in *Foreign Investment in the Petroleum and Mineral Industries: Case studies of Investor-Host Country Relations* (Baltimore: Johns Hopkins University Press, 1971), p. 48.

20. Ibid., pp. 49ff.

21. The "terms of the takeover" are summarized in Mark Bostock and Charles Harvey, eds., *Economic Independence and Zambian Copper: A Case Study of Foreign Investment*, Praeger Special Studies in International Economics and Development (New York: Praeger, 1972), pp. 219–239. Analyses are presented by Mark Bostock and Charles Harvey, "The Takeovers," in ibid., pp. 145–187; John Niehuss and Peter Slinn, "Some Legal Aspects of the Zambian Takeover," in ibid., pp. 243–255; J. G. Potter, "The 51 Per Cent Nationalisation of the Zambian Copper Mines," in *Towards Economic Independence*, ed. Faber and Potter, pp. 91–127; and Antony Martin, *Minding Their Own Business* (London: Hutchinson, 1972), pp. 180–183.

ernmental agency, MINDECO, which acquired 51 percent of the shares, appointed six directors, while the minority shareholding group appointed five directors. The leading governmental director, who was the chief executive officer of MINDECO, served as chairman of both NCCM and RCM. However, the management contracts provided that the managing director of each operating company would be nominated by the minority (i.e., corporate) shareholders. These contracts also stipulated that each operating company would be managed in accordance with previous standards of efficiency in order to ensure the continued "optimization of production and profit." What is more, the agreements were drawn to give the minority directors "a veto over certain key decisions with respect to the financial and capital programs of RCM and NCCM."[22] Failure on the part of the government or its agencies to comply with various terms of the nationalization and management agreements could have resulted in a judgment to the effect that ZIMCO securities (issued to compensate the former majority shareholders) were "immediately due and payable."[23] Finally, in the event of an irreconcilable dispute between majority and minority directors, the matter would have been referred for arbitration to the International Center for the Settlement of Investment Disputes (ICSID), an affiliate of the World Bank. As Bostock and Harvey observed, "the implications are clear":

> Other investors in Zambia—including the World Bank itself and the IMF—whose money could very well be needed to bridge a period of low copper prices would be unlikely to ignore any refusal by Zambia to abide by a ruling of ICSID. In other words, the mining companies have successfully ensured that their own private agreement is an inseparable part of the whole complex of Zambia's international financial relations. Zambia has always been dependent upon its international borrowing powers because of the instability of its export earnings, even if this dependence has been potential rather than actual in recent years. As a result, Zambia's reputation for financial rectitude, whether in deals with private or with official lenders, has always been important. What the mining companies have done is to formalize this situation

22. Niehuss and Slinn, p. 251, where the types of decision subject to this veto are specified.

23. Ibid. "Although it is normal practice for loan agreements to make the entire loan due and payable immediately upon breach of *financial* conditions, this penalty is unusual for breach of *nonfinancial* conditions. Nevertheless, this is what has been done" (Bostock and Harvey, p. 151).

further by ensuring that Zambia earns as much disapproval as possible from as many people as possible for breach of these particular agreements.[24]

With respect to the issue of investment for mine expansion, which President Kaunda had emphasized in his explanation of the rationale for nationalization, Bostock and Harvey concluded that the takeover arrangement did not gain "control" for the government, since the minority directors "must approve all expansion plans" and "have no obligation to do so unless the project is commercially viable."[25] Similarly, James Fry, an economic adviser to the Zambian government, asserted that in Zambia, as in Zaire, nationalization of the mines has "transferred little real power to the governments. . . . In Zambia the companies maintain control over all their key decisions, and there can be little prospect of change for at least ten years, that is, until the time when the present contracts expire."[26]

Until 1973 this emphasis on the conservative and, by implication, deceptive character of the nationalization arrangement was thought to be unduly harsh by both company officials and many Zambian leaders.[27] On both sides, it was understood that a delicate balance had been maintained since nationalization, a balance that could be upset easily by poor diplomacy on the part of the minority shareholders. Management officials acknowledged the possibility of serious disagreements with government over the issues of mine expansion and rationalization among others. But they hoped to avoid formal disagreements and privately expressed their willingness to abandon certain of their rights under the nationalization agreements in order to preserve good relations and avert confiscatory action by the government before the management contracts were due to expire. One official remarked to this writer that the minority directors' veto was the kind of right that could be exercised "only once." Its existence, he thought, could help the man-

24. Bostock and Harvey, p. 151.

25. Ibid., p. 154.

26. James Fry, "Economic Independence in Zambia: A Review Article," *African Social Research*, no. 13 (June 1972), p. 210. This comment appears in the context of a criticism of M. L. O. Faber's thesis (in the essay cited in n.4); Fry supports the viewpoint of Alvin W. Wolfe (see n. 3 above).

27. Thus Dominic Mulaisho, managing director of MINDECO and chairman of both operating companies, criticized Bostock and Harvey for having underestimated the potentially great importance of governmental efforts to rationalize company procedures. *The Times of Zambia*, Business Review, June 16, 1972.

agement companies in bargaining. "If it did not exist," he said, "we might resist a bit less than we do."

In August 1973 President Kaunda suddenly expressed his government's dissatisfaction with various provisions of the nationalization agreements. He announced that Zambia would immediately redeem the outstanding ZIMCO securities and that the mining companies would no longer be entitled to their privileged status with respect to exchange control regulations and taxation. Henceforth, he declared, NCCM and RCM would provide for their own management and technical services. Zambia's shareholding in these companies would be transferred from MINDECO to the minister of finance. (MINDECO would retain various small mine holdings, including a colliery.) Operational responsibility for NCCM and RCM would be vested in the minister of mines and mining development, who would become chairman of both companies; and the government would appoint the managing director of each. Finally, the government would establish a new, wholly owned marketing company.[28]

Kaunda's abrupt repudiation of the 1969 agreements exposed the real insubstantiality of the formal control that had been vested in the minority shareholding interest. Such control was shown to be of little account in the face of a determined exercise of state power. To be sure, the challenge to company rights under the agreements arising from unilateral action by the Zambian government activated legal defenses that were written into the agreements. As in Chile, where, during the 1960s, Kennecott Copper Corporation had taken care to entrench its management contract with guarantees that would make unilateral nationalization (which occurred in 1971) costly to the government, the Zambian companies now raised serious legal objections to the government's notice of early termination.[29] The Zambian government did not seem to appreciate that company rights under the management and sales agreements would not automatically expire upon the

28. Republic of Zambia, *Address by His Excellency the President, Dr. K. D. Kaunda at the Press Conference on the Redemption of ZIMCO Bonds,* August 31, 1973. The president appointed a negotiating committee to implement these decisions.

29. On Kennecott's effective strategy in Chile, see Theodore H. Moran, "Transnational Strategies of Protection and Defense by Multinational Corporations: Spreading the Risk and Raising the Cost for Nationalization in Natural Resources," *International Organization* 27 (Spring 1973): 273–287. Moran suggests that AMAX and RST may have learned from this example. Ibid., p. 284.

redemption of the outstanding bonds and loan stock.[30] As a result, protracted negotiations, leading to new arrangements for marketing, management, and related matters, had not been concluded when this study was completed in 1974.[31]

Whatever new pattern of control emerges, we may suspect that the concept of "control" itself may be too mechanical to convey the deeper meaning and significance of "power." "Control" may suggest that power inheres in formal organizations that appear to exercise dominance: for example, the state (the traditional institution of final dominance) or a supranational business group, coordinated by interlocking directorships and serviced by intergovernmental financial institutions and their affiliates. The significant controversy concerning the possession of power in postcolonial central Africa, with Wolfe and Fry perceiving dominant power in the corporate enterprise system while Faber and Ostrander insist upon the emergent states, appears to have been conducted on just such grounds with inconclusive results. It is time to suggest that the terms of this controversy may have been formulated upon a faulty premise—the commonplace opinion that the source of power is institutional rather than social. An alternative formulation may prove to be more rewarding.

REVOLUTION FROM ABOVE

At the time of independence, Zambia was sorely deficient in both educated citizens and the organizational resources required to accomplish the bold nationalist goals of the governing party. The independence movement had enlisted every substantial African interest in an intense struggle against white-settler rule.[32] Its success had greatly stimulated the natural aspirations of the people. Yet the means at hand were woefully insufficient for the purposes of an enlightened and progressive government. And the burdens of underdevelopment were greatly increased by economic hardships resulting from the continuing international dispute over Rhodesia.

To build up its capacity for vigorous and effective action in furth-

30. See chap. 2.
31. However, a state marketing company had been established and a Zambian director appointed. Zambians had also been designated as managing directors of NCCM and RCM.
32. See chap. 1.

erance of rapid development, the government has resorted to a strategy of organizational revolution. Since independence Zambia's economic and social landscape has been thoroughly transformed. As a result of measures taken between 1968 and 1970, the government is estimated to have acquired "nominal control of well over 80 per cent of all economic activity,"[33] including a 51 percent ownership stake in the giant copper industry. Indeed, Zambia has experienced a breathtaking revolution from above.

Educational development has been crucial to this transformation. In 1965 there were about 17,200 students enrolled in secondary schools throughout Zambia.[34] The University of Zambia was inaugurated in 1966 with an enrollment of 312 students.[35] By 1971 secondary school enrollment had more than trebled to 54,260, while the university's enrollment had risen to slightly more than 1,750.[36] The Second National Development Plan projected an increase in secondary school enrollment to 74,000 by 1976, while enrollment at the university would rise to more than 3,000. It has been estimated that approximately 7,000 Zambians will earn university degrees during the 1970s; more than 90 percent of them will be earned at the University of Zambia.[37]

University graduates enter upon three main avenues of employment: the civil service, the teaching service, and the parastatal sector consisting of statutory bodies and state-owned companies. Nearly all students are supported by the government and required by the terms of their scholarships to work in the public sector for a specified period, up to three years, depending upon the field of study. In 1965 there were about 2,460 Zambians in the two senior divisions of the civil service, comprising 42 percent of the total. By 1968, the Zambian component had increased by nearly 70 percent to about 7,660—67 percent of the total number of civil servants.[38] Likewise, between 1966 and 1968 the number of Zam-

33. M. L. O. Faber, "Introduction," in *Towards Economic Independence*, ed. Faber and Potter, p. 11.

34. Republic of Zambia, *Ministry of Education Annual Report, 1965* (Lusaka, 1967), p. 42.

35. Republic of Zambia, *First National Development Plan 1966–1970* (Lusaka, 1966), p. 60.

36. Republic of Zambia, *Second National Development Plan, January, 1972–December, 1976* (Lusaka, 1971), pp. 130, 138.

37. Republic of Zambia, Office of the Vice-President, *Zambian Manpower* (Lusaka, 1969), p.53.

38. Dennis L. Dresang, "The Civil Service in Zambia" (unpublished paper, 1969).

bian teachers rose by 33 percent, from about 8,700 to 11,600, while remaining at about 82 percent of the total number of teachers.[39] Yet it is in the parastatal sector that the revolution from above has made its most distinctive impact.

The term "parastatal" has been defined as follows: "A parastatal organisation is not an integral part of the Government but an institution, organisation or agency which is wholly or mainly financed or owned or controlled by the Government."[40] An official study has identified three distinct types of parastatal bodies. The "commercial" type is incorporated under the Companies Ordinance to pursue a commercial undertaking, for example, the seminationalized mining companies and other enterprises in the ZIMCO group. The "semicommercial" type is created by statute to provide a public service on a business basis, for example, rail transport. In addition, there are "noncommercial" parastatal bodies established by statute to perform various public functions.[41] Figure 2 presents an outline of the parastatal sector, which was found to comprise 134 organizations "of one kind or another" in 1970.[42] As Sheridan Johns has observed, parastatal bodies in Zambia "generate roughly one half of the national income and employ about one fourth of the country's wage earners. Their activities reach into almost all spheres of Zambian life from mining, industry, transport, and agriculture to health, research, social welfare, and youth training."[43] Since Zambia has undertaken to industrialize in accordance with precepts that appear to require state participation up to at least 51 percent in the vast majority of large-scale enterprises,[44] the parastatal sector may be expected to grow and further consolidate its dominant position in the economy.

39. Republic of Zambia, Central Statistical Office, *Statistical Year-Book 1969*, (Lusaka, 1970), p. 50.
40. Republic of Zambia, Cabinet Office, *Report of the Committee Appointed to Review the Emoluments and Conditions of Service of Statutory Boards and Corporations and State-Owned Enterprises*, Lusaka, March 1970, p. 5.
41. Ibid., pp. 10–12.
42. Ibid., p. 15.
43. Sheridan Johns, "Para-Statal Bodies in Zambia: Problems and Prospects," in *Socioeconomic Development in Dual Economies: The Example of Zambia*, ed. Heide and Udo Ernst-Simonis (Munich, 1971), p. 218.
44. Along with his 1968 announcement to the effect that INDECO would acquire controlling interests in numerous foreign firms (See chap. 2), President Kaunda also declared that potential "business barons" in Zambia would have to accede to predominant state participation in the ownership of their enterprises. Republic of Zambia, *Zambia Towards Economic Independence*, Address of His Excellency Dr. K. D.

The incomes earned by administrative- and professional-grade employees of the civil service, teaching service, and parastatal bodies are well above the income levels of the industrial work force. In 1970 university graduates entering the civil and teaching services were paid basic salaries of K1,800 to K1,900 in addition to various other financial benefits.[45] This level was nearly 40 percent higher than the average income of mine workers and nearly three times as great as the average income received by wage earners outside the mining sector.[46] University graduates entering the parastatal sector received salaries that were substantially higher than civil service pay rates, although the fringe benefits (subsidized housing, medical insurance, leave pay, pensions, consumer loans, etc.) to which they are entitled were much less generous.[47] An official inquiry found that most graduates of the University of Zambia in 1969 preferred employment in the parastatal and private sectors to the civil service. This preference was attributable to higher pay scales for "middle management" outside of the civil service, where the opportunity for rapid advancement seems to be less promising than in the burgeoning lines of commercial (including state) enterprise.[48]

At the top of the civil service administrative scale in 1970, permanent secretaries (numbering approximately twenty-five) received basic salaries of K6,760 in addition to allowances. Net income at this level, after the payment of income tax, pension contribution, and subeconomic rent, came to more than K5,000.[49]

Kaunda, President of the Republic of Zambia, to the National Council of the United National Independence Party, at Mulungushi, April 19, 1968 (Lusaka, n.d.), p. 33. The following year he announced that the state would acquire majority ownership in all mining enterprises. Republic of Zambia, *Towards Complete Independence*, Address by His Excellency the President, Dr. K. D. Kaunda, to the UNIP National Council held at Matero Hall, Lusaka, August 11, 1969 (Lusaka, n.d.), pp. 29–39. However, in certain large enterprises involving foreign investment and management, for example, the production of explosives, the state has been satisfied with less than majority ownership.

45. Republic of Zambia, *Report of the Commission Appointed To Review the Salaries, Salary Structure and Conditions of Service of the Zambia Public Service* (Lusaka, 1971), pp. 27, 30.

46. See chap. 4.

47. Republic of Zambia, *Report of the Committee To Review the Emoluments* (1970), pp. 56–66.

48. Ibid., p. 57 and app. H.

49. Republic of Zambia, *Report of the Commission to Review the Salaries* (1971), p. viii. The salary for this position was increased to K9,000 in 1971; but fringe benefits were correspondingly cut so that take-home pay came to K5,001. Ibid.

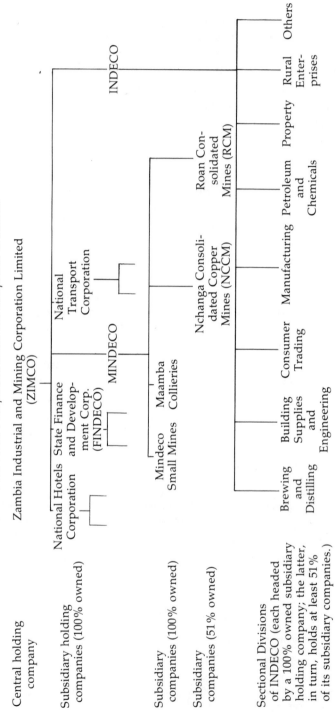

Figure 2. *An Outline of the Parastatal Sector*

A. *Commercial bodies incorporated under the Companies Ordinance*

Central holding company

Zambia Industrial and Mining Corporation Limited (ZIMCO)

Subsidiary holding companies (100% owned)

National Hotels Corporation — State Finance and Development Corp. (FINDECO) — National Transport Corporation — MINDECO — INDECO

Subsidiary companies (100% owned)

Mindeco Small Mines — Maamba Collieries

Subsidiary companies (51% owned)

Nchanga Consolidated Copper Mines (NCCM) — Roan Consolidated Mines (RCM)

Sectional Divisions of INDECO (each headed by a 100% owned subsidiary holding company; the latter, in turn, holds at least 51% of its subsidiary companies.)

Brewing and Distilling — Building Supplies and Engineering — Consumer Trading — Manufacturing — Petroleum and Chemicals — Property — Rural Enterprises — Others

B. *Partial listing of other parastatal organizations*

Semicommercial bodies established by statute (selected examples):

Zambia Airways Corporation
Zambia Railways
Zambia Electricity Supply Corporation (ZESCO)
National Agricultural Marketing Board (NAMBOARD)
Daily Produce Board
Cold Storage Board

Noncommercial bodies established by statute (selected examples):

National Council for Scientific Research
National Museums Board
Zambia National Provident Fund
Workmen's Compensation Fund Control Board
National Food and Nutrition Commission
Flying Doctor Service

Substantially higher salaries were paid to Zambian executives at top management levels in the parastatal and private sectors.[50] In the eyes of many able persons at the outset of their careers, these financial peaks appear to be attainable goals. Not only high income but great social prestige is also the reward of higher education and high-level employment. In Zambia, as in many another newly developing country, an organizational revolution spurred by material incentives is the forcing house for class formation on a nationalist basis.[51]

The Managerial Bourgeoisie

In his moving critique of social inequality and poor economic performance in the newly independent African states, the French agronomist, René Dumont, has written that "a new type of bourgeoisie is forming in Africa . . . a bourgeoisie of the civil service."[52] Among students of the existing socialist societies, the idea of a bureaucratic class is highly controversial.[53] With respect to the study of nonsocialist countries, where private enterprise bulks large in economic life, the concept of a "bureaucratic" or "state" bourgeoisie is ultimately misleading. Yet it would be useful to devise an apt term for the dominant classes of those underdeveloped countries that maintain market economies. Any such term or category should reflect the coexistence of a newly developing

50. The maximum salary reported for a Zambian chief executive in the parastatal sector was K10,000. *Report of the Committee To Review the Emoluments* (1970), p. 67. In the operating mines (as distinct from the state holding company, MINDECO) the highest ranking Zambians were personnel superintendents, for which office the minimum salary in 1972 was K6,000 in addition to rent-free housing and other perquisites.

51. I have previously described this process in Nigeria. See my *Nigerian Political Parties: Power in an Emergent African Nation* (Princeton: Princeton University Press, 1963); and "Contradictions in the Nigerian Political System," *The Journal of Modern African Studies* 3 (1965): 201–213.

52. René Dumont, *False Start in Africa*, 2d ed., rev., trans. Phyllis Nauts Ott (New York: Praeger, 1969), p. 81.

53. Thus Charles Bettelheim asserts the rise of a new "state bourgeoisie" in the Soviet Union (Paul M. Sweezy and Charles Bettelheim, eds., *On the Transition to Socialism* [New York and London: Monthly Review Press, 1971], p. 43), as did Milovan Djilas (*The New Class* [New York: Praeger, 1959]). By contrast, the inherent impermanence of bureaucratic class power in the Soviet Union is argued by Herbert Marcuse (*Soviet Marxism* [New York: Vintage Books, 1961], p. 100), and Isaac Deutscher (*Marxism in Our Time* [Berkeley, California: Ramparts Press, 1971], pp. 204–205); see also Leon Trotsky, *The Revolution Betrayed*, trans. Max Eastman (1937; New York: Pioneer Publishers, 1945).

and dependent private enterprise sector with a preponderant yet protective public sector. In this circumstance, which is widespread in the "Third World," businessmen, bureaucrats, leading politicians, and members of the learned professions constitute a new ruling class. I suggest the term "managerial bourgeoisie" to designate this class. Inasmuch as this term clearly refers to the private business elite as well as the managers of public enterprises and high governmental officials, it may be preferred to either "bureaucratic" or "state" bourgeoisie. Moreover, this term, in contrast with the term "entrepreneurial bourgeoisie," reflects the apparent disposition of bourgeois elements in newly developing countries to manage the production and distribution of wealth rather than to create new wealth-producing enterprises.[54]

In all societies, "revolutions from above" are prone to develop deeply conservative tendencies. In the newly developing countries of Africa, modern conservatism, as distinct from traditionalism, connotes a disposition to arrest the transformation of an organizational revolution into a social revolution or shift in the class content of power. In Zambia, as elsewhere, the bourgeoisie takes care to contain radicalism and maintain its position as the predominant class.

For an example of behavior tending to consolidate the bourgeoisie as a class we may refer to Dennis Dresang's discussion of "entrepreneurialism" in the civil service.[55] This concept involves two distinct but related patterns of behavior. First, senior civil servants are encouraged by a relatively decentralized and "fragmented" administrative system to exercise a considerable degree of independent judgment and discretion in the formulation and implementation of departmental policies. Second, demonstrated entrepreneurial talent in the administrative service often leads to a financially lucrative career in the business world. Dresang suggests that opportunities of this kind are actively sought by many public officials.

---

54. Cf. Martin Kilson's interesting perspective on the "emergent African bourgeoisie" ("African Political Change and the Modernization Process," *The Journal of Modern African Studies* 1 [1963]: 425–440. esp. p. 439).

55. Dennis L. Dresang, "Entrepreneurialism and Development Administration in Zambia," *The African Review* 1 (January 1972): 104–107; see also his "Entrepreneurialism and Development Administration," *Administrative Science Quarterly* 18 (March 1973): 76–85.

Increasing pressure to Zambianise senior positions in private
businesses has opened a whole new set of opportunities for
many civil servants in addition to those within the bureaucracy. Indeed, almost half of the 83 Zambian civil servants inter-
viewed by the author said that they anticipated leaving the
civil service before normal retirement age for a role in the
private sector.[56]

Even the mining companies, including both the parastatal operating companies and the private management companies, complain
that it is difficult for them to retain the services of their senior and
well-paid Zambian employees in the face of more lucrative offers
from other firms. Exchanges of high-level personnel between the
various organizations of the private and state sectors tend to unify
the interests of the predominant class. Inevitably, the values of the
business world, which are inimical to social revolution, and
bureaucratic values of a similar conservative stamp permeate the
bourgeoisie as a whole.

In addition to intersectoral careers and close personal relationships between public officials and business managers, the Zambian
policy of "partnership" between parastatal organizations and
foreign companies serves to promote the class interests of the
bourgeoisie. Leading members of the Zambian bourgeoisie are
constantly tempted to imbibe the capitalistic and managerial attitudes of their foreign business associates. Some, as we have remarked, may look ahead to careers in the wider business world.
Given the obviously bourgeois life styles of individuals in this elite
social stratum, they may be expected to embrace an elitist ideology.
In Zambia, as elsewhere in the Third World, state enterprise as the
predominant form of production may not have a socialist outcome.[57] Indeed the opposite effect may be expected, as the
influence of international capitalism functions to reinforce imma-
nent tendencies toward embourgeoisment of the state bureaucratic elite.

56. Dresang, "Entrepreneurialism and Development Administration in Zambia," p. 105.
57. Algeria, where a pattern of 51 percent state participation in the oil industry
has been established, is a parallel case. In a revealing study, Ian Clegg shows how,
in the name of "socialism," Algerian state enterprise is controlled by a "bureaucratic
bourgeoisie" to promote ruling class interests. *Workers' Self-Management in Algeria*
(New York and London: Monthly Review Press, 1971); see also Paul A. Beckett,
"Algeria vs. Fanon: The Theory of Revolutionary Decolonization and the Algerian
Experience," *The Western Political Quarterly* 26 (March 1973): 5–27.

Thus far, the virtues of "permanent partnership" with foreign business groups have been extolled by Zambian leaders who are not in principle favorably disposed toward capitalist doctrines. In his inaugural statement as chairman of the Zambia Industrial and Mining Corporation, President Kaunda declared:

> As with the national economy, ZIMCO is therefore also destined to grow from strength to strength. In order that this growth may continue unfettered ZIMCO is going to need money and technical expertise and this is where our philosophy of permanent partnership as against transient partnership is in our opinion particularly suitable to our situation. We need to augment our domestic skills with the sophisticated technical knowhow of other countries. We need partners in progress.[58]

However, the idea of "permanence" is not at all inconsistent with change in the nature of the partnership agreements. For example, the management contracts negotiated in 1969 served to ensure smooth mining operations during the initial period of state participation. They also contributed to the maintenance of international and local expatriate confidence in the stability of Zambian economic conditions. Eventually, having established her bona fides in the business world, Zambia decided to change the form of partnership by dispensing with management contracts. Although Zambia does not as yet possess the national expertise required to manage the industry and must continue to employ expatriate managers, engineers, and other technicians, the ardent desire of Zambians for "self-management," as opposed to the management contract method, is unmistakable. In this respect, the national bourgeoisie yields to no group or class in the intensity of its nationalism.

From an international capitalist standpoint, the national bourgeoisie is the local wing of a transnational class. Within a host country for foreign investments, the managerial bourgeoisie consists of a local wing, which is normally nationalistic, and a corporate international wing that tolerates and patronizes local nationalism. It is the singular failing of many analyses to mistake this modern outlook for the ethnocentric chauvinism of past colonial rulers. To be sure, chauvinistic primitives are far from extinct

58. Zambia Industrial and Mining Corporation Limited, *Chairman's Statement*, 1971.

in the world of international business; they may even be numerous in countries like Zambia, where large-scale industry developed as part of a system of colonial and racial domination. Yet the truly representative members of the corporate international bourgeoisie are relatively free from the debilitating effects of national and racial chauvinism. The most impressive and successful executives appear to have been chosen to serve their companies in Zambia partly because they exemplify a catholicity of outlook that meshes well with the human environment. This has been remarkably true with respect to officials of the Anglo American Corporation's head office in Lusaka, most of whom are white South Africans who have in the past and could in the future function effectively within the white supremacist environment of that country.

No one explanation will adequately account for the ability of many white Southern Africans (including British nationals of Rhodesian and South African background) to function effectively in various walks of Zambian life, notably in the business, administrative, educational, and professional spheres. Not a few of them, who deplore racial oppression in their own countries, or countries of origin, appear to value the opportunity to lead constructive lives in a nonracial society. Yet the Anglo American Corporation phenomenon and, to a lesser extent, that of RST, reveal something more than personal choice with respect to career opportunity and life style. The leading officials of these companies are cosmopolitan by training and inclination, but that virtue is also a professional necessity of corporate international life. Raymond Vernon has remarked that prudent multinational businessmen follow the rule: "when in Rome do as the Romans do."[59] In speaking of officials who serve multinational corporations in diverse national environments, it may not be unreasonable to suggest a parallel with the Roman Empire. The legal system of Imperial Rome was founded upon the universalist principles of Stoic philosophy. Stoicism taught that all men were brothers in reason despite their widely differing circumstances. It also promoted the ideal of public service.[60] Like the administrators of the Roman Empire, the servants of today's corporate international empire are likely to be temperamental stoics—intellectually cool, urbane, tolerant of divergent

59. Vernon, p. 147.

60. George H. Sabine, *A History of Political Theory*, rev. ed. (New York: Holt, 1950), pp. 148–173.

viewpoints, committed to the cause of economic rationality, and ever hopeful that right reason will prevail.[61]

In the case of the Anglo American Corporation, a stoical attitude may facilitate one's disassociation from the sordid facts of South African society, where the parent company lives, and alternative identification with the "Greater Group," as an object of fealty. These closely paraphrased remarks by white officials of the Anglo American Corporation in Zambia may indicate the spirit of their service.

My first identification is with the Corporation; as far as I am concerned it just happens to be South African. When I am sent to Johannesburg, I will be going to the Corporation rather than the Republic. I genuinely regard myself as being a white African, and I will not like having to live in a racially stratified community. But I will go there and I am sure that things will change in South Africa. I will work for it, not by demonstration or heroics but in the normal course of life.

My first loyalty is to Anglo. Harry Oppenheimer sent me here and there is something I can do for the Group in this place. Harry picks his men carefully and it is extremely rare to have a direct conflict with the home office. I cannot think of one case in which advice based on local expertise has been overruled. If I could not live with Group policies in this country, I would ask to be transferred and they would send me where my views would not conflict with the environment.

I feel as though I belong to the company more than any country. I really believe in [the late]Ernest Oppenheimer's definition of the company's aim. ["To make profits for its shareholders but to do so in such a way as to make a real contribution to the welfare of the countries where it operates." From the Introduction to annual reports of the Anglo American Corporation of South Africa.]

61. Howard V. Perlmutter postulates the "geocentric man" as the ideal executive of the multinational corporation. "The Tortuous Evolution of the Multinational Corporation," in *World Business: Promise and Problems,* ed. Courtney C. Brown (New York: Macmillan, 1970), pp. 81–82. The theme of transnational universalism in relation to multinational enterprise is developed by several other contributors to this volume, namely, George W. Ball, Courtney C. Brown, Richard Eells, and Frank Tannenbaum.

In the case of Roan Selection Trust, there was no entity comparable to Anglo American's "Greater Group" with which managerial employees might identify. Efforts to extend the operations of this company to Chile and Australia were frustrated by exchange control restrictions imposed by the government of the Federation of Rhodesia and Nyasaland in 1961.[62] RST was best described as a Rhodesian (later Zambian) company, owned mainly by Americans, under British and Commonwealth management. Prior to nationalization, the RST management had been aware that the dominant shareholder, American Metal Climax, which held 42.3 percent of RST shares, was anxious to reduce its holding because it feared "political risks" in the Zambian environment. In 1968–1969, AMAX attempted without success to sell half of its shareholding to a German company.[63] When the Zambian government acted to acquire majority ownership of the mines, the board of RST, excluding AMAX representatives, hoped to reorganize the company as an international mining house (see chapter 2). This idea was abandoned reluctantly for financial reasons, and RST was taken over entirely by AMAX, a company known to be wary of "political risks" in Zambia. Hence it may be noted that in a New York address, the managing director of MINDECO stressed the shift in Zambia's "political attitude toward the mining industry" as a result of state participation and reaffirmed the Zambian government's commitment to "the concept of partnership."[64] Similarly, Sir Ronald L. Prain, who served as RST's chief executive for twenty-five years, while commending the new practice of governmental participation in the ownership of mines in the copper exporting countries, has also stated that the political climate for investments in the developing countries compares favorably with that of the industrial countries.[65] Were Prain's viewpoint to prevail at AMAX, the ties of the Zambian bourgeoisie to corporate internationalism would be considerably strengthened.

62. U.S., Court of Appeals for the Third Circuit, *Brief of Defendants-Appellants American Metal Climax, Inc., and Roan Selection Trust Limited* in *Kohn* v. *American Metal Climax, Inc., et al.*, February 22, 1971, p. 10.

63. Ibid., p. 11.

64. D. C. Mulaisho, "Address to the New York Section of the American Institute of Mining, Metallurgical and Petroleum Engineers," September 21, 1972 (mimeo.).

65. *The Future Availability of Copper Supplies,* An address to The Institute of Metals, Autumn Meeting, Amsterdam, 1970, pp. 6, 10.

A Class Analysis

During the latter stages of the African people's struggle against colonial and white settler rule, sectional and class differences were overridden by those who championed the common national interest. Subsequently antagonisms that were inherent in Zambian society came to the fore. As a result of the inherited pattern of economic development, with commerce, industry, and commercial agriculture heavily concentrated in the Copperbelt and along the line-of-rail, the process of class formation has been closely related to the circumstance of sectional privilege. Donald Rothchild's summary of recent data is conclusive on this point.

> In 1969 the line of rail provinces accounted for 84 per cent of the total number of employees and 91 per cent of total earnings from employment. Manufacturing activity was heavily concentrated in the line of rail provinces; even though half Zambia's population lived in the non-line of rail provinces, only two per cent of the total work force found employment there. This imbalance was also reflected in average African earnings in the public and private sectors. Average earnings of K935 in Copperbelt Province were well above the national average of K789; annual earnings in North-Western Province (K404), Northern (K430), and Western Province (K483), however, were well below the average figure.[66]

Just as Zambian economic development has been skewed drastically by an extreme geographical concentration of modern technology, so too has the development of the Zambian proletariat been shaped conically from the commanding height of the mine workers. As Michael Burawoy says, the Zambian mine workers are "a labour elite" or "aristocracy"—"the average income of a mineworker is approximately twice the national average for 'local' employees."[67] The special-interest orientation of organized mine workers within the Zambian nationalist movement is a well

66. Donald Rothchild, "Rural-Urban Inequities and Resource Allocation in Zambia," *Journal of Commonwealth Political Studies* 10 (1972): 224 and sources cited at p. 240.

67. Michael Burawoy, "Another Look at the Mineworker," *African Social Research,* no. 14 (December 1972), pp. 267, 276–280. Elsewhere he cites figures of K1,248 and K789 as the respective average incomes of black mine workers and black workers in all other industries. Burawoy, *The Colour of Class on the Copper Mines,* Zambian Papers, No. 7, University of Zambia Institute for African Studies (Manchester: Manchester University Press, 1972), p.2.

documented historical fact.[68] Recently, Burawoy and others have shown that the ruling party elicits far less enthusiasm from the mine workers than from other, less advantaged, sections of the proletariat: "UNIP remains predominantly a people's party deriving its support from the poorer sections of the Zambian communities. Studies seem to suggest that it is very much more powerful in the squatter townships than in the mine townships."[69] Yet the wage earning class as a whole shares in the relative prosperity of urban Zambia.[70] While it is true, as Burawoy says, that ever since independence, "Government has feared the power of the mineworkers,"[71] the danger perceived arises from the strength of organized labor as a whole and not that of the mine workers only. Various means have been devised to ensure that the potential power of the unions will not be unleashed in opposition to official policies that call for wage restraint and the intensification of labor. Such means include compulsory affiliation of all unions with a supervisory central labor organization, restrictions on the right to strike, a procedure for compulsory arbitration, and the introduction of "works councils" designed to improve industrial discipline.[72]

The Zambian bourgeoisie is no less diversified than is the proletariat. It includes the white collar class or traditional "salariat," teachers, members of the learned professions, and businessmen. Its apex or ruling section is identified in this study as the "managerial bourgeoisie." A rough estimate of the size of this group in 1970, taking into account some 8,000 to 10,000 senior civil servants and fewer than 500 university graduates, might be 25,000 persons in addition to their immediate families—a total of some 100,000 to 125,000 persons in a population of approximately 4,100,000, or between 2 and 3 percent. Should the size of this group treble in ten years (during which time 7,000 Zambians are expected to earn university degrees),[73] it would still constitute no more than 5 to 7 percent of the nation.

68. Literature cited at chap. 4 n.1.

69. Burawoy, "Another Look at the Mineworker," p. 279, citing another study by A. Pandawa.

70. See chap. 4.

71. Burawoy, *The Colour of Class on the Copper Mines,* p. 78.

72. These objects are covered by *The Industrial Relations Act,* No. 36 of 1971; and see chap. 4.

73. See n. 37.

The Balance of Power.—Government policies since independence have operated to nurture the growth and consolidate the position of the bourgeoisie. The "revolution from above" in state enterprise, with its elitist connotations, is directly relevant to the growth of the managerial bourgeoisie. This trend is reinforced by two other developments: the acquisition of large farms, previously under absentee European ownership, by Zambians;[74] and the spread of "entrepreneurialism"[75]—an opportunist pattern of behavior on the part of senior public officials—which links the state bureaucracy ever more firmly to the private sector. The end result is an institutional environment and climate of opinion that are propitious for the operations of multinational corporations. The latter, in turn, must be willing to form partnerships with the local bourgeoisie on terms that satisfy at least two basic requirements: they must facilitate the "revolution from above" through management training programs and other policies designed to stimulate local development; they must observe the "doctrine of domicile" by permitting their local subsidiaries to act in accordance with host-country policies in preference to the conflicting policies of other states. Where such partnerships exist, the managerial bourgeoisie consists, as we have said, of both local and corporate international sections.

---

74. President Kaunda has given this valuable insight into the origins of a potentially significant land-owning class: " . . . while much has been said . . . about colleagues and comrades who own farms, the criticisms have ignored two important factors; first, that it is easy to know who owns a farm but it is not so easy to know who owns a commercial enterprise or who owns shares in an enterprise; second, that there are also colleagues who have vast tracts of land held and used under customary law. Our colleagues who have bought farms are paying heavily for them and are for the moment benefiting little. Those of us who run farms on land held under traditional custom are benefiting more. At any rate, we are developing land under customary law using the financial facilities, using our ability to borrow from banks. This we are able to do because of our commanding position as leaders. With the passing of time together with our ability to use all the facilities available to us but not to neighbors, this land will become our family property because we have developed it. This will stop other people from using part of that same piece of land and, indeed, if anything they will tend to move away. The end result will be exactly the same as that of a colleague who has bought himself a farm. Both the one who has bought a farm and the one who has used customary law to acquire land have been using the privileged position in which society has placed them to their own personal advantage and probably also to that of their own family" (Kenneth Kaunda, "The Responsibilities of Leadership" [an address to the UNIP National Council], *Third World* 2 [March 1973]: 13–14).

75. See above, pp. 199–200.

It may be objected that the managerial bourgeoisie delineated by this analysis is far too divided internally to carry much analytical weight. Despite our contention that crucial and truly representative elements of the corporate international wing are well disposed toward cooperation with the local wing, a serious objection must be overcome. Assuming a cosmopolitan rather than chauvinistic outlook on the part of the corporate international elite, can it be reconciled with the staunchly parochial nationalism of the local bourgeoisie? If not, there is small probability of transnational class cohesion.

In fact, parochial nationalism on the part of the ruling class in a newly developing country may be entirely consistent with the broad interests of the corporate international bourgeoisie. Insofar as parochial nationalism blocks the formation of wider political unities among neighboring underdeveloped countries, it fortifies international capitalism by reducing the potential viability of anticapitalist alternatives. The doctrine of domicile does imply a large measure of flexibility on the part of multinational corporations in their efforts to straddle conflicting political ideologies. To the extent that corporations are able to do this, they may well promote peaceful change within politically turbulent regions such as Southern Africa. But they do so, to the greatest possible extent, on a nonsocialist basis: in all countries, they promote the growth of the bourgeoisie as a class.

At this point, the question of control may be reconsidered in a new light. Previous attempts to clarify this issue by means of institutional analysis have resulted in a disagreement between those who hold that predominant power lies with the multinational corporations and those who say that it lies with the postcolonial state. The relevant evidence presented in this chapter may be summarized thus: On one hand, the "doctrine of domicile" and some of the evidence concerning "formal control" tend to show that the corporations are adapting imaginatively and effectively in terms of their own long-range interests to the new political order. On the other hand, a "revolution from above" has enabled the Zambian section of the managerial bourgeoisie to control the conditions of partnership with foreign corporations and consolidate its autonomous power. These conclusions do oversimplify the findings of this study, but they fairly suggest that in terms of institutional analysis it is extremely difficult to say where the balance of power lies in the relationship between the Zambian state and the mining companies. From an institutional standpoint, we can only say that each side has gained important objectives by means of an arrangement that is subject to regular review.[76]

From the standpoint of class analysis, however, power may be said to lie with the managerial bourgeoisie. Conflicts within this class, especially between its local and corporate international wings, may be expected to occur in the normal course of events. However, means for reconciling such conflicts are being perfected, and neither wing is disposed to undermine the basis of its survival in Zambia. The local wing would not wish to jeopardize the economic and technical support that it receives from international capitalist sources for its chosen strategy of development.[77] The corporate international wing represents a world-scale social force, arising primarily but not exclusively within the industrialized capitalist countries. It seeks to devise and perfect institutions that will protect its sphere of operations in many countries. The multinational corporation is one such institution and should be understood in terms of transnational class development. In this process, the bourgeoisie, true to its epoch-making tradition, has taken the lead.

Within Zambia, all sections of the national bourgeoisie have benefited from nationalistic economic policies designed mainly to

76. In a comment to the author, Robert H. Bates refines the issue of power in this relationship as it appears in the perspective of institutional analysis thus: "You seem to say that there are two ways of inferring power in the relationship between the firms and the government. One is by observing a short run series of encounters between the two parties in bargaining sessions within a given institutional setting. A second is to observe a change over time of the values or the ethos of the parties—what they are after in these bargaining sessions—and of the institutional setting within which these encounters take place. And while the companies may lose out to the state in the short run bargaining series, over the long run they may be transforming the ethos of the state and the institutions of the state in a way that is favorable to their economic interests. To observe and keep a record of the outcomes of the short term encounters would thus be to miss out on the data that would indicate the long term prevalence of the companies and what they stand for."

77. For example, in 1973, Zambia borrowed $150 million from two international banking consortia, led by Japanese and American bankers. These loans enabled the Zambian government to settle its compensation debts and revoke the nationalization agreements several years ahead of schedule. In 1973, the Zambian government also received several loans, totalling $189.5 million, from the World Bank to finance agricultural and educational projects, capital goods imports, and an extension of the Kafue hydroelectric project. *World Bank/IDA 1973 Annual Report*, pp. 29, 56, 58; and International Bank for Reconstruction and Development press release nos. 73/40, 73/53.

redress racial grievances. Measures introduced in 1968 and supplemented in succeeding years serve to promote Zambian private enterprise at the expense of "resident expatriate enterprise," which is traditionally both European and Asian. These measures, including the reservation of certain fields of enterprise—both retail and wholesale trading, building material industries, and transportation—to Zambian citizens and restrictions on commercial borrowing by expatriate businessmen, have put Zambians in control of the small-business sector.[78] By doing away with a major portion of the previously dominant alien segment of the local bourgeoisie, these policies have greatly strengthened the mass base of the national bourgeoisie.[79]

Despite this commitment to the promotion of Zambian private enterprise, the official party and state doctrine, authored by President Kaunda and termed "humanism,"[80] is hostile to capitalism, which Kaunda equates with economic greed and exploitation. "Let me emphasize," Kaunda has said, "that I want Zambian business to expand and to prosper. But for goodness sake, I do not propose to create Zambian capitalism here. This is incompatible with my conception of Humanism."[81] Evidently, Kaunda believes that Zambia can enjoy the advantages of creative enterpreneurship without giving rise to a social order that breeds class privilege and an acquisitive social ethic.[82] He has also prescribed a Code of Leadership, which stipulates that no party leader or "senior public ser-

78. The most complete exposition of these measures is contained in three addresses by President Kaunda: Zambia Towards Economic Independence, pp. 23–31; Towards Complete Independence, pp. 8–13; and "Take Up the Challenge . . . ," pp. 58–61.

79. A significant portion of the alien segment of the local bourgeoisie survives. Resident expatriate businessmen, like other foreign businessmen, are encouraged to form joint ventures as minority owners with Zambian businessmen in approved productive (but not distributive) enterprises. Such companies are not subject to discriminatory restrictions on local borrowing. Republic of Zambia, Towards Complete Independence, Address by . . . K. D. Kaunda, p. 12. The several hundred remaining expatriate farmers should also be noted, in addition to the large number of resident expatriates in various professional callings.

80. See chap. 1.

81. Republic of Zambia, Zambia Towards Economic Independence, Address by . . . K. D. Kaunda, p. 32.

82. Kaunda has often expressed his awareness of the dilemmas that are implied in this approach. The following quotation is illustrative: "We find that the entrepreneur can, in certain sectors of the economy, be of great benefit to Zambia now. If we insist on controlling everything through the State, we shall restrain our development. We do not have the administrative skills in sufficient quantity to be able to develop and control everything centrally. For example, there is a physical limit to

vant" may be associated in any way with capitalist enterprises.[83] While Zambian businessmen will be nurtured by the state, they are to be excluded from positions of public trust.

Kaunda's humanism is bound to create ideological strain within the bourgeoisie. But it is not incompatible with the development of that class under existing conditions; moreover, it is directly relevant to the great national problem of rural retardation, which threatens to undermine the emergent social order. Kaunda has said that "humanism in Zambia is a decision in favor of rural areas."[84] In practice, this implies a redistribution of national wealth away from urban areas to the needier rural districts.[85] Thus far, the redistributive policies of the Zambian government have appeared to make far greater demands upon the wage earning class than the bourgeoisie.[86] The urban workers may wonder why they alone (from their viewpoint) should be called upon to sacrifice for the

the number of industrial projects that can be supervised. It is for this reason that the State concentrates on large-scale industrial development. In the in-between area of the large projects, in the gaps, the small-scale entrepreneurs can often be the most efficient method of development, the most economical in terms of manpower skills. . . . We have now cleared the way for the development of joint enterprises between Zambians and expatriates. We are actually seeking to encourge small and medium-scale development through entrepreneurs.

"The fundamental clash between capitalists and a noncapitalist society seems more likely than ever. No one is more aware of the problem than I. Once you introduce a man to capitalism, he may acquire a taste for it, a taste for accumulating more and more for himself. He may acquire an individualistic approach. Do we not run the risk of opening Pandora's box by letting out and encouraging this element of free capitalism? Will we not find in, say, ten years' time, that this capitalism is so entrenched that we are unable to eradicate it? Or more sinister still, will we not find that we have become tainted, and have lost the desire to eradicate it? It is a risk we are taking, but we must create the means to control capitalism, to make it work for us, not against us" (*Towards Complete Independence*, Address by . . . K. D. Kaunda, pp. 59–60).

83. Republic of Zambia, *"Take Up the Challenge . . . ,"* Speeches [by] K. D. Kaunda, p. 52; and Kaunda, "The Responsibilities of Leadership," pp. 11–16. The code of leadership, published in 1973, prohibits the receipt of more than one salary or the ownership of businesses, farms, or rented houses by leaders of the party, officials of the national or local governments, civil servants, managers of the Zambia police and defense forces, and others in public employment, including the academic and administrative officers of educational institutions. *African Research Bulletin,* Political, Social and Cultural Series 10, 10 (November 15, 1973): 3014. This policy is similar to a Tanzanian precedent. See Julius K. Nyerere, *Freedom and Socialism* (Dar es Salaam: Oxford University Press, 1968), p. 249.

84. Republic of Zambia, *Zambia Towards Economic Independence,* Address by . . . K. D. Kaunda, p. 14.

85. Rothchild, pp. 222–242.

86. See chap. 4.

sake of rural development, while the bourgeoisie appears to be enriching itself. This may explain why the bourgeoisie is presently content to live within Kaunda's humanist ideological shell. It connotes class collaboration between the bourgeoisie and the peasantry at the expense of the proletariat.[87] If it works and rural development, as envisioned by Kaunda, becomes a reality, humanism will be difficult to challenge directly and openly; if not, the bourgeoisie may turn boldly to other doctrines and policies.[88]

87. Alan J. F. Simmance has observed that governmental subsidies to farmers are, for the most part, "designed to keep down the price of food to urban consumers at enormous national cost . . . . From K4 million in 1965, subsidies rose to a peak of K35 million in 1968 and have fluctuated between K18 and K23 million in the years thereafter. They can hardly have cost less than the entire capital allocation to agriculture in the post-independence period and quite possibly a good deal more." Clearly, "the reduction or elimination of these heavy subsidies on basic foodstuffs would generate tremendous savings and significantly reduce the comparative attractiveness of urban life" (Urbanization in Zambia, An International Urbanization Survey Report to the Ford Foundation [New York: 1972], p. 15). The adverse effects of any such departure in policy would fall most heavily upon the urban poor—the residents of "squatter villages" or shanty towns, unorganized casual laborers, and the unemployed. The political tendency of this potentially volatile element might then coalesce more closely with that of the organized workers.

88. A potential challenge to Kaunda's emphasis on the primacy of rural development is posed by Valentine S. Musakanya, formerly secretary to the cabinet, minister of state for technical and vocational training, and governor of the Bank of Zambia. Musakanya's position, shared by "a scattering of well-placed civil servants and businessmen," is well summarized by Rothchild: "These men articulate the interests and outlook of the urban, industrial, and commercial sectors and place heavy emphasis on building on existing bases of strength. Emphasizing the scarcity of national resources, they argue that in Zambia's particular circumstances 'development must start from the centres of population and the already industrialized areas and spill over to the rural areas.' They assume that the modern sector will demonstrate the capacity for self-sustained growth and that this sector can be effectively Zambianized over the years. But they raise serious questions about the application of the principle of reallocative equity to urban-rural relations. Musakanya is quite blunt on the latter point: ' . . . the rural areas have the human material neither to [pursue] nor sustain a development effort, and such development as is created has only temporary effect as it depends largely on urban manpower and materials. Thus rural development efforts are not only expensive, but from the outset doomed to minimum return.' His solution is to allocate resources to those areas 'where the mental and physical equipment is available' to utilise them in full—the urban and periurban areas and certain secondary intensive development zones selected for their ability to yield high investment returns" ("Rural-Urban Inequities and Resource Allocation in Zambia," p. 233, quoting from Valentine Musakanya, "Where to Spend Our Scarce Resources," African Development [October 1970], p. Z. 18–20).

According to A. J. F. Simmance, "The protagonists of this viewpoint . . . see no need to compromise between 'intensive development zones' and the provision of basic services throughout the land but would abandon the latter in favor of the

Whither Zambia?—"Zambia's destination," says Kaunda, "is neither capitalism nor orthodox socialism."[89] Charles Harvey remarks that Kaunda's philosophy of humanism "specifically rejects the doctrines of socialism," despite its accommodation of "socialist policy elements."[90] Experience elsewhere teaches that a nondoctrinaire strategy of development, which relies upon a combination of private, cooperative, and state enterprise, under the auspices of a managerial bourgeoisie and in partnership with multinational corporations, is unlikely to build socialism. In the absence of a clear political purpose to the contrary, Zambia's organizational revolution may be expected to stop short of social revolution, in which case, bureaucratic rule will prevail. Providentially, from the democratic viewpoint, Kaunda himself has emerged as the archenemy of bureaucratic rule in Zambia. "We had more than sixty years of paternalism," he has said, "and there is no intention to bring it back under a different guise."[91]

Political ideas are generated by attempts to cope with the problems of society. In Zambia the most intractable of all problems arise from the relative stagnation of the rural economy and the resulting massive exodus of job seekers and their dependents to the towns. The chosen remedy involves an intensified effort to raise agricultural productivity and improve the quality of rural life. This, in turn, requires the elevation of morale and the maintenance of a

---

former. They argue that the people are abandoning the land already, so why throw good money after bad? They no longer believe in the village as the prime basis of African social life. Theirs is still a minority viewpoint but time, economic circumstance, and the facts of the rural/urban drift may yet be on their side" (*Urbanization in Zambia*, p. 45).

From this perspective, Kaunda's humanism, with its idealization of traditional rural values and commitment to the overriding importance of rural regeneration, may not seem to be very relevant.

89. Republic of Zambia, *"Take Up the Challenge . . . ,"* Speeches [by] K. D. Kaunda, p. 49.

90. "Economic Independence," in *Economic Independence and Zambian Copper,* ed. Bostock and Harvey, p. 5.

91. Republic of Zambia, *A Path for the Future,* Address by His Excellency the President, Dr. K. D. Kaunda, as Secretary-General of the United National Independence Party on the occasion of the Opening of the Sixth General Conference of the United National Independence Party, Mulungushi, May 8, 1971 (Lusaka, 1971), p. 33. James R. Scarritt, who has made a systematic study of elite values in newly independent Zambia, has observed that the egalitarian tendency of Kaunda's recent thought is likely to clash with the elitist attitudes and values of Zambian politicians and civil servants. "Elite Values, Ideology, and Power in Post-Independence Zambia," *African Studies Review* 14 (April 1971): 48–51.

high standard of social discipline in the countryside. These objectives, involving the basic attitudes of villagers, cannot be attained by bureaucratic means. They require a genuine commitment on the part of rural dwellers themselves to participate effectively in various development programs.

Toward the end of 1968, Kaunda announced that the state administration would be decentralized to invigorate the national development effort at provincial and local levels. However, this reform would not be allowed to compromise the ruling party's creed of strict centralization in the political sphere. Kaunda summarized his policy pithily as "decentralisation in centralism. This," he said, "is designed to take us a step further towards the achievement of our goal, which goal, for lack of a better word, I choose to call participatory democracy."[92]

The term "participatory democracy" was well chosen because it does correctly identify a core characteristic of Kaunda's personal political outlook. He is, at the very least, uneasy with the bureaucratic method of functional specialization in public affairs. "Through Humanism and Participatory Democracy," he has said, "we are endeavoring to create a situation in which . . . no individual or group of individuals shall be allowed to possess a monopoly of any form of power by which they can influence the direction or pace of development in the Nation in pursuance of their own interests." To his mind, the public interest is compromised whenever politicians monopolize political and bureaucratic power, or industrialists and businessmen monopolize economic and financial power, or soldiers monopolize military power, or technocrats and intellectuals monopolize knowledge (intellectual power), or pressmen and writers monopolize the power of the pen, or workers monopolize power through strikes, or chiefs monopolize the power of tradition.[93] Participatory democracy, he contends, should be practiced in every sphere of social life. Every enterprise should have a "workers' council" and accept the "con-

---

92. Republic of Zambia, *Zambia's Guideline for the Next Decade,* His Excellency the President, Dr. Kenneth Kaunda, Addressing the National Council of UNIP at Mulungushi, November 9, 1968 (Lusaka: 1968), p. 20. The administrative and political implications of this reform are discussed by William Tordoff, "Provincial and Local Government in Zambia," *Journal of Administration* 9 (January 1970): 23–35.

93. Republic of Zambia, *A Path for the Future,* Address by . . . K. D. Kaunda, p. 37.

cept of co-determination."[94] Similar committees should be set up within the civil service without, however, disrupting discipline.[95] Established intellectuals should not imagine that they have any monopoly of good ideas: "A real sound intellectual will rejoice in going to the villages and meeting his fellow intellectuals who may not have even rudiments of elementary book education."[96] Even the army should devise "a system which would enable the soldiers to practice participatory democracy and, at the same time, maintain firm and strict discipline."[97]

In 1971 parliament enacted the National Service and Home Guard acts. The former establishes the liability of citizens, both male and female, in particular those who have completed secondary education, to serve for a period of two years for training in "defense, production and mass work."[98] Ex-servicemen and ex-servicewomen become members of the Home Guard, remaining as such until the age of fifty-five. Kaunda's conception is akin to the revolutionary model of "a nation in arms": The regular army "will train the rest of the nation so that by 1980 everybody should be able to defend the Revolution."[99] This might be taken as an allusion to the possible danger of a rightist coup d'état as well as the danger of invasion by foreign enemies.

At the time of writing, participatory democracy—a state predicated on the reality of popular power—appears to be a distant goal, Kaunda's dream. The existing reality is bureaucratic control and crude social inequality. One may say, without fear of contradiction, that the vital interests of the bourgeoisie have been secured with far greater certainty than they may have been endangered by economic and political reforms adopted since 1968. Participatory democracy can be manipulated to serve the interests of the

94. Republic of Zambia, *"Take Up the Challenge . . . ,"* Speeches [by] K. D. Kaunda, p. 41. Unless exempted by the president, all enterprises that employ not less than one hundred persons are required to establish "works councils" under The Industrial Relations Act of 1971.

95. Ibid., p. 12.

96. Ibid., p. 15.

97. Ibid., p. 11.

98. However, students enrolled in institutions of higher education are permitted to serve for a minimum period of four months, after which they must pay a proportion of their posteducation earnings for a period of up to twenty months. Provision is also made for voluntary enlistments.

99. Republic of Zambia, *Zambia's Guideline for the Next Decade*, Kenneth Kaunda Addressing the National Council, p. 15.

bourgeoisie. This formula is occasionally and deviously prescribed by conservatives to reduce social conflict. It can be used by proponents of the existing social order to co-opt partially disaffected and potentially disruptive elements—workers, farmers, students, or soldiers—into existing institutions of corporate solidarity.[100]

Yet participatory democracy, candidly conceived, has a radical tendency that should not be minimized. It means that the standard of professionalism is replaced by the standard of participation. In all spheres, all functions may be performed by all people. Functional distinctions between party and civil service, party and army, army and civil service, are erased or blurred; the institutions of learning and justice may lose their distinctive measures of autonomy. All at once, the high income and professional classes that wield bureaucratic and financial power may be threatened by a potentially revolutionary coalition of workers, farmers, and soldiers. Should this happen in Zambia—and the formal declaration of a "One-Party Participatory Democracy" in 1973 may be fateful—new industrial forms might emerge from a creative struggle between bureaucratic and popular power.

100. See I. Clegg's summary of the European experience with workers' participation in management. *Workers' Self-Management in Algeria,* pp. 18–22.

BIBLIOGRAPHY

Works Concerning the Corporation—National
and Transnational—Cited in This Study

Alger, Chadwick F. "The Multinational Corporation and the Future International System." *The Annals of the American Academy of Political and Social Science* 403 (September 1972): 104–115.

Baran, Paul A., and Sweezy, Paul M. "Notes on the Theory of Imperialism." *Monthly Review* 21 (March 1966): 13–31.

Barber, Richard J. *The American Corporation: Its Power, Its Money, Its Politics.* New York: E. P. Dutton & Co., Inc., 1970.

Behrman, Jack N. *National Interests and the Multinational Enterprise: Tensions among the North Atlantic Countries.* Englewood Cliffs, N. J.: Prentice-Hall, 1970.

Berle, Adolf A., Jr. *Power Without Property.* New York: Harcourt, Brace, 1959.

————. *The Twentieth Century Capitalist Revolution.* New York: Harcourt, Brace & World, 1954.

Berle, Adolf A., and Means, Gardiner C. *The Modern Corporation and Private Property.* Rev. ed. New York: Harcourt, Brace & World, 1968.

Brooke, Michael Z., and Remmers, H. Lee. *The Strategy of Multinational Enterprise: Organisation and Finance.* New York: American Elsevier Publishing Company, 1970.

Brown, Courtney C., ed. *World Business: Promise and Problems.* New York: The Macmillan Company, 1970.

Drucker, Peter F. *The New Society.* New York: Harper, 1950.

Dunning, John H., ed. *The Multinational Enterprise.* London: George Allen and Unwin, 1971.

Epstein, Edwin M. *The Corporation in American Politics.* Englewood Cliffs, N. J.: Prentice-Hall, 1969.

Evans, Peter B. "National Autonomy and Economic Development: Critical Perspectives on Multinational Corporations in Poor Countries." In *Transnational Relations and World Politics.* Edited by Robert O. Keohane and Joseph S. Nye. Cambridge, Mass.: Harvard University Press, 1971. Pp. 325–342.

Galbraith, John Kenneth. *The New Industrial State.* New York: Houghton Mifflin, 1967.

Galloway, Jonathan F. "Multinational Enterprises as Worldwide Interest Groups." *Politics and Society* 2 (Fall 1971): 1–21.

Girvan, Norman. "Multinational Corporations and Dependent Underdevelopment in Mineral Export Economies." *Social and Economic Studies* 19 (December 1970): 490–526.

Goodsell, Charles T. *American Corporations and Peruvian Politics.* Cambridge, Mass.: Harvard University Press, 1974.

Hacker, Andrew, ed. *The Corporation Take-Over.* Garden City, N. Y.: Anchor Books, 1965.

Huntington, Samuel P. "Transnational Organizations in World Politics." *World Politics* 25 (April 1973): 333–368.

Hymer, Stephen. "The Multinational Corporation and the Law of Uneven Development." In *Economics and World Order from the 1970's to the 1990's.* Edited by Jagdish N. Bhagwati. New York: Macmillan, 1972. Pp. 113–140.

Jacoby, Neil H. "The Multinational Corporation." *The Center Magazine* 3 (May 1970): 37–55.

Kindleberger, Charles P., ed. *The International Corporation.* Cambridge, Mass.: The M. I. T. Press, 1970.

Latham, Earl. "The Body Politic of the Corporation." In *The Corporation in Modern Society.* Edited by Edward S. Mason. Cambridge, Mass.: Harvard University Press, 1969. Pp. 218–236.

Lilienthal, David E. *The Multinational Corporation.* New York: Development and Resources Corporation, 1960.

Litvak, Isaiah A., and Maule, Christopher J. "The Multinational Firm: Some Perspectives." In *The Multinational Firm and the Nation State.* Edited by Gilles Paquet. Don Mills, Ontario: Collier-Macmillan Canada, 1972. Pp. 20–34.

Mason, Edward S., ed. *The Corporation in Modern Society.* Cambridge, Mass.: Harvard University Press, 1959.

Mikesell, Raymond F., et al. *Foreign Investment in the Petroleum and Mineral Industries: Case Studies of Investor-Host Country Relations.* Published for Resources for the Future, Inc. Baltimore and London: Johns Hopkins Press, 1971.

Modelski, G. "The Corporation in World Society." In *The Year Book of World Affairs 1968.* Edited by George W. Keeton and Georg Schwarzenberg. London: Stevens, 1968. Pp. 64–79.

Moran, Theodore H. "Transnational Strategies of Protection and Defense by Multinational Corporations: Spreading the Risk and Raising the Cost for Nationalization in Natural Resources." *International Organization* 27 (Spring 1973): 273–287.

Paquet, Gilles, ed. *The Multinational Firm and the Nation State.* Don Mills, Ontario: Collier-Macmillan Canada, 1972.

Perlmutter, Howard V. "The Tortuous Evolution of the Multinational Corporation." In *World Business: Promise and Problems.* Edited by Courtney C. Brown. New York: The Macmillan Company, 1970. Pp. 66–82.

Pinelo, Adalberto. *The Multinational Corporation as a Force in Latin American Politics: A Case Study of the International Petroleum Company in Peru.* Praeger Special Studies in International Economics and Development. New York: Praeger Publishers, 1973.

Sturm, Hobert P., and Wormuth, Francis D. "The International Power Elite." *Monthly Review* 11 (December 1959): 282–287.

Sweezy, Paul M., and Magdoff, Harry. "Notes on the Multinational Corporation." *Monthly Review* 21 (October 1969): 1–13; (November 1969): 1–13.

United Nations. Department of Economic and Social Affairs. *Multinational Corporations in World Development.* UN Doc. ST/ECA/190. New York: 1973.

Vernon, Raymond. *Sovereignty at Bay: The Multinational Spread of U. S. Enterprises.* New York: Basic Books, 1971.

Waltz, Kenneth N. "The Myth of National Independence." In *The International Corporation.* Edited by Charles P. Kindleberger. Cambridge, Mass.: The M. I. T. Press, 1970. Pp. 205–223.

West, Richard. *River of Tears: The Rise of the Rio Tinto-Zinc Mining Corporation.* London: Earth Island, 1972.

Other General Works Cited in This Study

Bachrach, Peter, and Baratz, Morton. "The Two Faces of Power." *American Political Science Review* 56 (1962): 947–952.

Bell, J. Bowyer. *The Myth of the Guerrilla: Revolutionary Theory and Malpractice.* New York: Alfred A. Knopf, 1971.

Deutsch, Karl W. *The Nerves of Government.* New York: The Free Press, 1966.

Deutscher, Isaac. *Marxism in Our Time.* Berkeley, Calif.: Ramparts Press, 1971.

Djilas, Milovan. *The New Class.* New York: Praeger, 1959.

Jalée, Pierre. *The Pillage of the Third World.* New York: Monthly Review Press, 1968.

Kaplan, Morton A. "Systems Theory." In *Contemporary Political Analysis.* Edited by James C. Charlesworth. New York: The Free Press, 1967. Pp. 150–163.

Lenin, V. I. *What Is To Be Done?* New York: International Publishers, 1943.

Lynd, Robert S. "Power in American Society as Resource and Problem." In *Problems of Power in American Democracy.* Edited by Arthur Kornhauser. Detroit: Wayne State University Press, 1959. Pp. 1–45.

McConnell, Grant. *Private Power and American Democracy.* New York: Vintage Books, 1966.

Macpherson, C. B. *The Real World of Democracy.* London: Oxford University Press, 1966.

Marcuse, Herbert. *Soviet Marxism.* New York: Vintage Books, 1961.

Myrdal, Gunnar. *An International Economy.* New York: Harper and Bros., 1956.

————. *Asian Drama: An Inquiry into the Poverty of Nations.* 3 vols. New York: Random House, 1968.

Orzak, Louis H. "The Dusseldorf Agreement: A Study of the Organization of Power and Planning." *Political Science Quarterly* 65 (September 1950): 393–414.

Sabine, George H. *A History of Political Theory.* Rev. ed. New York: Henry Holt, 1950.

Sweezy, Paul, and Bettelheim, Charles. *On the Transition to Socialism.* New York and London: Monthly Review Press, 1971.

Trotsky, Leon. *The Revolution Betrayed.* Translated by Max Eastman. 1937 Reprint. New York: Pioneer Publishers, 1945.

Works Concerning Central and Southern Africa,
and the Copper Industry, either Cited
or Consulted in the Preparation of This Study

"Africa's Biggest Business." *News/Check,* September 1, 1967, pp. 13–18.

Allan, William. *The African Husbandman.* Edinburgh: 1965.

Alport, Lord. *The Sudden Assignment.* London: Hodder and Stoughton, 1965.

Anglin, Douglas G. "Confrontation in Southern Africa: Zambia and Portugal." *International Journal* 25 (Summer 1970): 497–517.

Austin, Dennis. *Britain and South Africa.* London: Oxford University Press, 1966.

Baldwin, Robert E. *Economic Development and Export Growth: A Study of Northern Rhodesia, 1920–1960.* Berkeley and Los Angeles: University of California Press, 1966.

Bancroft, J. Austen. *Mining in Northern Rhodesia: A Chronicle of Mineral Exploration and Mining Development.* Arranged and Prepared by T. D. Guernsey. London: The British South Africa Company, 1961.

Barber, James. *Rhodesia: The Road to Rebellion.* London and New York: Oxford University Press, 1967.

Barber, William J. *The Economy of British Central Africa: A Case Study of Economic Development in a Dualistic Society.* London: Oxford University Press, 1961.

Barnes, J. A. *Politics in a Changing Society: A Political History of the Fort Jameson Ngoni.* Cape Town: Oxford University Press, 1954.

Bates, Robert H. *Patterns of Uneven Development: Causes and Consequences in Zambia.* The Social Science Foundation and Graduate School of International Studies, University of Denver, Monograph Series in World Affairs. Denver, Colo., 1974.

————. *Unions, Parties, and Political Development: A Study of Mineworkers in Zambia.* New Haven and London: Yale University Press, 1971.

Bernfield, Seymour S., in collaboration with Hochschild, Harold K. "A Short History of American Metal Climax, Inc." In *1887–1962 American Metal Climax, Inc. World Atlas.* Chicago: Rand McNally and Company, 1962.

Bohm, Peter. *Pricing of Copper in International Trade: A Case Study of the Price Stabilization Problem.* Stockholm: The Economic Research Institute, 1968.

Booth, Judge William H. "Report: International Commission of Jurists." Windhoek, Namibia, March 1972. Mimeographed.

Bostock, Mark, and Harvey, Charles, eds. *Economic Independence and Zambian Copper: A Case Study of Foreign Investment.* Praeger Special Studies in International Economics and Development. New York: Praeger, 1972.

Bostock, R. M., Murray, D. H., and Harvey, C. *Anatomy of the Zambia Copper Nationalisation.* An Occasional Paper by Maxwell Stamp (Africa) Limited. Reprinted from *African Development.* London, 1970.

Bowman, Larry W. *Politics in Rhodesia: White Power in an African State.* Cambridge, Mass.: Harvard University Press, 1973.

————. "The Subordinate State System of Southern Africa." *International Studies Quarterly* 12 (September 1968): 231–261.

Brackenbury and Co., M. C. *Dealing on London Metal Exchange 1966.* M. C. Brackenbury and Co., 1966.

Bradley, Kenneth. *Copper Venture: The Discovery and Development of Roan Antelope and Mufulira.* London: Mufulira Copper Mines Limited and Roan Antelope Copper Mines Limited, 1952.

Brelsford, W. V. *The Tribes of Zambia.* 2d ed. Lusaka: Government Printer, 1965.

Brown, Martin S., and Butler, John. *The Production, Marketing, and Consumption of Copper and Aluminum.* Praeger Special Studies in International Economics and Development. New York: Praeger, 1968.

Burawoy, Michael. "Another Look at the Mineworker." *African Social Research,* no. 14 (December 1972), pp. 239–287.

——. *The Colour of Class on the Copper Mines: From African Advancement to Zambianization.* Zambian Papers, No. 7. Manchester: Manchester University Press on behalf of The Institute for African Studies, University of Zambia, 1972.

Caplan, Gerald L. "Barotseland: The Secessionist Challenge to Zambia." *The Journal of Modern African Studies* 6 (October 1968): 343–360.

——. *The Elites of Barotseland, 1878–1969.* Berkeley, Los Angeles, London: University of California Press, 1970.

Cervenka, Zdenek, ed. *Land-locked Countries of Africa.* Uppsala: The Scandinavian Institute of African Studies, 1973.

Clausen, Lars. "On Attitudes Towards Industrial Conflict in Zambian Industry." *African Social Research,* no. 2 (December 1966), pp.117–138.

Clegg, Edward. *Race and Politics: Partnership in the Federation of Rhodesia and Nyasaland.* London: Oxford University Press, 1960.

Coleman, Francis L. *The Northern Rhodesia Copperbelt 1899–1962: Technological Development up to the End of the Central African Federation.* Manchester: Manchester University Press, 1971.

Colson, Elizabeth. *The Social Consequences of Resettlement.* Kariba Studies IV. Manchester: Manchester University Press, 1971.

Colson, Elizabeth, and Gluckman, Max, eds. *Seven Tribes of British Central Africa.* London: Oxford University Press, 1951.

Coombe, Trevor. "The Origins of Secondary Education in Zambia." Parts I, II, and III, *African Social Research,* no. 3 (June 1967), pp. 173–205, no. 4 (December 1967), pp. 283–315, and no. 5 (June 1968), pp. 365–405.

Courtney, Winifred, and Davis, Jennifer. *Namibia: United States Corporate Involvement.* The Africa Fund (associated with the American Committee on Africa) published in cooperation with The Programme to Combat Racism of the World Council of Churches. New York, March 1972.

Creighton, T. R. M. *The Anatomy of Partnership: Southern Rhodesia and the Central African Federation.* London: Faber, 1960.

Curtin, T. R. C. "Total Sanctions and Economic Development in Rhodesia." *Journal of Commonwealth Political Studies* 7 (July 1969): 126–131.

Davidson, J. W. *The Northern Rhodesian Legislative Council.* London: Faber and Faber, 1948.

Davis, D. Hywel, ed. *Zambia in Maps.* London: University of London Press, 1971.

Davis, J. Merle, ed. *Modern Industry and the African: An Enquiry into the Effect of the Copper Mines of Central Africa upon Native Society and the Work of Christian Missions.* 2d ed. With a new Introduction by Robert I. Rotberg. London: Frank Cass & Co., 1967.

De Vletter, D. R. "Zambia's Mineral Industry and Its Position Amongst World's Major Copper Producers." *Geologie en Mijnbouw* 51 (May-June 1972): 251–263. Special Zambia Issue.

————. Director, Metals and Minerals Development Unit. "Mining Costs." Mimeographed. Ministry of Lands and Mines, April 24, 1968.

Dotson, Floyd, and Dotson, Lillian O. *The Indian Minority of Zambia, Rhodesia, and Malawi.* New Haven: Yale University Press, 1968.

Dresang, Dennis L. "Entrepreneurialism and Development Administration." *Administrative Science Quarterly* 18 (March 1973): 76–85.

————. "Entrepreneurialism and Development Administration in Zambia." *The African Review* 1 (January 1972): 91–117.

————. "The Civil Service in Zambia." Mimeographed. 1969.

Drysdall, A. R., and Langevad, E. J. Republic of Zambia, Ministry of State Participation, Geological Survey Department. *The Mines and Minerals Act, 1969, and The Mineral Tax Act, 1970.* Economic Report No. 26. Lusaka: 1970.

Elkan, Walter. *Migrants and Proletarians: Urban Labour in the Economic Development of Uganda.* London: Oxford University Press, 1960.

Elliott, Charles, ed. *Constraints on the Economic Development of Zambia.* Nairobi: Oxford University Press, 1971.

Epstein, A. L. *Politics in an Urban African Community.* Manchester: Manchester University Press on behalf of the Rhodes-Livingstone Institute, Northern Rhodesia, 1958.

Faber, M. L. O., and Potter, J. G., eds. *Towards Economic Independence: Papers on the Nationalisation of the Copper Industry in Zambia.* University of Cambridge Department of Applied Economics, Occasional Paper 23. Cambridge: The Cambridge University Press, 1971.

Fagan, Brian M., ed. *A Short History of Zambia (from the Earliest Times until A. D. 1900).* Nairobi: Oxford University Press, 1966.

Fortman, Bastiaan de Gaay, ed. *After Mulungushi: The Economics of Zambian Humanism.* Nairobi: East Africa Publishing House, 1969.

Franck, Thomas M. *Race and Nationalism: The Struggle for Power in Rhodesia–Nyasaland.* New York: Fordham University Press, 1960.

Franklin, Harry. *Unholy Wedlock: The Failure of the Central African Federation.* London: George Allen and Unwin, 1963.

Fry, James. "Economic Independence in Zambia: A Review Article." *African Social Research,* no. 13 (June 1972), pp. 207–216.

Gann, L. H. *A History of Northern Rhodesia: Early Days to 1953.* London: Chatto & Windus, 1964.

————. *The Birth of a Plural Society: The Development of Northern Rhodesia under the British South Africa Company, 1894–1914.* Manchester: Manchester University Press, 1958.

————. "The Northern Rhodesian Copper Industry and the World of Copper: 1923–1952." *The Rhodes-Livingstone Journal* 18 (1955): 1–18.

Garlick, W. G. "How the Copperbelt Orebodies Were Formed." *Horizon* (August 1959), pp. 10–19.

Gelfand, Michael. *Northern Rhodesia in the Days of the Charter: A Medical and Social Study, 1878–1924.* Oxford: Basil Blackwell, 1961.

Gertzel, Cherry; Mutukwa, Kasuka; Scott, Ian, and Wallis, Malcolm. "Zambia's Final Experience of Inter-Party Elections: The By-Elections of December 1971." *Kroniek van Afrika* (June 1972), pp. 57–77.

Gervasi, Sean. *Industrialization, Foreign Capital and Forced Labour in South Africa.* Unit on Apartheid, Department of Political and Security Council Affairs, United Nations, ST/PSCA/Ser.A/10. New York, 1970.

Good, Robert C. *U. D. I.: The International Politics of the Rhodesian Rebellion.* Princeton: Princeton University Press, 1973.

Gray, Richard. *The Two Nations: Aspects of the Development of Race Relations in the Rhodesias and Nyasaland.* London: Oxford University Press, 1960.

Gregory, Theodore. *Ernest Oppenheimer and the Economic Development of Southern Africa.* Cape Town: Oxford University Press, 1962.

Grundy, Kenneth W. "The 'Southern Border' of Africa." In *African Boundary Problems.* Edited by Carl Gösta Widstrand. Uppsala: The Scandinavian Institute of African Studies, 1969. Pp. 119–160.

Haefele, Edwin T., and Steinberg, Eleanor B. *Government Controls on Transport: An African Case.* Washington, D. C.: The Brookings Institution, 1965.

Hall, Richard. *The High Price of Principles: Kaunda and the White South.* London: Hodder and Stoughton, 1969.

———. *Zambia.* New York: Praeger, 1965.

Hance, William, ed. *Southern Africa and the United States.* New York: Columbia University Press, 1968.

Hanna, A. J. *The Beginnings of Nyasaland and North-Eastern Rhodesia, 1859-95.* Oxford: The Clarendon Press, 1956.

———. *The Story of the Rhodesias and Nyasaland.* 2d rev. ed. London: Faber and Faber, 1965.

"Harry Oppenheimer's Industrial Africa." *Fortune* (May 1960), pp. 152-165.

Hazlewood, Arthur. "The Economics of Federation and Dissolution in Central Africa." In *African Integration and Disintegration: Case Studies in Economic and Political Union.* Edited by Arthur Hazlewood. London: Oxford University Press, 1967. Pp. 185–250.

Hazlewood, Arthur, and Henderson, P. D. *Nyasaland: The Economics of Federation.* Oxford: Basil Blackwell, 1960.

Heath, K. C. G. "Making a Desert Give up Its Treasures." *Optima* 17 (June 1967): 75–82.

———. "New Patterns of World Mining." *Optima* 19 (March 1969): 15–31.

Heisler, Helmuth. "A Class of Target-Proletarians." *Journal of Asian and African Studies* 5 (July 1970): 161–175.

Hellen, John A. *Rural Economic Development in Zambia, 1890–1964.* African Studies Center of the Ifo Institute for Economic Research, Munich, Afrika-Studien No. 32. Munich: Weltforum Verlag, 1968.

Henderson, Ian. "The Origins of Nationalism in East and Central Africa: The Zambian Case." *Journal of African History* 11 (1970): 591–603.

Herfindahl, Orris C. *Copper Costs and Prices: 1870–1957.* Published for Resources for the Future, Inc. Baltimore: The Johns Hopkins Press, 1959.

Hochschild, Harold K. "The Copper Mining Industry of Northern Rhodesia." Paper read at discussion group on "Overseas Business, Economic Development and the Cold War," Harvard Business School Association, 50th Anniversary Conference, September 5, 1958. Mimeographed.

Horrell, Muriel. *South-West Africa.* Johannesburg: South African Institute of Race Relations, 1967.

"The House That Harry Builds." *The Financial Mail of Zambia,* July 22, 1966, pp. 217–220.

Houser, George M. "Statement to the UN Council for Namibia." Mimeographed. New York: January 19, 1972.

"How Safe Is Zambia's Copper." *Business and Economy of Central and East Africa* (July 1967): pp. 8–10.

Jackman, Mary Elizabeth. *Recent Population Movements in Zambia.* Zambian

Papers, no. 8. Manchester: Manchester University Press, on behalf of the Institute for African Studies, University of Zambia, 1973.

Johns, Sheridan. "Para-Statal Bodies in Zambia: Problems and Prospects." In *Socioeconomic Development in Dual Economies: The Example of Zambia.* Edited by Heide and Udo Ernst-Simonis. Munich: 1971. Pp. 217–251.

Jolly, Richard. "The Seers Report in Retrospect." *African Social Research,* no. 11 (June 1971), pp. 1–26.

Kapferer, Bruce. *Strategy and Transaction in an African Factory.* Manchester: Manchester University Press, 1972.

Kaunda, Kenneth. *A Humanist in Africa: Letters to Colin Morris from Kenneth Kaunda, President of Zambia.* London: Longmans, Green, 1966.

———. "The Responsibilities of Leadership." *Third World* 2 (March 1973): 11–16.

———. *Zambia Shall Be Free: An Autobiography.* London: Heinemann, 1962.

———. "Zambia's Aim—Loyalty between Government and People." *Optima* 16 (June 1966): 59–64.

———. *Humanism in Zambia and a Guide to Its Implementation.* Lusaka: Government Printer, n.d.

Kay, George. *A Social Geography of Zambia.* London: University of London Press, 1967.

Keatley, Patrick. *The Politics of Partnership.* Penguin Books, 1963.

Legum, Colin, and Legum, Margaret. *South Africa: Crisis for the West.* London: Pall Mall Press, 1964.

Legum, Colin, ed. *Zambia: Independence and Beyond: The Speeches of Kenneth Kaunda.* London: Nelson, 1966.

Legum, Colin, and Drysdale, John, eds. *Africa Contemporary Record: Annual Survey and Documents, 1968–69.* London: Africa Research Limited, 1969.

———. *Africa Contemporary Record: Annual Survey and Documents, 1969–70.* Exeter: Africa Research Limited, 1970.

Legum, Colin, and Hughes, Anthony, eds. *Africa Contemporary Record: Annual Survey and Documents, 1970–71.* London: Rex Collings, 1971.

———. *Africa Contemporary Record: Annual Survey and Documents, 1971–72.* London: Rex Collings, 1972.

Leys, Colin. *European Politics in Southern Rhodesia.* Oxford: The Clarendon Press, 1959.

Leys, Colin, and Pratt, Cranford, eds. *A New Deal in Central Africa.* New York: Praeger, 1960.

Lombard, C. Stephen. "Agriculture in Zambia since Independence." *East Africa Journal* 8 (March 1971): 17–19.

———. "Farming Co-operatives in the Development of Zambian Agriculture." *The Journal of Modern African Studies* 19 (July 1972): 294–299.

———. *The Growth of Co-operatives in Zambia, 1914–71.* Zambian Papers, no. 6. Manchester: Manchester University Press on behalf of the Institute for African Studies, University of Zambia, 1971.

Long, Norman. *Social Change and the Individual.* Manchester: Manchester University Press, 1968.

Maimbo, Fabian J. M., and Fry, James. "An Investigation into the Change in Terms of Trade between the Rural and Urban Sectors of Zambia." *African Social Research,* no. 12 (December 1971), pp. 95–110.

Makings, S. M. "Agricultural Change in Northern Rhodesia/Zambia, 1945–1965." *Stanford Food Research Institute Studies* 6 (1966): 195–247.

Martin, Antony. *Minding Their Own Business: Zambia's Struggle against Western Control.* London: Hutchinson, 1972.

Mason, Philip. *Year of Decision: Rhodesia and Nyasaland, 1960.* London: Oxford University Press, 1960.

Meebelo, Henry S. *Reaction to Colonialism: A Prelude to the Politics of Independence in Northern Zambia, 1893–1939.* Manchester: Manchester University Press, 1971.

Meredith, Martin. "Zambia: Kaunda on Top." *Africa Report* 15 (May 1970): 5–6.

Mitchell, J. Clyde. *The Kalela Dance: Aspects of Social Relationships among Urban Africans in Northern Rhodesia.* The Rhodes-Livingstone Papers, no. 27. Manchester: Manchester University Press, 1956.

Mitchell, J. Clyde, ed. *Social Networks in Urban Situations.* Manchester: Manchester University Press, 1969.

Mitchell, James. "Electricity Supply in Zambia." Mimeographed. Copperbelt Power Company, 1968.

Molteno, Robert. "Zambia and the One Party State." *East Africa Journal* 9 (February 1972): 6–18.

Mtshali, B. V. "Zambia's Foreign Policy." *Current History* 58 (March 1970): 148–153, 177–179.

Mulaisho, D. C. "Address to the New York Section of the American Institute of Mining, Metallurgical and Petroleum Engineers." September 21, 1972. Mimeographed.

Mulford, David C. *The Northern Rhodesia General Election, 1962.* Nairobi: Oxford University Press, 1964.

———. *Zambia: The Politics of Independence, 1957–1964.* London: Oxford University Press, 1967.

Musakanya, Valentine. "Where To Spend Our Scarce Resources." *African Development* (October 1970), pp. Z. 18–20.

Mwaanga, Vernon J. "Zambia's Policy toward Southern Africa." In *Southern Africa in Perspective.* Edited by Christian P. Potholm and Richard Dale. New York: The Free Press, 1972. Pp. 234–241.

Mwanakatwe, J. M. *The Growth of Education in Zambia since Independence.* Nairobi: Oxford University Press, 1968.

Newman, Barry. "Namibia: A Major Test for the UN." *The Wall Street Journal*, March 24, 1972.

Ohadike, Patrick O. *Development of and Factors in the Employment of African Migrants in the Copper Mines of Zambia 1940–66.* Zambian Papers, no.4. Manchester: Manchester University Press, on behalf of the Institute of Social Research, University of Zambia, 1969.

Oppenheimer, H. F. "Sir Ernest Oppenheimer: A Portrait by His Son." *Optima* 17 (September 1967): 95–103.

Ostrander, F. Taylor. "The Place of Minerals in Economic Development." A talk as presented to the Council of Economics at the 92nd Annual Meeting of the American Institute of Mining, Metallurgical and Petroleum Engineers, Dallas, Texas, February 27, 1963.

———. "The Role of Foreign Private Capital in Africa." In *Southern Africa in Transition.* Edited by John A. Davis and James K. Baker. Published for the American Society of African Culture. New York: Praeger, 1966. Pp. 347–361.

———. "Zambia in the Aftermath of Rhodesian UDI: Logistical and Economic Problems." *African Forum* 2 (Winter 1967): 50–65.

Ostrander, F. Taylor, and Kloman, Erasmus. "The Corporate Structure of Rhodesian Copperbelt Mining Enterprise." Mimeographed. New York: American Metal Climax, Inc., 1962.

Phillipson, D. W. *Historical Notes on Political Development in Zambia.* Lusaka: Government Printer, 1972.

Pinkney, E. T. "Torco: The Key to 'Unyielding' Copper Ores." *'Optima* 17 (June 1967): 83–87.

Prain, Ronald L. "Building on a Mineral Foundation in Central Africa." Mimeographed. 1957.

———. *The Copperbelt of Northern Rhodesia.* The Henry Morley Lecture. London: The Royal Society of Arts, 1955.

———. *The Future Availability of Copper Supplies.* An Address to The Institute of Metals, Autumn Meeting, Amsterdam, 1970.

———. *The International Outlook for Copper.* American Metal Market Forum, London, 1971.

———. "The Problem of African Advancement on the Copperbelt of Northern Rhodesia." Transcript of Address Given by Ronald L. Prain, O. B. E. at a Joint Meeting of the Royal African Society and the Royal Empire Society, London, November 26, 1953.

———. *Selected Papers.* London: The Rhodesian Selection Trust Group, 1958, 1961. Vol. 1, *1953–1957;* Vol. 2, *1958–1960.*

———. *Selected Papers..* London: The RST Group, 1964, 1968. Vol. 3, *1961-1964;* Vol. 4, *1964–1967.*

———. "Speech by Sir Ronald Prain at Kafue Polder Lunch," July 28, 1965. Mimeographed.

"Profile of Jean Vuillequez." *Horizon* (Copy).

"Profile: Sir Ronald Prain." *Optima* 23 (March 1973): 52–53.

Radmann, Wolf. "Intergovernmental Cooperation: The Case of Foreign Investments in Zambia and Chile." Presented at the Fourteenth Annual Meeting of the African Studies Association, Denver, November 1971.

Rake, Alan. "Railways Race for the Copper Trade." *African Development* (August 1971), pp. 9–11.

Ranger, T. O. *The Agricultural History of Zambia.* Lusaka: National Educational Company of Zambia, 1971.

Ranger, T. O., ed. *Aspects of Central African History.* London: Heinemann, 1968.

Rasmussen, Thomas. "Political Competition and One-Party Dominance in Zambia." *The Journal of Modern African Studies* 7 (October 1969): 407–424.

Raven, Faith. *Central Africa: Background to Argument.* London: The Africa Publications Trust, 1960.

Richards, Audrey I. *Land, Labour and Diet in Northern Rhodesia: An Economic Study of the Bemba Tribe.* London: Oxford University Press, 1939.

Robie, Edward H., ed. *Economics of the Mineral Industries: A Series of Articles by Specialists.* Seeley W. Mudd Series. New York: The American Institute of Mining, Metallurgical and Petroleum Engineers, Inc. 1959.

Romnicianu, Michel. "Management Agreements: Are They Really Necessary?" *Enterprise.* The Indeco Journal (First Quarter, 1972), pp. 8–11.

Rotberg, Robert I. *Christian Missionaries and the Creation of Northern Rhodesia, 1880–1924.* Princeton: Princeton University Press, 1965.

———. "The Lenshina Movement of Northern Rhodesia." *The Rhodes-Livingstone Journal* 29 (1963): 63–78.

———. *The Rise of Nationalism in Central Africa: The Making of Malawi and Zambia, 1873–1964.* Cambridge, Mass.: Harvard University Press, 1965.

———. "Tribalism and Politics in Zambia." *Africa Report* 12 (December 1967): 29–35.

Rothchild, Donald. "Intersectional Conflicts and Resource Allocation in Zambia." Paper read at the Fourteenth Annual Meeting of the African Studies Association, November 1971, Denver, Colorado. Mimeographed.

———. "Rhodesian Rebellion and African Response." *Africa Quarterly* 6 (1966): 184–196.

———. "Rural-Urban Inequities and Resource Allocation in Zambia." *Journal of Commonwealth Political Studies* 10 (1972): 222–242.

———.*Toward Unity in Africa: A Study of Federalism in British Africa.* Washington, D. C.: Public Affairs Press, 1960.

"Rural-Urban Terms of Trade in Zambia: Editorial Note." *African Social Research*, no. 12 (December 1971), pp. ix-x.

Sandbrook, Richard, "The Working Class in the Future of the Third World." *World Politics* 25 (April 1973): 448–478.

Scarritt, James R. "Elite Values, Ideology, and Power in Post-Independence Zambia." *African Studies Review* 14 (April 1971): 31–54.

———. "Political Values and the Political Process in Zambia." *Bulletin* (University of Zambia Institute for Social Research), no. 1 (1966), pp. 59–78.

———, and Hatter, John L. "Racial and Ethnic Conflict in Zambia." *Studies in Race and Nations*, 2, 2 (1970–1971): 1–30. Center on International Race Relations, University of Denver.

Scott, Ian, and Molteno, Robert. "The Zambian General Elections." *Africa Report* 14 (January 1969): 42–47.

Sicely, E. M. "The Development of the Kafue Flats." An Address to the Zambian Association for National Affairs, June 25, 1965. Mimeographed.

Simmance, Alan J. F. *Urbanization in Zambia.* An International Urbanization Survey Report to the Ford Foundation. New York: February 1972.

Skelton, Alex. "Copper." In *International Control in the Non-Ferrous Metals.* By William Yandell Elliott et al. New York: Macmillan, 1937. Pp. 363-536.

Skinner, Walter E., comp. *Mining Industry Year Book.* London: annual.

Sklar, Richard L. "Zambia's Response to U. D. I." *Mawazo* 1 (June 1968): 11–32.

Slinn, Peter. "Commercial Concessions and Politics during the Colonial Period: The Role of the British South Africa Company in Northern Rhodesia, 1890–1964." *African Affairs* 70 (October 1971): 365-384.

Soremekun, Fola. "Kenneth Kaunda's Cosmic Neo-Humanism." *Geneve-Afrique* 9, 2 (1970): 1–28.

———. "The Challenge of Nation-Building: Neo-Humanism and Politics in Zambia, 1967–1969." *Geneve-Afrique,* 9, 1 (1970): 1–39.

Stokes, Eric, and Brown, Richard, eds. *The Zambesian Past: Studies in Central African History.* Manchester: Manchester University Press, 1966.

Strauss, S. D. "Marketing of Nonferrous Metals and Ores." *Economics of the Mineral Industries: A Series of Articles by Specialists.* Edited by Edward H. Robie. Seeley W. Mudd Series. New York: The American Institute of Mining, Metallurgical, and Petroleum Engineers, Inc., 1959. Pp. 275-298.

Stanford Research Institute, Management and Social Systems Area. *Final Report Tanzania-Zambia Highway Study I: Summary Report.* Prepared for Republics of Zambia and Tanzania and U. S. Agency for International Development.

Sutcliffe, R. B. "The Political Economy of Rhodesia Sanctions." *Journal of Commonwealth Political Studies.* 7 (July 1969): 113–125.
————. "Zambia and the Strains of UDI." *The World Today* 23 (December 1967): 506–511.
Sutulov, Alexander. *The Soviet Challenge in Base Metals.* Salt Lake City: The University of Utah Printing Services, 1971.
Thompson, C. H., and Woodruff, H. W. *Economic Development in Rhodesia and Nyasaland.* London: Dennis Dobson, 1954.
————. "Provincial and Local Government in Zambia." *Journal of Administration* 9 (January 1970): 23–35.
    438–445.
Tordoff, William. "Provincial and Local Government in Zambia." *Journal of Administration* 9 (January 1970): 23–35.
Tordoff, William, ed. *Politics in Zambia.* Manchester: Manchester University Press, 1974; Berkeley, Los Angeles, London: University of California Press, 1974.
United Nations Association of the U. S. A. *Southern Africa: Proposals for Americans.* A Report of a National Policy Panel established by the United Nations Association of the U. S. A. New York, 1971.
United Society for Christian Literature. *Black Government: A Discussion between Kenneth Kaunda and Colin Morris.* Lusaka: United Society for Christian Literature, 1960.
Vilakazi, Absolom L. "Non-Governmental Agencies and Their Role in Development in Africa: A Case Study." *African Studies Review* 13 (September 1970): 169–202.
Waldstein, Nan S. "The Struggle for African Advancement within the Copper Industry of Northern Rhodesia." Mimeographed. Cambridge, Mass.: Center for International Studies of the Massachusetts Institute of Technology, 1957.
Watson, William. *Tribal Cohesion in a Money Economy: A Study of the Mambwe People of Northern Rhodesia.* Manchester: Manchester University Press, 1958.
Weiss, Ruth. "Strife in Zambia." *Venture* 24 (April 1972): 19–24.
Welensky, Sir Roy. *Welensky's 4,000 Days: The Life and Death of the Federation of Rhodesia and Nyasaland.* London: Collins, 1964.
West, Michael. "Price Stability for Copper: The Prospects and Problems." *Optima* 23 (September 1973): 149–158.
Williams, Shirley. *Central Africa: The Economics of Inequality.* Fabian Commonwealth Bureau. London: Fabian Society, 1960.
Willis, A. J. *An Introduction to the History of Central Africa.* 2d ed. London: Oxford University Press, 1967.
Wilson, Godfrey, and Wilson, Monica. *The Analysis of Social Change.* Cambridge: Cambridge University Press, 1945; paperback ed., 1968.
Wolfe, Alvin W. "Capital and the Congo." In *Southern Africa in Transition.* Edited by John A. Davis and James K. Baker. Published for the American Society of African Culture. London: Pall Mall, 1966. Pp. 362–377.
————. "The African Mineral Industry: Evolution of a Supranational Level of Integration." *Social Problems* 2 (Fall 1963): 153–164.
World Council of Churches. *Cabora Bassa and the Struggle for Southern Africa.* London, 1971.
Young, C. E. "Rural-Urban Terms of Trade." *African Social Research,* no. 12 (December 1971), pp. 91–94.

Young, Ralph A. "Zambia's Independence Constitution." Mimeo-graphed. The University of Zambia, Department of Political Science.
Yu, George T. "Working on the Railroad: China and the Tanzania-Zambia Railway." *Asian Survey* 11 (November 1971): 1101–1117.
"Zambia after the Mufulira mine disaster." *African Development* (December 1970), p.8.

Zelniker, Shimshon. "Changing Patterns of Trade Unionism: The Zambian Case, 1948–1964." Ph.D. dissertation, University of California, Los Angeles, 1970.
Zulu, J. B. *Zambian Humanism: Some Major Spiritual and Economic Challenges.* Lusaka: National Educational Company of Zambia, 1970.

Other Works Relating to Africa Cited in This Study

Amsden, Alice Hoffenberg. *International Firms and Labour in Kenya: 1945-70.* London: Frank Cass, 1971.
Beckett, Paul A. "Algeria vs. Fanon: The Theory of Revolutionary Decolonization and the Algerian Experience." *The Western Political Quarterly* 26 (March 1973): 5–27.
Berg, E. J. "Backward-Sloping Labor Supply Functions in Dual Economies: The Africa Case." *The Quarterly Journal of Economics* 75 (August 1961): 468–492.
Berg, Elliot J., and Butler, Jeffrey. "Trade Unions." In *Political Parties and National Integration in Tropical Africa.* Edited by James S. Coleman and Carl G. Rosberg, Jr. Berkeley and Los Angeles: University of California Press, 1964. Pp. 340–381.
Clegg, Ian. *Workers' Self-Management in Algeria.* New York and London: Monthly Review Press, 1971.
De Gregori, Thomas R. *Technology and the Economic Development of the Tropical African Frontier.* Cleveland: The Press of Case Western Reserve University, 1969.
Dumont, René. *False Start in Africa.* Translated by Phyllis Nauts Ott. 2d rev. ed. New York: Praeger, 1969.
Gott, Richard. *Mobutu's Congo.* Fabian Research Series No. 266. London: Fabian Society, 1968.
Green, Reginald H., and Seidman, Ann. *Unity or Poverty: The Economics of Pan-Africanism.* Baltimore: Penguin Books, 1962.
Hailey, Lord. *An African Survey.* Rev. ed. London: Oxford University Press, 1957.
Hance, William. *The Geography of Modern Africa.* New York: Columbia University Press, 1964.
Kilson, Martin. "African Political Change and the Modernisation Process." *The Journal of Modern African Studies* 1 (1963): 425–440.
Lewis, W. Arthur. *Politics in West Africa.* London: George Allen and Unwin, 1965.
Lofchie, Michael F. "Observations on Social and Institutional Change in Independent Africa." In *The State of the Nations: Constraints on Development in Independent Africa.* Edited by Michael F. Lofchie. Berkeley, Los Angeles, London: University of California Press, 1971. Pp. 261–283.
Nyerere, Julius K. *Freedom and Socialism.* Dar es Salaam: Oxford University Press, 1968.

Sklar, Richard L. "Contradictions in the Nigerian Political System." *The Journal of Modern African Studies* 3 (1965): 201–213.

———. *Nigerian Political Parties: Power in an Emergent African Nation.* Princeton: Princeton University Press, 1963.

———. "Political Science and National Integration—A Radical Approach." *The Journal of Modern African Studies* 5 (1967): 1–11.

Governmental Documents and Publications Cited or Consulted

Congo, The Democratic Republic of the, Ministere Des Affaires Etrangers. "Final Joint Communique." Mimeographed. July 16, 1966.

International Bank for Reconstruction and Development; International Development Association. *World Bank/IDA Annual Report.* Washington, D. C., 1973.

International Labour Office, United Nations Development Programme, Technical Assistance Sector. *Report to the Government of Zambia on Incomes, Wages and Prices in Zambia: Policy and Machinery.* The Cabinet Office. Lusaka, 1969.

Lusaka Inter-Governmental Copper Conference. Papers submitted by the Zambian mining companies, LICC/WP (MC)/1–10. Mimeographed.

———. Press Releases. Mimeographed.

Northern Rhodesia. "Agreement between the Government of Southern Rhodesia and the Government of Northern Rhodesia relating to the Rhodesia Railways." *Northern Rhodesia Gazette,* December 13, 1963.

———. *The British South Africa Company's Claims to Mineral Royalties in Northern Rhodesia.* Lusaka: Government Printer, 1964.

———. *Mine Townships.* Chapter 121 of the Laws. Lusaka: Government Printer, 1961.

———. *Report of the Board of Inquiry Appointed to Inquire into the Advancement of Africans in the Copper Industry in Northern Rhodesia.* Lusaka: Government Printer, 1954.

———. *Report of the Commission Appointed to Inquire into the Mining Industry in Northern Rhodesia.* Lusaka: Government Printer, 1962.

———. *Report of the Commission Appointed to Inquire into the Stoppage in the Mining Industry in Northern Rhodesia in July, 1957, and to Make Recommendations for the Avoidance and Quick Settlement of Disputes in the Industry.* Lusaka: Government Printer, 1957.

———. *Report of the Commission Appointed to Inquire into the Unrest in the Mining Industry in Northern Rhodesia in Recent Months.* Lusaka: Government Printer, 1956.

———. *Report of the Commission of Inquiry into Unrest on the Copperbelt, July-August, 1963.* Lusaka: Government Printer, 1963.

———. *Report of the Committee Appointed to Inquire into the Participation of Africans in Local Government in Municipal and Township Areas.* Lusaka: Government Printer, 1960.

Republic of Zambia. *Address by His Excellency Dr. Kenneth D. Kaunda, President of the Republic of Zambia, to the Mulungushi Conference and A Guide to the Implementation of Humanism in Zambia.* Presented to the Annual General Conference of the United National Independence Party at Mulungushi August 14–20, 1967. Lusaka: Government Printer, n.d.

———. *Another Link is Forged: Inauguration of the Zambia-Tanzania Railway Project, October 26 and 28, 1970.* Lusaka, n.d.

———. *Constitution of Zambia (Appendix 1 to the Laws of Zambia).* Lusaka: Government Printer, n.d.

———. "The Employment Act, 1965." *Supplement to the Republic of Zambia Government Gazette, dated the 1st October, 1965.*

———. *Government Paper on the Report of the Commission of Inquiry into the Mining Industry (Brown Report, 1966).* Lusaka: Government Printer, 1966.

———. *The Industrial Relations Act, 1971,* No. 36 of 1971. Lusaka: Government Printer, n.d.

———. *Mines and Minerals, Chapter 329 of the Laws of Zambia.* Lusaka: Government Printer, n.d.

———. *The Nation Is You.* Address to, and Resolutions of, the National Council of the United National Independence Party at Mulungushi Hall, Lusaka, March 4–6, 1972. Lusaka: Government Printer, 1972.

———. *The Progress of Zambianization in the Mining Industry.* Lusaka: Government Printer, 1968.

———. *Prospects for Zambia's Mining Industry.* Lusaka: Mindeco Ltd., 1970.

———. *Report of the Commission Appointed to Review the Salaries, Salary Structure and Conditions of Service of the Zambia Public Service (including the Zambia Police) and the Defense Force.* Government Paper No. 1 of 1971. Lusaka: Government Printer, 1971.

———. *Report of the Commission of Inquiry into the Mining Industry, 1966.* Lusaka: Government Printer, 1966.

———. *Report of the National Commission on the Establishment of a One-Party Participatory Democracy in Zambia.* Lusaka, October, 1972.

———. *Report of the National Commission on the Establishment of a One-Party Participatory Democracy in Zambia: Summary of Recommendations Accepted by Government.* Government Paper No. 1 of 1972. Lusaka: Government Printer, 1972.

———. *Towards Self-Sufficiency Through Development, Progress Report, 1970.* Tabled by His Excellency the President (Dr. K. D. Kaunda) during the Address to Parliament on the Opening of the Third Session of the Second National Assembly, January 8, 1971. Lusaka: Neczam, 1971.

———. Bank of Zambia. *Report and Statement of Accounts for the Year Ended December 31st 1971.* N.p., n.d.

———. Cabinet Office. *Manpower Report.* Lusaka: Government Printer, 1966.

———. Cabinet Office. *Report of the Committee Appointed To Review the Emoluments and Conditions of Service of Statutory Boards and Corporations and State-Owned Enterprises.* Lusaka, March 1970.

———. Cabinet Office. *Zambia Towards Economic Independence.* Address by His Excellency Dr. K. D. Kaunda, President of the Republic of Zambia, to the National Council of the United National Independence Party, at Mulungushi, April 19, 1968. Lusaka: Government Printer, n.d.

———. Central Planning Office, Office of the President. *An Outline of the Transitional Development Plan.* Lusaka: Government Printer, 1965.

———. Central Statistical Office. *Statistical Year-Book.* 1967, 1968, 1969. Lusaka: Government Printer, 1967, 1969, 1970.

———. Development Division, Office of the Vice-President. *Zambian Manpower.* Lusaka: Government Printer, 1969.

———. Indeco Limited. *Annual Report, 1972.*

———. The Industrial Development Corporation of Zambia Limited. *Annual Report,* 1966, 1968–1969.

————. Metal Fabricators of Zambia Limited. *Beginning of an Industry.* N.p., n.d.

————. Mindeco Limited. *Zambia's Mining Industry.* Lusaka, n.d.

————. Mindeco Limited. *Annual Report,* 1971, 1972.

————. Mindeco Limited. *Executive Chairman's Statement,* 1971.

————. Ministry of Development and Finance. *Economic Report, 1969.* Lusaka: Government Printer, 1970.

————. Ministry of Development Planning and National Guidance. *Second National Development Plan, January 1972–December 1976.* Lusaka, December 1971.

————. Ministry of Education. *Annual Report for Year 1965.* Lusaka: Government Printer, 1967.

————. Ministry of Finance. *Economic Report,* 1966, 1967, 1971. Lusaka: Government Printer, 1966, 1968, 1971.

————. Nchanga Consolidated Copper Mines Limited. *Annual Report,* 1971, 1972, 1973. With statements by the Chairman, Mr. D. C. Mulaisho.

————. Office of National Development and Planning. *First National Development Plan 1966–1970.* Lusaka, 1966.

————. Office of the Vice President. Finance Division. *Economic Report 1968.* Lusaka: Government Printer, 1969.

————. Parliament. *Parliamentary Debates,* First and Second National Assemblies. Lusaka: Government Printer, 1964–1972.

————. Permanent Mission of the Republic of Zambia to the United Nations. *Address by His Excellency the President, Dr. K. D. Kaunda, at the Press Conference on the Redemption of ZIMCO Bonds.* State House, Lusaka, August 31, 1973. N.p., n.d.

————. Roan Consolidated Mines Limited. *Annual Report,* 1970, 1971, 1972. With statements by the Chairman, Mr. D. C. Mulaisho.

————. Roan Consolidated Mines, Ltd. *Annual Report,* 1973. With statement by the chairman, the Hon. H. Mulemba, MP.

————. Roan Consolidated Mines Limited and Nchanga Consolidated Copper Mines Limited. *Zambia's Copper Mining Industry.* N.p., n.d.

————. Zambia Industrial and Mining Corporation Limited. *Annual Report 1971.*

————. Zambia Industrial and Mining Corporation Limited. *Chairman's Statement, 1971.*

————. Zambia Information Services. *A Path for the Future.* Address by His Excellency the President, Dr. K. D. Kaunda, as Secretary-General of the United National Independence Party on the occasion of the Opening of the Sixth General Conference of the United National Independence Party, Mulungushi, May 8, 1971. Lusaka: Government Printer, 1971.

————. "President Kaunda's Press Conference," May 12, 1966, "Background," No. 12/66.

————. "Statement of Kishasa Railway Talks," July 15, 1966, "Background," No. 16/66.

————. *"Take Up the Challenge . . ."* Speeches made by His Excellency the President, Dr. K. D. Kaunda, to the United National Independence Party National Council, Mulungushi Hall, Lusaka, November 7–10, 1970. Lusaka: Government Printer, n.d.

————. *Towards Complete Independence.* Address by His Excellency the President, Dr. K. D. Kaunda, to the UNIP National Council held at Matero Hall, Lusaka, August 11, 1969. Lusaka: Government Printer, n.d.

————. *Zambia's Guideline for the Next Decade.* His Excellency the President, Dr. Kenneth Kaunda, Addressing the National Council of UNIP at Mulungushi, November 9, 1968. Lusaka: Government Printer, n.d.

Rhodesia Railways. *Reports and Accounts 30 June 1965.*

Southern Rhodesia. *Documents Relating to the Negotiations between the United Kingdom and Southern Rhodesian Governments, November 1963-November 1965,* Cmnd. 2807, Southern Rhodesia. London, 1965.

"Summary of Information Arising from the Zambia/Congo Inter-Government Discussions Held in Kinshasa on 12th/14th July, 1966." Mimeographed.

United Kingdom. British Parliament. *Hansard,* vols. 718. 721.

————. *Report of the Advisory Commission on the Review of the Constitution of Rhodesia and Nyasaland.* Cmnd. 1148–50. London: H. M. S. O., 1960.

————. *Report of the Nyasaland Commission of Inquiry.* Cmnd. 814, London: H. M. S. O., 1959.

United States. Court of Appeals. *Brief of Defendants-Appellants American Metal Climax, Inc., and Roan Selection Trust Limited* in *Harold E. Kohn, Trustee,* v. *American Metal Climax, Inc. and Roan Selection Trust Limited,* United States Court of Appeals for the Third Circuit, February 22, 1971.

————. Court of Appeals. *Harold E. Kohn, Trustee, et al.* v. *American Metal Climax, Inc., et al.,* United States Court of Appeals for the Third Circuit, Opinion of the Court, March 31, 1972.

————. Department of the Interior. Bureau of Mines. *Copper.* Preprint from the 1969 Bureau of Mines Minerals Yearbook. Washington, D.C.: Government Printing Office, n.d.

————. *Mineral Industry Surveys on Copper,* 1967–1970, and monthly. Washington, D. C., 1967–71.

————. Department of State. Office of External Research. "Conference on the Multinational Corporation." Mimeographed. Proceedings, February 14, 1969.

————. House of Representatives. *Activities of Private United States Organizations in Africa.* Hearings before the Subcommittee on Africa of the Committee on Foreign Affairs, 87th Cong., May 8, 11, 12, 16, 26, and June 1, 1961. Washington, D. C.: Government Printing Office, 1961.

United Nations. *Charter of the United Nations and Statute of the International Court of Justice.*

————. *Report of the Secretary-General in pursuance of resolution 253 (1968).* UN Doc. S/8786/Add.2, 10 October 1968.

————. *Report of the Security Council Special Mission Established Under Resolution 326 (1973).* UN Docs. S/10896, 5 March 1973 and S/10896/Add. 1, 6 March 1973.

————. S/RES/277 of 18 March 1970.

U. N., Development Program. *Activities of the United Nations and Its Family of Agencies in Zambia.* Lusaka, 1967.

U. N., Development Program. "Possible Support for Zambia." Lusaka, 1967.

U. N., Development Program. "United Nations Development Programme Technical Assistance Activities." Mimeographed. Lusaka, February 1967.

U. N., Economic and Social Council. *Report of the Ad Hoc Working Group of Experts Prepared in Accordance with Resolution 7 (XXVII) of the Commission on Human Rights.* E/CN.4/1076, 15 February 1972.

U. N., Economic Commission for Africa. *The Multinational Corporations in Africa.* (Africa Contemporary Record Current Affairs Series.) London: Rex Collings, 1972.

U. N., Economic Commission for Africa; Food and Agriculture Organization. *Report of the UN/ECA/FAO Economic Survey Mission on the Economic Development of Zambia.* Ndola, 1954.

U. N., Security Council. *Official Records,* S/PV. 1331, S/PV. 1336. New York, 1966.

Nongovernmental Documents and Publications, Cited or Consulted

American Committee on Africa. "Strike in Namibia." Mimeographed. New York, January 7, 1971.

American Metal Climax, Inc. *AMAX, Annual Report.* 1965-1973.

———. *Notice of Annual Meeting of Shareholders* and *Proxy Statement,* April 5, 1972.

———. *Report on Tsumeb Corporation Limited.* New York, February 25, 1974.

———. "Statements Concerning African Developments—1960–1965." Mimeographed.

Anglo American Corporation. *The Anglo American Corporation Group in Zambia.* N.p., n.d.

Anglo American Corporation (Central Africa) Limited. *Announcement to Shareholders.* Lusaka, November 17, 1969.

———. "Reply to Questionnaire Submitted to Anglo American Corporation (Central Africa) Limited by the Ministry of Lands and Mines." January 1968. Mimeographed.

Anglo American Corporation of South Africa Limited, *Annual Report.* 1965-1973.

———. *Statement by the Chairman, Mr. H. F. Oppenheimer.* Annual, 1967-1974.

Anglo American Corporation and Roan Selection Trust. "Statement of Case on Behalf of the Anglo American Corporation Group of Companies and the Roan Selection Trust Group of Companies." Brown Commission of Inquiry, May 1966.

Barclays Bank D. C. O. *Barclays Overseas Survey.* Annual, 1969–1972. London, n.d.

Barclays Bank International Limited. *Barclays International Review.* Monthly.

Botswana RST Limited. *Prospectus.* April 21, 1972.

———. *To the Holders of Ordinary Shares and Ameri-Depositary Receipts of Botswana RST Limited.* A Letter from R. L. Prain, Chairman, November 30, 1971.

Charter Consolidated Limited. *Annual Report and Accounts,* 1967. With statement by the chairman.

Chibuluma Mines Limited, *Statement by the Chairman, Sir Ronald L. Prain,* 1956, 1957, 1958.

Copper Industry Service Bureau. File 70.9.3. Amalgamation of Mine and Public Townships.

————. File 90.14.9A. Zambianization Committee from January 1967.
————. File 90.14.9B. Progress of Zambianization in Mining Industry.
————. File 100.20. Zambia Mineworkers' Union, General.
————. File 100.47. African Staff Association.
————. File 130.1.14. Origins of the Labour Force as at 31 December 1966.
————. *Mindeco Mining Year Book of Zambia, 1970, 1971, 1973*. Kitwe, n.d.
————. Productivity Seminar Papers, January 1968. Mimeographed.
————. *RST and Anglo American Corporation Mining Year Book of Zambia, 1969*. Kitwe, n.d.
————. *Copperbelt of Zambia Mining Industry Year Book, 1964–1968*. Kitwe, n.d.
DeBeers Consolidated Mines Limited. *1966 Annual Report*. With statement by the chairman, Mr. H. F. Oppenheimer.
International Confederation of Free Trade Unions, African Research Office. "Financial Position of the Northern Rhodesian Copper Mines, 1959–1963." Mimeographed. SPEC/06/64. Kampala, 1964.
International Confederation of Free Trade Unions. "The Copper Mining Industry of Northern Rhodesia." Mimeographed. SPEC/01/1963. Kampala, 1963.
Mufulira Copper Mines Limited. *Statement by the Chairman, Mr. (Sir) R. L. Prain*, 1953, 1954, 1955, 1956, 1957, 1958.
Namibia Support Group. "United States Complicity in Underdevelopment in Namibia: The Tsumeb Corporation." Mimeographed. New York, 1972.
Nchanga Consolidated Copper Mines Limited. *Annual Report, 1966, 1967*.
Northern Rhodesia Educational Trust, the, Ndola, n.d.
Northern Rhodesia Mine Workers' Union. "African Advancement Proposals." Chingola Printers, 1960.
Rhodesian Anglo American Limited. *Statement by the Chairman, Mr. H. F. Oppenheimer, 1960–1964*.
Rhodesian Selection Trust Group of Companies. *Statement by the Chairman, Sir Ronald L. Prain, 1959–1963*.
Rhodesian Selection Trust Limited. *Statement by the Chairman, Mr. (Sir) R. L. Prain, 1954, 1955, 1956, 1957, 1958*.
Rhokana Copper Refineries Limited. *Annual Report, 1966, 1967*.
Rhokana Corporation Limited. *Annual Report, 1966–1967*.
Roan Antelope Copper Mines Limited. *Statement by the Chairman, Mr. (Sir) R. L. Prain, 1953, 1954, 1955, 1956, 1957, 1958*.
Roan Selection Trust. "Analysis of donations made by the Roan Selection Trust group of companies over the 8 year period to 30th June, 1967, following recommendations by the Advisory Committee on Appeals." Typescript.
————. "Hercules Copper Airbridge: The Lockheed 382B Hercules for the Zambian Mining Industry." Mimeographed. AER 366, February 1, 1966.
————. *Kafue Flats, A Development Plan*. Public Relations Department of the RST Group of Companies on behalf of the Kafue Pilot Polder Trust.
————. "Lockheed Hercules Operating Experience in Zambia." Mimeographed. May 11, 1967.
————. "Reply to Questionnaire Submitted to RST by the Ministry of Lands and Mines." Mimeographed. January 1968.
Roan Selection Trust Limited. Addresses by the Chairman, Sir Ronald L. Prain, to Informal Meetings of Shareholders, and Reports of Proceedings of Informal Meetings of Shareholders (Stockholders) in London and New York, 1964–1968.

———. *Annual Report.* 1965–1969.

———. *Explanatory Statement for Meetings of Shareholders to be Held on 6th August, 1970,* and *Appendices to Explanatory Statement of Roan Selection Trust Limited.* June 30, 1970.

———. *State Participation in the Zambian Mining Industry.* A statement to shareholders by the Chairman, Sir Ronald L. Prain. November 17, 1969.

———. *Statement to Shareholders of Roan Selection Trust Limited by the Chairman, Sir Ronald L. Prain.* August 22, 1969.

RST Group. *An Introduction to RST.* N.p., 1964.

———. *Working with RST in Zambia.* Revised. N.p., 1966.

RST Group of Companies. *Education and Training Report 1964.* n.p., n.d.

———. *Statement by the Chairman, Sir Ronald L. Prain,* 1964–1969.

"Summary of the Mining Industry's Contribution to Contingency Planning." Mimeographed.

United National Independence Party. "Constitution of the United National Independence Party." Mimeographed.

Zambia Broken Hill Development Company Limited. *Annual Report.* 1966, 1967, 1968, 1969, 1970.

———. *Explanatory Statement,* April 26, 1971.

———. *Scheme of Arrangement for the acquisition of a 51 per cent interest in the mining undertaking of The Zambia Broken Hill Development Company Limited by Mindeco Limited.* Circular to Shareholders. Lusaka, June 15, 1971.

Zambia Copper Investments Limited. *Annual Report.* 1971, 1972, 1973.

———. *Review by the President, Mr. M. B. Hofmeyr,* in *African Development* (November 1970), pp. 20–21.

Zambian Anglo American Limited. *Annual Report.* 1965–1969. With statements by the chairman, Mr. H. F. Oppenheimer.

———. *Annual Report.* 1971, 1972, 1973.

———. *Statement by the President, Mr. H. F. Oppenheimer.* September 1971.

Miscellaneous Sources

African Development. London, monthly.

Africa Research Bulletin. Economic Financial and Technical Series. Exeter, England, monthly.

Africa Research Bulletin. Political Social and Cultural Series. Exeter, England, monthly.

Business and Economy of Central and East Africa. Ndola, 1967–1968, monthly.

Business Week. New York, weekly.

The Financial Mail of Zambia (Ndola) 1966–1967.

The Financial Times (London).

The Fortune Directory: The 200 Largest Industrials outside the U. S. and the 50 Largest Banks outside the U. S. Annual.

The Fortune Directory: The 500 Largest U. S. Industrial Corporations and the 50 Largest Banks, Merchandising, Transportation, Life-Insurance, and Utility Companies. Annual.

Metals Week. New York: weekly.

Moody's Bank and Finance Manual. New York: Moody's Investors Service, Inc., annual.

Moody's Industrial Manual. New York: Moody's Investors Service, Inc., annual.

The New York Times.

The Times (London).

The Times of Zambia (Ndola).

The Times of Zambia, Business Review (Ndola).

The Wall Street Journal (New York).

"Zambia Economic Survey," *African Development* (October 1972), pp. Z1-Z42.

The Zambia Mail (Lusaka).

"Zambia: Six Years After," *African Development* (October 1970), Zambia Supplement.

Index

Abercorn, 12

"African advancement," 104–109

African mineworkers' union, 96; formation of, 102; and mine townships, 133; nonpolitical tendency of, 107–108; and non-Zambian Africans, 116; and participative management, 123–124. *See also* Labor relations

African National Congress, 15, 17, 21, 144

American Metal Climax, Inc. (AMAX), 5; apprehension concerning Zambia, 204; assets and income of, 51; association with Mitsui, 73; association with Phelps Dodge, 95; diverse interests of, 48; formation of, 48; investment in Botswana, 177; investment in Namibia, 172–176, 186; investment in South Africa, 48, 186; sources of African income, 148–149; takeover of RST, 49 and n. *See also* Hochschild, Harold; Hochschild, Walter; MacGregor, I. K.; Ostrander, F. Taylor; Roan Selection Trust Limited

American Metal Company Limited, 47, 48

Ametalco Group, 84–86

Anglo American Corporation Group: and agriculture in Zambia, 127; attitude of officials in Zambia, 202–203; compensation to, 59, 60; and copper fabrication, 94–95; and copper pricing, 78; corporate structure of, 30–32, 41–42, 44–45; expenditure for education in Zambia, 128; as the "Greater Group," 203; group system of, 43, 165; holding in RST Group, 34; investment in Angola and Mozambique, 169–171; investment in Botswana, 177; investment in Namibia, 172; Japanese loan to, 70, 88; labor relations in Northern Rhodesia, 106; management of, 85n; managerial attitudes concerning Rhodesian crisis, 165–169; output of, 68–70; reported size of, 51; in Rhodesia, 142, 144; and Rhodesian crisis, 165, 185; sales policy, 78; value of assets in Zambia, 40. *See also* Copper marketing; Labor relations; Zambia, contingency planning

Anglo American Corporation of Rhodesia Limited (AMRHO), 165, 167–168

Anglo American Corporation of South Africa Limited, 5, 42–47, 51–52; bulwark of Imperial capital, 46; chairman's statement, 166; chairmen of, 53; directorate of, 46; diverse interests of, 46; origin of, 43; political orientation of, 52; sources of income, 46. *See also* Oppenheimer, Ernest; Oppenheimer, Harry F.

Angola, 19, 159, 169

Angolan rail route. *See* Benguela Railway

Anmercosa Sales Limited, 83, 85

Apprenticeship, 26, 115

Arnold, Guy, 153

Australia, 48, 204

Baldwin, Robert E., 10, 100, 103, 105, 119

Baluba Mines Limited, 33, 42, 71, 72. *See also* RST Group

Bancroft Mines Limited, 31, 41. *See also* Anglo American Corporation Group

Banda, Dr. H. Kamuzu, 16

Barber, William J., 14

Barotseland, 17, 21, 35

Bates, Robert H., 102, 107, 110, 117, 209n

Bemba, 8, 22

Benguela Railway, 157–163

Berle, Adolf A., 1, 6, 7

Bermuda, 41

Bostock, Mark, 189, 190

Botswana, 155, 177

Botswana RST Limited, 48, 49

Bourgeoisie: composition in Zambia, 206; corporate international, 201–203, 207–209; effect of governmental policies upon, 207, 209–210, 215; managerial, 198–204, 213; national, 210; revolutionary, 110; as a transnational class, 209. *See also* Class; Managerial bourgeoisie

British government: colonial labor policy of, 104; and proposal to partition Northern Rhodesia, 17; settlement of claims to mineral rights, 35–38. *See*